LIBRARY OF
NEW TESTAMENT STUDIES

615

formerly the Journal for the Study of the New Testament Supplement series

Editor
Chris Keith

Editorial Board
Dale C. Allison, John M. G. Barclay, Lynn H. Cohick, R. Alan Culpepper,
Craig A. Evans, Robert Fowler, Simon J. Gathercole, Juan Hernandez Jr., John
S. Kloppenborg, Michael Labahn, Love L. Sechrest, Robert Wall, Catrin H. Williams,
Britanny Wilson

Studies in Canonical Criticism
Reading the New Testament as Scripture

Robert W. Wall

LONDON • NEW YORK • OXFORD • NEW DELHI • SYDNEY

T&T CLARK
Bloomsbury Publishing Plc
50 Bedford Square, London, WC1B 3DP, UK
1385 Broadway, New York, NY 10018, USA
29 Earlsfort Terrace, Dublin 2, Ireland

BLOOMSBURY, T&T CLARK and the T&T Clark logo are trademarks of
Bloomsbury Publishing Plc

First published in Great Britain 2020
This paperback edition published in 2021

Copyright © Robert W. Wall, 2020

Robert W. Wall has asserted his right under the Copyright, Designs and Patents Act, 1988,
to be identified as Author of this work.

For legal purposes the Acknowledgments on p. xiii constitute an extension
of this copyright page.

All rights reserved. No part of this publication may be reproduced or
transmitted in any form or by any means, electronic or mechanical,
including photocopying, recording, or any information storage or retrieval
system, without prior permission in writing from the publishers.

Bloomsbury Publishing Plc does not have any control over, or responsibility for, any
third-party websites referred to or in this book. All internet addresses given in this
book were correct at the time of going to press. The author and publisher regret any
inconvenience caused if addresses have changed or sites have ceased to exist, but can
accept no responsibility for any such changes.

A catalogue record for this book is available from the British Library.

Library of Congress Control Number: 2019956626

ISBN: HB: 978-0-5676-9363-1
PB: 978-0-5677-0482-5
ePDF: 978-0-5676-9364-8
eBook: 978-0-5676-9366-2

Series: Library of New Testament Studies, volume 615
ISSN 2513-8790

Typeset by Newgen KnowledgeWorks Pvt. Ltd., Chennai, India

To find out more about our authors and books visit www.bloomsbury.com
and sign up for our newsletters.

For
Stephen E. Fowl
Friend, Colleague, Exemplar

Contents

Foreword	viii
Acknowledgments	xiii
Abbreviations of Secondary Sources	xiv
Introduction	1
Part I The Fourfold Gospel	5
1 A Canonical Reading of a Gospel Pericope: Matthew 2:7-15 (2012)	7
Part II The *Apostolos*: Acts and the Catholic Epistles Collection	21
2 A Canonical Approach to the Unity of Acts and Luke's Gospel (2010)	23
3 The Unifying Theology of the Catholic Epistles (2003–13)	41
4 Probing 2 Peter: The Role of a "Neglected" Letter in the NT (2016)	73
Part III The Pauline Letters Collection and Hebrews	91
5 Reading the Pauline Pastorals in Canonical Context (2012)	93
6 A Canonical Approach to the *Paratext* of Hebrews (2019)	127
Part IV The Revelation of John	147
7 The Church in John's Revelation (2015)	149
Works Cited	167
Index of Authors	175
Index of Biblical Figures	178
Index of Scriptures	179

Foreword

I am especially pleased to offer my support for Professor Robert W. Wall's important contribution to a canonical understanding of the New Testament (NT) writings; the present collection provides evidence of this. Following the Old Testament (OT) pioneers in canonical criticism, James A. Sanders and Brevard Childs, with an appropriate hermeneutic that focuses on the function of the canonical text, Wall has contributed many publications that have had a significant impact on the implications of this focus for understanding the NT from a similar hermeneutic. He rightly recognizes that what Sanders and Childs did for our understanding of the OT also has significant implications for current interpretations of the NT. He correctly argues that reading the NT canonically is significantly different from simply reading it as instructive ancient historical religious literature. Wall's leadership in this field of inquiry was well established with his earlier *The New Testament as Canon: A Reader in Canonical Criticism* (LNTS 76) in 1992, which justly received not only considerable positive scholarly responses but also similar pastoral responses. That distinguished him as the emerging leader in this field of inquiry for NT studies. Then and now he has focused on the *function* of the NT as a "canonical" or authoritative collection of writings that reflected not only the content and essence of the Church's emerging faith but also the life to that community of followers of Jesus who eventually became widely known as "Christians."

Unlike some interpreters of the NT, he has neither ignored the critical issues surrounding the biblical texts nor minimized the different perspectives in them but has rather emphasized the "canonical conversations" in the NT and their implications for current Christian communities.[1] Namely, he encourages open dialogue about the contents of the NT and the implications of this for faith. He allows for diversity in NT contents rather than twisting the message of the NT authors to make them say the same thing. Interestingly, the early churches in the second century condemned Tatian's attempt to harmonize the Gospels in his *Diatessaron* (also called *The Gospel of the Mixed*) because, in part, they recognized that forcing all of the Gospels to say the same thing eventually destroys the distinctive message and contribution of each Evangelist. Wall recognizes that there is not one NT theology but rather multiple theologies and emphases. He shows how careful "canonical criticism" does not ignore the multiple voices and perspectives in the NT but rather encourages a "canonical conversation" without forcing uncritical harmonizations or hermeneutics on a collection of writings that have considerable harmony despite some diversity. Long ago (1973),

---

[1] See, for example, Robert W. Wall, "The Significance of a Canonical Perspective of the Church's Scripture," in L. M. McDonald and J. A. Sanders, eds., *The Canon Debate* (Peabody, AM: Hendrickson, 2002 and Baker Academic, 2011), pp. 528–40.

the distinguished NT scholar George Eldon Ladd produced *A Theology of the New Testament* (revised and updated by D. H. Hagner in 1993) that became the standard textbook on the theology of the NT. It was superbly written but was often criticized for not making clear that the NT has multiple theologies, not just one. Ladd would certainly agree with that observation and made it clear in his classes, but it was not as clear in his first edition. In the revised edition, David Wenham wrote an important Appendix that makes clear that it is inappropriate to flatten out the distinctions in the NT through over-harmonization but that the distinctions cannot overlook the considerable unity within the disunity in the NT. I should note personally that Ladd corrected me years ago when I was his student for my attempts to make every voice of the Bible to say the same thing. He was right, but he did not make that as clear in his first edition as it was in Hagner's subsequent revision. There is a theology in the NT that the writers would agree with, but there are also multiple distinctive messages. Wall happily does not ignore or hide NT distinctions but deals with them positively without eroding the unity of the NT message. All of the Evangelists affirm the uniqueness of Jesus who confirmed to them that he was the promised messianic figure whose identity was affirmed in his resurrection.

Although most of the chapters in this volume are previously published, Wall has updated them and added a new study on the canonical implications of the paratextual elements of the NT letter, "To the Hebrews." As with all his other studies, it shows considerable awareness of the value of this letter for Christian faith and living. He rightly sees that authors of the NT saw in their not yet clearly defined First scriptures (later designated "Old Testament" scriptures) a new understanding of Jesus that clarified to them his identity and that continues to inform the faith of the followers of Jesus to this very day. In my view, Wall has rightly anchored his understanding of the NT writings in their value for understanding the faith that gave rise to those writings along with their continuing value for interpreting and understanding Christian faith.

In his opening essay on Gospel criticism, Wall acknowledges the difference in reading the Gospel of John (or any of the Gospels) as a "canonical" Gospel, namely as the *fourth* Gospel, instead of how it was written and read at first simply as the only Gospel known to a particular community of followers of Jesus. Christians regularly read it now as the "Fourth Gospel" instead of as the only Gospel known to the first community that received it. More precisely, does it matter if we read it as the *Fourth* Gospel in a way that complements theologically the other canonical Gospels as an apostolic witness to the historical Jesus or as the only Gospel of the particular community that first received it? Does it matter that the Fourth Gospel, with one primary exception (John 5:28–29), does not focus on the future coming Kingdom of God but rather much more on the new life that is a present reality now and experienced in the Christ who brings abundant life to all who come to him (John 10:10; 11:25–26; 20:30–31)? For the Synoptics, the Kingdom is here in the present activity of Jesus (Luke 10:9–11; 17:20–21; cf. Matt 10:7; 12:28) but yet it is also a future reality that will be coming soon (Mark 9:1; Matt 16:28; Luke 9:27). Moreover, Wall follows the canonical form of the NT's fourfold Gospel tradition in speaking of Matthew's priority (rather than Mark's), which actually reflects manuscript evidence of the Gospel's reception by the earliest Christians.

As one who has also served both in the academy and in the church, I am well aware that Christians generally view their Bible as a relevant message from God that teaches us not only what to believe but also how to live. Rob Wall's approach is essential *for the church* and also for those who acknowledge the NT writings as scripture with a relevant word from God that addresses the critical issues of humanity in every generation. I regularly conclude my presentations on the formation of the Bible by emphasizing the importance of scripture as "canon," that is, as an authoritative Word from God (see, e.g., *The Formation of the Biblical Canon*, 2:358). If the Bible is only a collection of ancient religious texts understood in their historical context and viewed within that context to explain the religious traditions that emerged *in that context*, it is not yet a biblical "canon." The very notion of *canon* always implies an authoritative role of these ancient texts *in communities of faith*.

In these collected essays, Wall focuses primarily (but hardly exclusively) on the final form of the NT, especially its final text, order, and arrangement of canonical collections within the broader NT collection, and not on the chronological order of the compositional origins of its individual writings. What is made much clearer in this collection is that by shifting the historical project from a primary interest in the well-known prolegomena of the production of different NT books, the primary concern of modern biblical criticism, to the phenomena of their subsequent formation into discrete collections of books and then eventually into a NT canon, Wall is able to demonstrate how the ancient church wanted its readers—and by analogy subsequent generations of Bible readers—to interpret and practice the NT as scripture. Wall's shift of historical emphasis produces a shift also in hermeneutical gravitas, elevating what we might learn about the potential of textual meaning from the church's earliest reception of these writings. For Wall and most church members today, that is an essential ingredient in understanding of the Bible as the church's scriptures. He does not minimize the origin and context of the texts that comprise the Bible but emphasizes the function of those texts in the communities of faith that received them as sacred texts.

I have agreed with Wall here and with the earlier work of both James Sanders and Brevard Childs who were concerned that the function of the ancient texts not be lost in the pursuit of historical critical activity of scholars. I noted earlier in a critique of Childs that while I agreed with his approach in focusing on the *received canonical text* of the Church and with his stress that the function of the biblical canon and its theology cannot be limited strictly to a descriptive role of the historical development and setting of the biblical texts, a context with which he was quite familiar, he appeared to me at times to ignore the importance of that historical context for understanding the canonical import of the texts in question (see my *The Biblical Canon: Its Origin, Transmission, and Authority*, 2011, pp. 465–74). The early church fathers often showed considerable interest in that historical context and welcomed only those books in their NT collections that were closest in time to Jesus and the Apostles. It appears that in some cases the authorship of those writings was later attributed to specific authors to connect them with the apostolic community (Mark and Luke). Sometimes apostolic authorship was attributed to an apostle (Hebrews, 2 Peter, and perhaps others) that reflects several church fathers' concern over the historical setting of its religious texts. The message of the texts in question was also deemed relevant to the emerging church's identity and mission, namely whether their message cohered with the sacred tradition handed down in the churches from their first century setting. Eventually, some texts that were earlier deemed valuable to the churches in their identity and mission later no longer were considered as relevant or *adaptable* to the church's ever-changing circumstances. Over time, many of those texts ceased functioning as scripture in a majority of churches but often not for centuries, for example, Shepherd of Hermas, 1–2 Clement, Didache, Epistle of Barnabas, and others also less known.

By the middle to the end of the second century, many of the NT texts had gained considerable acceptance in many churches and, by that time, those closest to Jesus, the apostles, and apostolic names were attached not only to some of them (the Gospels, Paul, and some of the Catholic Epistles) but also to many writings now called NT Apocrypha, and apostolic figures were made use of to advance the perspectives posited in these later Christian texts. The emergence of pseudonymous writings attributed to well-known apostolic names emerged in the second and third centuries in most, if not in all, cases intended to employ those names to obtain acceptance of those writings in the churches. Some churches initially welcomed those texts as sacred scripture believing that apostolic persons had written them since by that time apostolic authorship had become an important criterion for acceptance. The churches wanted to anchor their faith in the witness of Jesus (Gospels) and those closest to him (Epistles). At first, apostolic authorship was not a criterion for acceptance since initially the canonical Gospels were not cited by their authorship but rather simply as the words of Jesus. Since Jesus was the Lord of the church (Rom 10:9, passim), it is most likely that the Gospels that reflect on his life, message, and fate were viewed as compelling testimony for the churches from the beginning of their circulation in the churches. Second-century evidence from citations shows that generally the Gospels were simply cited as the word and activity of Jesus rather than by the name of individual Evangelists who wrote the gospels. That was largely the case until the last half of the second century.

Other writings received widespread acceptance in the second century, especially those letters attributed to Paul, but with only a few exceptions, most of the citations did not refer to Paul's writings as scripture until the latter part of the second century. By then many other writings began to appear in apostolic names and in similar NT genres, namely, gospels, acts, letters, and apocalypses. Eventually the writings that were believed to be pseudonymous writings were rejected, and that often took time for churches to recognize their pseudonymous origin. Most of this rejection took place in the third and fourth centuries, but not all of it. Irenaeus, for example, rejected *The Gospel according to Judas* and several gnostic texts in the late second century. Some of the pseudonymous writings continued to circulate in churches for centuries, but most were rejected by the end of the fourth century. The proto-orthodox traditions reflected in the earliest Christian writings eventually carried the day for most churches and they have had continuing relevance for Christian faith, life, and mission throughout church history. Of course, not everything that Paul wrote survived antiquity (1 Cor 5:9; Col 4:16), but what did survive has had considerable relevance for all ancient and later churches.

In the essay that is new to this collection, Wall ably shows that the elements added to the letter of Hebrews during the canonical process (e.g., its title, its initial placement in the Pauline corpus, its "invincible anonymity") reflect its ongoing practical relevance to Christian congregations despite questions of its authorship. It is quite possible that its authorship was attributed to Paul to secure its place in the biblical canon and the early church fathers were uncertain about its authorship for centuries. This book was most likely *first* placed among Paul's writings by Pantaenus of Alexandria (ca. 170) and subsequently was attributed to Paul by Clement of Alexandria (see Eusebius, *HE* 6.14.2-4) and circulated with Paul's letters (P^{46}), but doubts about its authorship continued for centuries and its location among Paul's writings was not stable. However, despite continuing questions about its authorship by notable church fathers, especially Tertullian, Origen, Augustine, and Jerome, few came to reject it because its message continued to be relevant and adaptable for subsequent generations of Christians who were facing loss and persecution and were tempted to depart from their faith for a more secure place. Christians in challenging circumstances have been encouraged by the message of Hebrews to faithfully follow Jesus, the pioneer or *archegos* of their faith, in uncertain times knowing that he is the only stability in an unstable world and he does not change (13:8), and in this life we have here "no lasting city" so are enjoined to seek the city that is to come (13:14). That message has remained relevant and canonical in every generation since Hebrews was first penned and later cited despite the uncertainty of its authorship. For those of us who do not accept Pauline authorship of the book, it is nevertheless a witness to us that God had more talented and inspired children in the first century than we first thought. The location of Hebrews in Christian Bibles has never been the same in all Bibles, but its message is central to the Christian faith and coheres well with the first-century sacred traditions that stabilized the churches from the beginning.

Finally, Wall rightly emphasizes the critical elements of NT interpretation and its authoritative antecedent scriptures for the church and states clearly that the OT "supplies the New Testament with its normative theological markers, while the New Testament witness to the risen Messiah supplies the subject matter for a Christian hermeneutic by which the Old Testament becomes Christian scripture."[2] This perspective is clearly Christian and deserves our favorable acknowledgment.

The usefulness and value of this volume cannot be underestimated. Wall recognizes that traditional biblical scholarship is inextricably bound to historical-critical assumptions about history and textual exegesis, but the results of that cannot have the final word about the value and function of the biblical literature for believing communities of faith. The scriptures are always "canon" for the church. I support Professor Wall's canonical enterprise and appreciate this opportunity to encourage him in his continuing pursuit of the canonical function of the church's scriptures that has resulted in numerous volumes that he has written for both the Church and for biblical scholars. Whatever else biblical scholars reveal through critical evaluation of the biblical text, the authority and relevance of that text for faith and life cannot be ignored.

Lee Martin McDonald
The Divinity College, Acadia University
Wolfville, Nova Scotia (Canada)

---

[2] Ibid., 536–7.

Acknowledgments

I acknowledge with gratitude the following journals and books in which earlier versions of this collection's chapters were originally published. I have revised each chapter and added introductory comments to each chapter not only to acknowledge its original publication but also to indicate its relationship to my current understanding and practice of a canonical approach to the theological interpretation of scripture.

1. "A Canonical Reading of a Gospel Pericope: Matthew 2:7–15" expands "The Canonical View," in *Biblical Hermeneutics: Five Views*, ed. Beth Stovell and Stanley E. Porter (Downers Grove, IL: InterVarsity Press, 2012), 111–31.
2. "A Canonical Approach to Acts and Luke's Gospel" is reprinted by permission from *Rethinking the Reception and Unity of Luke-Acts*, ed. Andrew Gregory and C. Kavin Rowe (Columbia: University of South Carolina Press, 2010), 172–91.
3. "The Unifying Theology of the Catholic Epistles" combines a sequence of three revised excerpts from the following: "Toward a Unifying Theology of the Catholic Epistles: A Canonical Approach," in *Catholic Epistles and the Tradition*, BETL 176, ed. Jacques Schlosser (Leuven: Peeters, 2004), 43–71; "The James of Acts and the Letter of James," in *The Catholic Epistles and Apostolic Traditions*, ed. Karl-Wilhelm Niebuhr and Robert W. Wall (Waco, TX: Baylor University Press, 2009), 127–52; and *Reading the Epistles of James, Peter, John and Jude as Scripture: The Shaping and Shape of a Canonical Collection*, ed. David R. Nienhuis and Robert W. Wall (Grand Rapids, MI: Eerdmans, 2013), 40–69, 247–76.
4. "Probing 2 Peter: the Role of a 'Neglected' Letter in the New Testament" combines revised excerpts from the "Epilogue," in *Muted Voices of the New Testament: Readings in the Catholic Epistles and Hebrews*, LNTS 587, ed. Katherine Hockey, Madison Pierce, and Francis Watson (London: T&T Clark, 2017), 199–210; and from "What if no 2 Peter?," in *Der zweite Petrusbrief und das Neue Testament*, WUNT 397, ed. Wolfgang Grünstäudl, Uta Poplutz and Tobias Nicklas (Tübingen: Mohr-Siebeck, 2017), 37–54.
5. "Reading the Pauline Pastorals in Canonical Context" is excerpted from *1 and 2 Timothy & Titus*, THNTC (Grand Rapids, MI: Eerdmans, 2012), 2–40.
6. "Images of Church in John's Revelation" is reprinted by permission from *Why the Church?*, Reframing New Testament Theology (Nashville, TN: Abingdon Press, 2015), 141–60.

Abbreviations of Secondary Sources

AB	Anchor Bible
ANTC	Abingdon New Testament Commentaries
AYBRL	Anchor Yale Bible Reference Library
BBR	Bulletin for Biblical Research
BETL	Bibliotheca ephemeridum theologicarum lovaniensium
BibInt	Biblical Interpretation
BJRL	Bulletin of the John Rylands University Library of Manchester
CBQ	Catholic Biblical Quarterly
CNTT	Cambridge New Testament Theology
CSS	Cistercian Studies of Scripture
GBS	Guides to Biblical Studies
GLB	Aus der Geschichte der lateinischen Bibel
HTR	Harvard Theological Review
Int	Interpretation
JBL	Journal of Biblical Literature
JETS	Journal of the Evangelical Theological Society
JSNT	Journal for the Study of the New Testament
JSNTSup	Journal for the Study of the New Testament: Supplement Series
JSS	Journal of Semitic Studies
JTI	Journal of the Theological Interpretation of the Bible
LNTS	Library of New Testament Studies
LSTS	Library of Second Temple Studies
NGS	New Gospel Studies
NIB	New Interpreter's Bible
NICNT	New International Commentary of the New Testament
NIGNT	New International Greek Testament Commentary
NovTSup	Novum Testamentum Supplements
NTC	New Testament in Context
NTL	New Testament Library
OSHT	Oxford Studies in Historical Theology
PRSt	Perspectives in Religious Studies
SB	Stuttgarter Bibelstudien
SBL	Society of Biblical Literature
SBLRBS	Society of Biblical Literature Resources for Biblical Study
SBT	Studies in Biblical Theology
SNTS	Society for New Testament Studies
SNTSMS	Society for New Testament Studies Monograph Series
SP	Sacra pagina

STI	Studies in the Theological Interpretation of the Bible
THNTC	Two Horizons New Testament Commentaries
WBC	Word Biblical Commentary
WUNT	Wissenschaftliche Untersuchungen zum Neuen Testament
ZNW	Zeitschrift für die neutestamentliche Wissenschaft und die Kunde der älteren Kirche

Introduction

In 1992, Professor Eugene E. Lemcio and I published *The New Testament as Canon: A Reader in Canonical Criticism* (LNTS 76), a collection of our studies that intended to demonstrate the relatively new interpretive strategy identified then by the rubric "canonical criticism." One of its pioneering practitioners, James A. Sanders, contributed the foreword to that first volume to locate our collection—even if sometimes uneasily so—within the general framework of this new criticism. In fact, Professor Sanders was the first to call it "canonical criticism." More than twenty-five years later, I have gathered a selection of my more recent studies in canonical criticism to form a second collection that samples studies from each volume of the New Testament canon. The present collection suffers from the same issues that characterize all single-authored *Sammlungen* of this kind: a redundancy of ideas, sources, responses to questions and challenges, and so on. But I press on, trusting that readers will detect changes in nuance and application and know that my good intention is to help students and interested colleagues trace the development of one way of reading the Bible that is concentrated by the very idea of a textual canon and proffers them cues for interpreting it gleaned from its historic formation, final literary form, and ongoing function as the church's scripture.[1]

In practice, my approach to theological exegesis has always attempted to receive and rework the ideas of Professor Sanders along with those of the late Brevard Childs who introduced a complement interpretive strategy, often called "the canonical approach." I have done so to forge practices of biblical interpretation that center on the idea and implications of the production and performances of the church's two-testament Bible. It was actually Professor Childs who forged the principal characteristics of canonical criticism more than fifty years ago. His initial efforts instantiated an opposition to the essential presumption of modern biblical criticism that theological exegesis must be regulated exclusively by the communicative intentions and literary forms of their

---

[1] This more theological and functional idea of a biblical canon and its application in the wider field of theological interpretation of the church's two-testament scripture extends beyond North America to include an international collegium of biblical and literary scholars. I have benefited in particular from the interdisciplinary work of Scandinavian scholars such as Tomas Bokedal and Einar Thomassen, the perceptive contributions of my long-standing New Testament colleague, Karl Wilhelm-Niebuhr (Friedrich-Schiller University, Jena, Germany), and the colleagues who participated in the SNTS seminar on the Catholic Epistles we cochaired to whom I owe a special note of gratitude.

ancient authors/editors with their first readers and social worlds in mind. Only those analogies carefully drawn between criticism's reconstruction of the situations of the authorial audience and those situations that face and shape contemporary Bible readers have practical currency for today's church. The studies gathered in that first collection and now in this second share an essential agreement with Childs's negative response to a particular species of historical criticism that fixes the normative meaning of biblical texts in the minds of their authors or editors at the moment of the text's composition in antiquity. I would only point out that his response is freighted both by a theology of scripture that leans on Karl Barth and by more practical considerations since the historical prolegomena that determine a text's "original meaning" are mostly indeterminate and largely without a scholarly consensus. This conclusion, of course, hardly implicates a complete disregard of historical criticism but rather a shift away from the epistemic hegemony of methods concentrated at a biblical text's compositional (or authorial) origins in determining its normative meaning, and toward the text's postbiblical reception—its editorial shaping and final canonical shape—as an ecclesial canon surfeit with potential meaning for current practice.

While modern criticism's enduring legacy surely will include the identification and close reading of scripture's multiple and diverse witnesses, I agree with Childs that the proper context to wrap around the studied text and its enduring conversations between these multiple witnesses is the entire two-testament biblical canon. Doing so prevents the preferential treatment of any one biblical witness—a canon within the Canon—or the harmonization of several into a single noncanonical witness (e.g., Tatian's *Diatessaron*) and exposes new textual interactions, most especially between the two testaments as well as between the canonical collections within each testament. In fact, Childs's rejection of the term "criticism" was deeply rooted in his worry that the methods and implicit epistemology of modern criticism's approach to the Bible lead interpreters to embrace a humanistic reception of its sacred texts that tends to attenuate their special nature as a trustworthy witness to God and to God's actions in the history of Israel and in Jesus Christ to liberate creation from the deadening, all-pervasive grasp of sin. This theological reference point stipulates that the Bible's ontology—its very nature—presumes exegetical practices that are inherently and purposefully theological. Not only does the Bible in its final literary form assume an ongoing theological role as a normative (or canonical) witness to God that is adaptable to the ever-changing social worlds of its current readers, but also the very phenomena that shaped this canonical witness were not arbitrary at all but providential and purposeful of this sacred end.

Professor Sanders, however, challenged Childs's distrust of biblical criticism while embracing his commitment to the Bible's canonical performances in the life of God's people. With Childs, Sanders agrees that the academy's Bible is the church's scripture—a sacred text that draws its faithful practitioners into loving communion with God and all their neighbors. But in contrast to Childs, Sanders objects to a privileging of scripture's final redaction as canonical. The hermeneutics of the canonical process, beginning with the movement of sacred traditions and the text's compositional history and the fluid history of its postbiblical textual transmission (i.e., manuscript evidence) and reception, envisages the history of a community's deeply spiritual engagement of its canonical texts in order to hear the multivalent word of the Lord God Almighty that addresses its own day. Sanders refers to this dynamism as "the adaptability–stability factor," which characterizes not only how biblical writers employed (i.e., "adapted") their own canonical (i.e., "stable") texts for a new day but also how the church continues to do so today when performing its canonical texts in worship, catechesis, mission, and personal devotions. Readers will doubtless detect my sometimes edgy struggle to bring the interpretive interests of the "canonical criticism" of Sanders and the "canonical approach" of Childs into my own interpretive work.

The use of "scripture" rather than "the Bible" in the subtitle of this volume intends to indicate the hermeneutical pressure placed not only on the biblical text's sacred role and historical transmission within an ecclesial setting but also on its theological content and referent. This said, readers will note that my more recent work increasingly expands and extends Childs's interest in the theological aesthetic of scripture's final two-testament form, even if continually informed by Sanders's more historical interests in the hermeneutics of the postbiblical canonical process, broadly defined, as well as in scripture's practical function in shaping the theological understanding of believing communities. I continue to press the point that our interpretive work, if guided by the intentions of those who produced biblical texts, should focus more on reconstructing the intentions of those communities that formed the Bible in a postbiblical social world (i.e., the second through the fifth centuries of early Christianity) rather than on the intentions of those who composed these same texts centuries earlier. In any case, scripture has no religious authority or hold on the faith community without the mediating practices of careful and diverse readers who help make plain the full meaning of the images, genres, and theologies of biblical texts so that their own faith communities better envision their present life with God and all their neighbors.

I would encourage readers to pay special attention to the "introductory notes" that frame each study included in this collection. The purpose of these additional "notes" is twofold: First, even a brief description of each study's original occasion may help clarify its purpose and content. Since I've revised every essay included in this collection, a bibliographical rubric is given to locate its original publication. (A new experiment in canonical hermeneutics, which treats the most prominent paratextual elements of Hebrews as properties of the letter's canonization and reception as scripture, is published in this collection for the first time.) Second, my effort to clarify the purpose of each essay allows the opportunity to respond to criticisms of those who have interacted with these studies in their own work. In particular, these notes help qualify the emphasis evinced in this body of work upon the postbiblical phenomena of a text's canonization as the center of its hermeneutical gravitas. In particular, my interest in the earliest reception history of biblical books, especially their formation into discrete canonical collections, is cued more by a theology of scripture than by a skepticism in the tools of modern criticism, which I own and practice.[2]

---

[2] I attempt to elaborate and secure this theology of scripture in conversation with my colleague, Professor Daniel Castelo, in *The Marks of Scripture: Rethinking the Nature of the Bible* (Grand Rapids, MI: Baker Academic, 2019). One of this project's core theological intuitions is this: the initial reception and recognition of any composition that eventually found its way into the biblical canon is received and recognized differently than its first recipients by subsequent readers for whom this same composition is now read as scripture. Bible scholars are interested in reconstructing—preferably

The repeated attempts to apply this group of essays to the life and faith of today's Christian church reflect more than a professional location in a church-related university and seminary; they reflect a grateful response at the end of a long career (some students would say *too* long!), and an abiding sense of vocation as a teaching scholar in service of God's people. I continue to confess scripture as formative of a people's discipleship of the risen One. Even in the sometimes difficult negotiation between the university classroom and scholars' guild, most Bible faculty at church-related institutions try not to separate their careful exegesis of biblical texts from their theological implication for the religious lives of all those who happen to come under their care. The one should inform the other, whether "to comfort the afflicted or to afflict the comfortable"—to use one of Professor Sanders's classic phrases!

There are many people to thank in bringing a collection like this one to publication. It is evident that I have stood, sometimes precariously so, on the shoulders of others over these last twenty-five years to find a way through the sometimes difficult terrain of contemporary biblical studies. Their names populate the footnotes of the pages that follow. Among them I especially thank Lee Martin McDonald for his indispensable contribution to our understanding of the formation of the church's biblical canon and for his collegial hospitality in contributing the foreword to this collection. He does so not only as a dear friend but also as a devoted mentor in all things "Canon"!

I often give God thanks and praise for the wonderful colleagues and conversation partners that share in our work together at Seattle Pacific University and Seminary. Their friendship and collegiality by turns have inspired me and have trained me so that all of us might flourish in our teaching and scholarship. One in particular, while not a member of our scripture faculty, is a friend and mentor to us all: Professor Stephen E. Fowl, Professor of Theology at Loyola University of Maryland. Steve has encouraged me over many years in so many ways that have been both spiritually healing and intellectually illuminating. He is a kindred spirit whose influence on my life is without measure and for whom I thank God daily. It is a privilege to dedicate this collection to him in modest tribute of our friendship.

---

to the extent the evidence allows—scripture's "history of reception." Germans have even created a technical name for this important historical criticism: *Wirkungsgeschichte*—a "history of effects." Several exceedingly important observations about the nature of biblical texts can be reasonably gleaned from a careful study of this history: biblical texts are multivalent and in varying degrees, they are adaptable to ever-changing social and religious locations, those locations evince the contextual nature of their interpretation, biblical texts are self-evidently not self-interpreting, and so on. But little thought has been given to a theological understanding of this historical phenomenon and to the various roles performed by God's Spirit within the community of interpretation to secure our intuition dogmatically. Our book is one attempt to fill this gap. In large measure, my own shift of interest—and where I might posit the principal historical prolegomena of biblical interpretation—has moved from the moment of an author's composition of a biblical text to the moment of the church's canonization of that text in its final canonical form. This intellectual move is predicated by a theological understanding of the church's postbiblical reception and recognition of it as scripture. Our book on "the nature of the Bible" attempts to chart some of this dogmatic landscape to sharpen our understanding of a theological interpretation of scripture.

Part One

The Fourfold Gospel

A Canonical Reading of a Gospel Pericope: Matthew 2:7-15 (2012)

Introductory notes: The following chapter is a revised excerpt from my contribution to Biblical Hermeneutics: Five Views, ed. Beth Stovell and Stanley E. Porter (Downers Grive, IL.: InterVarsity Press, 2012), pp. 111-31. The primary purchase of this book is to introduce, demonstrate, and then compare five different interpretive approaches to a single biblical set-text, Matthew 2:7-15. The contribution of each "view"—historical, literary, theological, philosophical, and canonical—is provided by a practitioner; I contributed the "canonical" view. This excerpt has been significantly revised to include both a new introduction and a "plain sense" reading of the selected Gospel pericope to help readers envisage how a canonical approach to the fourfold Gospel implicates a toolbox of historical and (mostly) literary criticisms without necessarily dislocating the text from its setting within the church's two-testament scripture. In doing so, I attempt to respond to a cautionary note sometimes sounded that the canonical approach to exegesis amounts to a "canonical fundamentalism"—a replacement methodology to modern biblical criticism. More properly understood, the canonical approach refocuses all the tools of historical and literary criticism by the orienting concerns of scripture's ecclesial address and by its ongoing performances that target the theological and moral formation of its particular communities of readers and auditors in their worship, catechesis, mission, and personal devotions.

Introduction

The following chapter seeks to demonstrate a canonical approach to a single Gospel pericope, Matthew 2:7-15. Matthew's placement within the fourfold Gospel and the Gospel's role within the two-testament biblical canon, however, provides a context for the exegesis of a single passage. A canonical approach to exegesis resists the kind of atomism that drills down on a single passage seemingly without an awareness of what surrounds it either within its compositional setting (i.e., Matthew's Gospel) or within canonical context (i.e., the NT's fourfold Gospel). My exegetical "probes" into Matthew 2:7-15 seek to wrap this context around the pericope to interpret a thicker meaning. The claim of Matthew's "priority," for instance, is not made on the basis of typical historical criticisms of a narrative of the Evangelist's life of Jesus first composed and then used as a source for the writing of other canonical Gospels. The consensus of Gospel criticism is that this historical priority belongs to Mark's Gospel. The claim of Matthew's priority when comparisons are made between the four canonical Gospels is because it's placed first among the four in the final canonical form of the whole Gospel. In a sense, this too is based upon historical precedent, since Matthew's was probably the first Gospel used as scripture in the worship and catechesis of early Christians (see below). But this observation begs the question: why Matthew? I would suggest two good reasons, both rhetorically adduced, for Matthew's canonical priority: first, its preface to the story of Jesus's messianic mission offers the NT reader the best transition from OT to the NT; and, second, its narrative architecture is well suited for uses as scripture in Christian worship and catechesis.[1]

The role of Matthew's introduction of Jesus (Matt 1–4) as an effective "canonical seam" is mentioned in most commentaries on the Gospel. What often goes unmentioned is the threat that this transitional narrative throttles: namely, a Marcion-like theology that marginalizes or dismisses altogether the OT witness to Israel's God as the oracles of an inferior god. Although not admitting this as a reason, many Christians today practice the church's two-testament Bible as though Marcion was right all along: the OT rarely is used in worship or instruction and when "scripture" or "church" is mentioned Christians have only the NT in mind.

Matthew's Gospel begins its testimony of Jesus by carefully locating him within Israel's biblical story, not only his genesis from Israel's family tree (Matt 1:1-16) but his identification as Israel's Messiah (Matt 1:21). Naturally, the Gospel bears witness to a number of surprises that prevents the religious leaders of Jesus's Judaism from recognizing him as their savior including, ironically, his own genesis from God as "Emmanuel" (Matt 1:18-20, 22-25).

While this "canonical seam" as I call it is best understood more generally as connecting the two testaments together by Matthew's constant references to fulfilled prophecy or allusions to OT Israel that Matthew's Jesus then embodies from his beginning, this may be more precisely understood by the final form of the OT in the Christian canon in which the collection of prophets (including Daniel) comes last. The narrative of this reordering from the Synagogue's *Tanakh* to follow the church's Greek translation of the OT (LXX) follows a complicated plotline and need not concern us here. My point is that Matthew's priority facilitates an interpretive rubric that reads the OT witness to God who promises to restore God's people. These promises according to the OT are realized because of Jesus's messianic work according to the NT. I might even allow that the OT book that concludes the various editions of the OT typically forges a "seam" that makes this point in more particular ways, whether Malachi (as in the church's present Bible), Daniel (as in Sinaiticus) or Sirach (as in Alexandrinus) or 2 Chronicles (as in *Tanakh*). When read by this prophecy-fulfillment rubric, each book that concludes the OT and stands juxtaposed with the NT in the Christian biblical canon presents readers with a profile of messiahship that is personified by Matthew's

---

[1] For a fluent articulation of this idea, see David R. Nienhuis, *A Concise Guide to Reading the New Testament* (Grand Rapids, MI: Baker Academic, 2018), pp. 17–31.

Jesus. There is a sense in which any intertextual reading of Matthew's Gospel, such as engaged in below, is an evocation of the relationship between the two testaments in a way that presents a faithful God's realization of promises made to Israel through the messianic agency of Jesus.

The early use of Matthew in Christian worship and catechesis is partly the result of its narrative structure: it is a carefully ordered Gospel. Although Krister Stendahl's conclusions about a "School of St. Matthew" track a different point, his argument that Matthew is the production of teachers who used it in training disciples to read and teach scripture after rabbi Jesus (following the "Great Commission" in which the risen Jesus commanded his disciples to teach others as he had taught them; Matt 28:20) seems pertinent here.[2] That is, whether or not the faculty of this School trained new disciples in Jesus's *pesher* hermeneutics of scripture, which does make sense of the Jesus tradition received in Luke 24:44-48, the final form and early reception of Matthew's Gospel reflects a pedagogical interest. The sermons of Matthew's Jesus, spread across the entire Gospel with related narrative units, effectively consolidates his instruction in discrete thematic units in a way that allows an orderly and comprehensive overview of what Jesus taught his disciples, which they in turn are to teach and "make disciples" of all nations. In this sense, the continuity that extends from OT to NT extends to present readers, who are responsible for proclaiming the biblical story of salvation into their own worlds.[3]

A Plain Sense Reading of Matthew 2:7-15

A canonical approach is less about a particular interpretive method and more about a way of thinking about scripture and its theological (rather than historical) referent, and how this approach shapes exegesis and its existential and ecclesial effects. Practitioners of the canonical approach in its various guises share the full array of biblical criticisms. In particular the proper beginning point of every modern strategy of biblical interpretation is the construction of a text's "plain sense."[4] Matthew 2:7-15 belongs to the First Gospel's infancy narrative (Matt 1-2), which introduces NT readers to Jesus as the Son of God Messiah. The plotline delivers on the narrator's promise to tell readers about the Messiah's origins (γένεσις; 1:18a) by connecting the narrator's clipped narratives of his birth in Bethlehem (2:1-6) and rescue there from Herod's treachery (2:7-15, 16-23) to the angelic and biblical prophecies of his birth (1:18b-25) and ancestry (1:2-17) by a cache of common motifs (dream, angel of the Lord, Joseph, fulfillment of biblical

---

[2] Krister Stendahl, *The School of St. Matthew and Its Use of the Old Testament* (Philadelphia: Fortress Press, 1968).

[3] David R. Bauer's study of the literary structure of Matthew's Gospel, elaborating the work of his mentor, Jack Kingsbury, nicely demonstrates its pedagogical purpose for the post-Easter community of disciples. He concludes that the purpose of its narrative structure is to provide this community with a canonical curriculum to use in its teaching mission in the world as commissioned by the risen Jesus in his departing speech (Matt 28:16-20); David R. Bauer, *The Structure of Matthew's Gospel: A Study in Literary Design*, LNTS 31 (Sheffield: Sheffield Academic Press, 1989).

[4] For an expansive description of biblical criticism's pursuit of a biblical text's "plain sense," with which I mostly agree, see John Barton, *The Nature of Biblical Criticism* (Louisville: Westminster/John Knox, 2007), pp. 69-116.

prophecy) and catchwords, including γεννάω ("to give birth;" cf. 1:2-16 and 2:1, 4) and τίκτω ("to conceive;" 1:21-25 and 2:2).[5] That is, the Jesus who is conceived in Matt 1 as "son"—of Abraham (1:1, 2), king David (1:1, 6), Mary (1:16)[6] and God (1:18, 23)—is this same "child" of Matt 2 (2:8, 9, 11, 13, 14, 20, 21) who is rescued from harm's way to rescue "his people from their sins" (1:21). Matt 1-2 form an integral whole that performs the role of preface to the gospel's telling of the Messiah's story.

Matt 2:1-6 supplies the approach into our text by its ominous introduction of two competing royal families. On the one hand is Jesus, son of king David (1:1, 6), whose royal purchase is indicated by his birthplace in Judean Bethlehem (2:1) in accordance with biblical testimony (2:5-6); and on the other hand is king Herod, whose "days" in Roman Palestine were ostensibly his (2:1). The tension between them is made clear to the reader by the arrival of "magi from the East" in Jerusalem, the epicenter of God's sacred universe where the biblical promise of salvation will be realized in due time. The arrival of these astrologers in the holy city raises questions about a "king of the Jews;"[7] their claim to be on an unlikely pilgrimage "to worship him" should provoke suspicion in the reader. Not only are the practices magi engage in forbidden by Israel's scripture (see Acts 8, 19), they are followers of stars rather than scripture. The constructive theological role of this unsettling element in the birth story of Israel's messiah is anticipated by Jesus's other title as "son of Abraham" (1:1), the father of Gentile proselytes, ancestor of the four Gentile women included in the opening genealogy (i.e., Tamar, Ruth, Rahab, Bathsheba).

While the gospel's universalist theme might explain the presence of magi in Jesus's birth story, their entrance into the narrative world also introduces readers to a persistent conflict between the Messiah's more nationalistic ambition to save the household of Israel from their sins and, failing this, to prepare a band of disciples "to make disciples of all nations" (Matt 28:19-20). Although there is no mention of their conversion in the pericope, the magi's worshipful response to Jesus—they had come to Jerusalem to "worship" (purpose indicated by use of infinitive aorist active from προσκυνέω) him (2:2) and did so when they found him (2:11) anticipates the Gentiles' positive response to the gospel.[8]

---

[5] A narrative gap, cued by the use of a conjunctive δὲ in 2:1, supposes that something happened between 1:25, which depicts Mary and Joseph awaiting Jesus's birth, and 2:1, which speaks of a time following his birth.

[6] The repetition of the aorist indicative of γεννάω in 1:16 and the change of its voice from active to passive when adding Mary to Jesus's family tree is critical for the exegete to observe, since it may well indicate that Mary is actually surrogate of God's Son who is conceived "through (ἐκ) the Holy Spirit" (1:18) rather than by a biological process. This subtle move would then provide the subtext of the verbal change from γεννάω to τίκτω (1:21, 23, 25), the repetition of which frames Matthew's initial biblical prophecy from LXX Is 7:14 (1:23) and so the gospel's central Christological claim: Jesus is conceived by God (and not by Joseph, so 1:25) to perform the role of God's Son-with-us, which is to save "his people from their sins" (1:21).

[7] An insider's query, if on a quest for the promised messiah, would more likely ask after "the king of Israel." And in fact Matthew deliberately repeats "Jews" (Ἰουδαῖος) again when narrating the discourse of Gentile outsiders at his crucifixion (27:11, 29, 37) before using it a last time in 28:15 to set unrepentant Israel "outside" the messianic community.

[8] C. F. D. Moule notes that Matthew uses προσκυνέω frequently in the entire narrative of Jesus's public ministry to intensify the ordinary sense of his "numinous presence" as a divine being who is "with us," and that this gospel depicts this sense from his infancy. I would add that this sensation not only

But the magi's real role is as Herod's foil. In the first place, the reader should be shocked by Herod's responsiveness to their claim. After all, they are outsiders "from the East" who are listed in scripture as among those whom Israel should avoid. Yet Herod in solidarity with "all of Jerusalem" becomes "frightened" (ταράσσω; cf. Matt 14:26) by their words. Why should any Jew be made restless by the prospect of the arrival of Israel's messianic ruler!? It is highly ironic that Herod convenes Jerusalem's magisterium—sharply stated by the narrator as "scribes of the people" (2:4; cf. 1:21)—for scripture's confirmation of the magi's secular wisdom (2:4-6); but then upon hearing it turns back to the magi (2:7) to plot evil rather than to respond faithfully to what God has made clear by the cooperation of star and scripture.

Nothing is said of Herod's motives in paying heed to the magi, in being alarmed by what they say about a king's "birth" or then rejecting its obligation. Nor is there any hint given that the scribes Herod calls upon for biblical confirmation of messiah's birthplace will one day come to accuse Jesus of abolishing the very scripture that bears witness to it (cf. 5:17-18; 3:15). The narrative approach to our text concentrates the reader on the irony that will come to shape the gospel's plotline: the very ones for whom the prophecy of a messianic ruler is given will reject him and even conspire against him.

The narrator's repetition of Τότε Ἡρῴδης (2:7, 16) marks out two stages of Herod's opposition, perhaps implying that his horrific plan of infanticide (2:16) was in mind all along. Initially he simply exchanges information with the magi in secret (cf. 1:19), advising them from scripture that Bethlehem is the messiah's birthplace. He then commissions them to find him there so that "I too can come and worship him." His use of the aorist subjunctive of προσκυνέω suggests disingenuousness: the real reason he will come is not to worship his rival but to kill him.

The magi are led by the star to "the place where the child was" (2:9). Neither the scribes nor Herod join them on the final leg of their pilgrimage; almost surely they do not need instructions to find Bethlehem, which is a short distance from Jerusalem. The relevant issue is to find "the place where the child was" to worship him, and for this they need a star (2:2). The extravagant joy the magi experience[9] when they find the right address in Bethlehem (2:10) seems odd, but is explained by their sighting of the child who is then worshiped with similar extravagance (2:11). They find him with "Mary his mother," an intimacy that is repeated in this chapter (2:11, 13, 14, 20, 21) to recall an Exodus trope (LXX Ex 4:19-20) and prepare the reader for the angel's cue of Jesus's exodus from Egypt (cf. 2:19-21; see below). The extravagant gifts the magi give

---

extends to supernatural powers (as in synoptic tradition) but even as here to Gentile outsiders; *The Origin of Christology* (Cambridge: Cambridge University Press, 1977), pp. 175–6. Ulrich Luz adds that in Matthew the "pointed usage" is directed at Jesus by his supplicants as an "appropriate attitude before the risen Lord"; *Matthew 1-7: A Commentary*, Hermeneia (Minneapolis: Fortress Press, 2007), p. 137. But, again, it is stunning that this congregation of supplicants Matthew convenes includes these astrologers from the East, which suggests of course that Messiah has come to save the world from sin and not just "his people."

[9] Two pairs, one for "joy" ἐχάρησαν χαρὰν and the other for "great" μεγάλην σφόδρα are combined to create the impression of a real and realized experience that the pilgrimage of the magi had reached its destination with expectation of blessing.

in worship match their extravagant joy in finding the king of the Jews. What we do not know from the text is why.

These shadowy figures from another country out east depart the narrative "by another way" because of a dream's warning, in a manner similar to their entrance into the narrative because of a star's direction. The use of the passive of χρηματίζω suggests that the dream is divinely given (2:22; cf. Acts 10:22) and, unlike Herod who is unresponsive to scripture's prophecy, the magi are prompt to obey its direction.

Following the rescue of the magi by a dream, the plotline returns to the holy family who are also rescued from Herod's evil, in this case by another visitation of "the angel of the Lord" (1:20) who advises Joseph that Herod is about to launch a seek-and-destroy mission that targets "the child." The repetition of an articular τὸ παιδίον (2:13, 20) rather than a more personal pronoun (e.g., "your child") in the angel's speeches is striking. The reader knows this particular "child" from Matthew 1 where he is introduced as God's Son with us. And so the abrupt change to "my son" in the prophetic proclamation of the Lord's word in 2:15 is expected. The righteous Joseph (cf. 1:19), again addressed by the Lord's guardian angel, is but his surrogate father.

His obedient response to the angel's instruction in 2:13 (cf. 2:20) is anticipated by his earlier response to the angel's command (1:24) and is clearly inscribed by its precise repetition in 2:14 (cf. 2:21): Joseph "rose and took the child and his mother ... and departed to Egypt." They remain there until Herod's death, at which time the angel cues their exodus out of Egypt back to Israel (2:19-21), where they settle in Nazareth to await the beginning of Jesus's messianic career (2:22-23).

Probe 1: The Synoptic Problem and Matthew's Priority

Little is known about the origin and date of Matthew's Gospel. It is an anonymous narrative composed without an address or clear statement of purpose. What seems clear from the available evidence is that the church recognized Matthew as one of four discrete yet integral "gospels of the apostles" by the time Irenaeus wrote *Adversus haereses* (ca. 175 CE). Every canon list includes this same fourfold Gospel and manuscript evidence from the mid-second century finds these same four Gospels copied together on single codices for wide use.[10] Because the Gospels originated and were preserved within particular Christian communities, one may reasonably assume that each circulated independently prior to their collection and canonization as members of a fourfold collection. Since this assumption is based upon sparse historical evidence, Brevard Childs puts the crucial point this way: "the major formal sign of canonical shaping of the collection is the juxtaposition of the four books with titles which introduce the books as witnesses to the one gospel."[11]

---

[10] Cf. Graham N. Stanton, "The Early Reception of Matthew's Gospel: New Evidence from Papyri?," in *The Gospel of Matthew in Current Study*, ed. David E. Aune (Grand Rapids: Eerdmans, 2001), pp. 42–61.

[11] Brevard Childs, *The New Testament as Canon: An Introduction* (Minneapolis: Fortress, 1984), p. 155.

The exegetical problem of reading Matthew's distinctive telling of the Messiah's birth is encountered most acutely when doing so within the bounds of the fourfold Gospel canon. The immense difficulty of doing so has occasioned two kinds of intellectual reductionisms. The most ancient and still most common is illustrated by Tatian's *Diatessaron*, which retells the Gospel story by first eliminating or glossing over redundant or contradictory details when exposed by comparing the four Gospels side-by-side. This initial reduction of Gospel content is typically followed by a harmonizing of the various episodes of Jesus's life into a single novel (i.e., a noncanonical) narration of events. In such a fabricated Gospel there is no Matthew or any other canonical telling of Jesus's birth story.

The reductionism of modern criticism moves interpreters in another direction by an emphasis and explanation that concentrate on the real differences between the four individual gospels—the very details that Tatian eliminates! The explanation of these differences typically refers readers to the diverse social worlds, narrators, occasions, sources, genre, and compositional histories (and prehistories) that produced each Gospel in turn. The net effect of this more atomistic approach to Gospel criticism is to better understand their origins but then also to isolate each Gospel from the others. In the case of Messiah's birth story, all the details distinctive to Matthew's narrative of Jesus's birth (e.g., centrality of Joseph, the Magi, Herod's infanticide, Jesus's escape into Egypt) are explained by the various factors in play when the Gospel was composed by a particular story-teller for a community of auditors. The marked differences between Matthew's story of Jesus's birth when compared to Luke's, or to its absence in Mark and John, is explained by the peculiarities of the composition of each.

No modern criticism illustrates this difficulty more clearly than the so-called "Synoptic Problem." Careful students of the fourfold Gospel observe that the first three Gospels—the so-called "synoptic gospels" because they share the same "optics"—plot a different story of Jesus than the Fourth Gospel. The solution typically given to solve this problem is to defend the chronological priority of Mark's Gospel. Most historians have concluded on very little evidence that the second Gospel was actually the first written and was then used by the authors of both Matthew and Luke (and simply neglected by John) as a primary source of their own stories of Jesus. Virtually every modern introduction to the Gospels, whether conservative or critical, begins its survey of the Synoptic Gospels with Mark and typically relocates John to a separate chapter often with the Johannine letters (ironically, a pattern typically followed by the ancient church).

The application of this solution to the "synoptic problem" with respect to the Gospel's infancy narrative begins with an explanation of why Matthew and Luke tell a story that Mark doesn't! The effect of this modern sequence of gospels led by Mark's chronological priority is to narrow the reading of Matthew's infancy narrative to an add-on of Mark's normative gospel intended to stage Matthew's distinctive portrait of Jesus in a way that Mark does not.[12] The point to make is that this pattern

---

[12] The groundbreaking collection that introduced and illustrates this point most clearly is Günther Bornkamm, Gerhard Barth, and Heinz Joachim Held, *Tradition and Interpretation in Matthew*,

of understanding the relationships between four individual gospels, while clarifying the distinctive contribution of each, may undermine the nature of their integral and complementary witness to a single fourfold Gospel.

This same "synoptic problem" extends to the relationship between Matthew and Luke both of which edit Mark's Gospel by adding different stories of Messiah's birth to stage different interpretations of his life for different readers and ends. While Gospel criticism has surely sharpened our understanding of the differences between individual gospels, it has expended little energy to "put humpty dumpty back together again."[13]

In contrast to the solution proposed to the "synoptic problem," which neglects John in any case, a canonical approach to this same problem is illumined by the postbiblical canonical process. For example, the title eventually given to the fourfold collection to cue the church's reading of a singular "Gospel" signifies the importance of their overall coherence, even as the titles given to each (e.g., "according to Matthew") signifies the distinctive witness of each to the one and only Messiah. These two paratextual markers suggest the Gospel is best received and read when both its coherence and diversity are carefully maintained.

More to the point of this first probe, the formation and final form of the NT's Gospel collection signifies Matthew's priority rather than Mark's; that is, if modern criticism grants Mark's priority on the basis of its date, a canonical approach grants Matthew's priority on the basis of its reception and canonization by the church. Édouard Massaux's impressive two-volume work that reconstructs the earliest history of Matthew's gospel prior to Irenaeus concludes that it was the most widely used and quoted Gospel throughout the second century,[14] a preference that extends into the third century.[15] By comparison, Augustine referred to Mark as Matthew's "epitomizer"—a kind of "reader's digest" version of Matthew's normative rendering of Jesus.[16] It is quite

---

NTL (Philadelphia: Westminster, 1963). In introducing his contribution on the miracle stories of Matthew, Held asks this programmatic question, "How are we to account for the fact that Matthew does not simply hand on the tradition as he receives it (from Mark) but retells it?" (165). What follows in his influential essay is a construction of Matthew as an innovative interpreter of miracle stories received from Mark to secure his belief in the risen Jesus's ongoing authority.

[13] For a helpful summary of this point, see Francis Watson, "The Fourfold Gospel," in *The Cambridge Companion to the Gospels*, ed. Stephen Barton (Cambridge: Cambridge University Press, 2006), pp. 34–52; his ideas are now more fully developed in his *The Fourfold Gospel: A Theological Reading of the New Testament Portraits of Jesus* (Grand Rapids: Baker Academic, 2016).

[14] Édouard Massaux, *The Influence of the Gospel Saint Matthew on Christian Literature before Saint Irenaeus*, ed. Arthus J. Bellinzoni, 5 vols., NGS-5 (Macon, GA: Mercer University Press, 1990). At the same time, I note Helmut Koester's criticism of Massaux's methodology, which considers only literary correspondence between written texts but not the possibility of shared oral traditions, in "Written Gospels or Oral Tradition?" *JBL* 113 (1994): 293–7. Dating the history of a text's reception "before Irenaeus" is especially crucial since it is he who originates the formal idea of a Christian biblical canon. Harry Y. Gamble says about Irenaeus that his discussion and use of certain Christian writings (e.g., Acts) indicates a "relative novelty" when elevating them to the same level as the "gospels of the prophets" that suggests he is the first to do so; "The New Testament Canon: Recent Research and the *Status Quaestionis*," in *The Canon Debate*, ed. L. McDonald and J. A. Sanders (Peabody, MA: Hendrickson, 2002), p. 277.

[15] Lee M. McDonald, *The Biblical Canon: Its Origin, Transmission, and Authority* (Peabody, MA: Hendrickson, 2007), p. 255.

[16] C. Clifton Black, *Mark: Images of an Apostolic Interpreter* (Columbia: University of South Carolina Press, 1994), pp. 127–35.

possible that the importance of Matthew's story of Jesus within earliest Christianity is due to its proximity to Israel's scripture (LXX), which remained through the first half of the second century the church's book. In any case, Stanton (ms. evidence) and Massaux (quotations and allusions) have cobbled together a probable early history of Matthew's reception and use as scripture that secures the claim of its priority in Christian worship and catechesis at that very moment when the oral traditions about Jesus were written down, edited, collected and fixed into a fourfold Gospel canon. The placement of Matthew at the head of the Gospel canon evinces the church's early recognition of its priority in introducing readers to the apostolic witness to Jesus.

The canonical effect of Matthew's placement within the fourfold Gospel is also to envisage a reading strategy. Simply put, Matthew is the Bible's introduction to Jesus; readers meet him there first. In this sense, Matthew performs the rhetorical role of a narrative frontispiece that frames a reading of the other three gospels.[17] When the Gospel's own canon-logic is followed, it's not through Matthew as a rewritten Mark that provides an entry point into the canonical story of Jesus but as the rewritten story of a faithful Israel antecedent (and constantly echoed) in the Old Testament story of Israel.[18] If Mark is picked up next and read as an "epitomized" Matthew, fresh impressions of Mark's Jesus are now possible. For example, precisely because Mark's story does not begin with an infancy episode or ancestral trope, the primacy of Jesus's messianic mission is emphasized. Rather than reading Matthew 1-2 as an episode added to Mark's prior Gospel, the New Testament reader is introduced to an infant Messiah in a way that elaborates the central claims about him that are assumed when reading the full fourfold Gospel from beginning to end.[19]

Probe 2: The Intertextuality of Matthew 2:7-15

A second exegetical probe is more text-centered: allusions and quotations of parallel texts within the fourfold Gospel and antecedent texts within the wider two-testament canon that add layers of meaning to a biblical text. The relationship between Matthew

---

[17] Curiously, in treating the fourfold Gospel as a collection, Childs reverts to historical criticism's verdict of Markan priority to detect the discrete theological contribution of Matthew to the canonical witness to Jesus based upon changes made from the Markan original (see his *Biblical Theology of the Old and New Testaments: Theological Reflection* [Minneapolis: Fortress Press, 1992], pp. 262–76). From a canonical perspective, whether based upon the final literary form of the fourfold Gospel (at least in the West) or upon the church's reception of Matthew before Mark, Matthew has priority and Mark should be read in light of Matthew's narrative, not the reverse (see below for the implications of this approach when treating the Gospel's infancy narrative).

[18] Childs, *New Testament as Canon*, 69–71. Cf. Ulrich Luz, *Matthew 1-7: A Continental Commentary*, trans. Wilhelm Linss (Minneapolis: Fortress Press, 1989), pp. 127–63.

[19] There may be still other impressions made upon the reader of Mark if she assumes the prior reading of Matthew's gospel. The material Mark seems to elaborate in comparison with Matthew, for instance, seems to fill in gaps that Matthew leaves out. Further, the quick-paced action of Mark's telling of the story may be read as buttressing Matthew's more didactic emphasis on Jesus's teaching ministry. Indeed, it is his interpretation of scripture that provokes unrest within Israel according to Matthew but his messianic actions that provoke similar unrest in Mark.

and other biblical texts is not only cued by their linguistic agreements but also by their evident use of common themes or typologies.[20]

In the first place, when readers follow a two-testament scripture's own canon-logic, they will approach the opening narrative of Matthew's Gospel with the Old Testament story of Israel fresh in mind. They will read Matthew's story of Jesus's birth and hear loud echoes of antecedent stories that replay the plotline of the biblical drama of Israel's primal history. Jesus is a type of Moses whose infancy tells of another Exodus, kingship, and exile. The repetition of ἀνακάμπτω (2:12, 13, 14) to indicate that Jesus's departure from Israel for Egypt was a flight from Herod's terror echoes its use in Exodus 2:15 of Moses's flight away from Pharaoh's threat and toward his encounter with God who calls him to lead Israel out of Egypt to the promised land. Indeed, the exodus is the principal *typos* echoed in shaping this pericope.

Thus, the announcement that Jesus had come to save his people from their sins (Matt 1:21) serves as a type of deliverance from slavery—from sin, not Roman occupation. Of course, the most prominent co-text is Hosea 11:1b, "out of Egypt I have called my son," which is quoted in v. 15 to concentrate Matthew's account of Jesus's beginnings as a new beginning for Israel similar to the Exodus/Mt. Sinai. Matthew's use of the MT's preference of sonship (וּמִמִּצְרַיִם קָרָאתִי לִבְנִי) over the LXX's more familial ἐξ Αἰγύπτου μετεκάλεσα τὰ τέκνα αὐτοῦ extends the exodus motif to Israel's king (so Num 24:8): the conflict between Herod and Jesus is between two kings and who of them is God's royal son (or David's son; cf. Matt 1:1; 2 Sam 7) and rightful heir to Israel's throne.

The fulfillment formula that introduces the Hosea quotation in v. 15 provides a Scriptural witness to a particular historical event—in this case, Herod's threat and the holy family's flight to Egypt. In doing so, the quoted co-text cues up a prophetic context that includes the entire Old Testament script, pointing to Israel's future reconciliation with God. In fact, the subsequent adumbration of the "out of Egypt" catchphrase in Hosea (11:1; 12:9, 13; 13:4) recalls Israel's previous encounters with God, most especially in the Exodus event, that leads inevitably to the climactic conclusion that Israel "has known no God but me and there is no savior besides me" (Hos 13:4). Set within this prophetic setting, Matthew's story of Jesus's infancy is testimony to God's fulfillment of a biblical promise made to Israel: Emmanuel is Israel's only hope. Since the magi's worship of Jesus (2:11) is suggestive of the gospel's advance beyond Israel into "all the nations" (Matt 28:19-20), Jesus's exile into Egypt (2:13-14), when interpreted by Hosea (2:15), implies that Jesus is a type of Israel sent out to enlighten and save the nations.

---

[20] Cf. Childs, *NT as Canon*, 161-5. Richard Bauckham's substantial argument that eyewitness memories lie behind the gospels (*Jesus and the Eyewitnesses: The Gospels as Eyewitness Testimony* [Grand Rapids: Eerdmans, 2006]) may well extend to the infancy narratives, thought by many to be literary fictions that serve a rhetorical or theological but not an historical purpose. If so, perhaps Mary is the source of Luke's tradition and Joseph of Matthew's given their pivotal characterization in each story. While all modern commentaries make note of this textual phenomenon, they develop its exegetical value differently. John Nolland, for example, argues that the Hosea quote does not confirm an implicit claim for Jesus's divine sonship made earlier in Matt 1, especially by the Emmanuel prophecy; rather, this quotation introduces this crucial theme into the gospel, which is developed more fully in Matt 3-4; *The Gospel of Matthew*, NIGTC (Grand Rapids: Eerdmans, 2005), 123.

Based upon this intertext, the historical events are recounted in Matthew 1-2 to testify to a faithful God's intention to save and restore Israel. Readers of the Hosea co-text will also know that obdurate Israel's response to God is typically one of unbelief; this impression will also prepare them for a reading of the Gospel in which unbelief is thematic. Finally, then, the fulfillment formula reminds the reader that what is central to Hosea is also central to the gospel. Hosea's rehearsal of Israel's encounter with God, itself a synthesis of the Old Testament testimony, continues in the story of Emmanuel whose offer of God's salvation is rejected once again by Gomer-Israel.

The exegete guided by the intertextuality of the canon also renders our set-text in Matthew within the bounds of a fourfold Gospel. They will observe this Gospel includes two infancy narratives whose independence is secured by an array of source and redaction-critical studies. They will know to resist harmonistic or historicist reductions of the two, while recognizing the common traditions they do share help sketch a unified narrative of Jesus's beginnings: the Messiah's name is given as "Jesus," his messianic vocation is predicted by an angel, and his family's residence is finally relocated to "Nazareth." Keeping this plotline in mind will help explain the political and religious conflict that follows in Jesus's public ministry.

When read after Matthew, however, Luke's infancy narrative elaborates the distinctive elements of the first. In some sense, the manner of Jesus's introduction to the reader by the magi and star, by Herod's infanticide, by the holy family's escape to Egypt and return to Israel instantiate "hidden and revealed elements" that frame a reading of Luke.[21] The character of the intertextual relationship between Luke and Matthew is not linguistically adduced, since Luke's "hidden and revealed elements" are independent of Matthew's; rather the nature of this intratext is typological and elaborative. For example, the arrival of Palestinian shepherds intensifies the universal scope of God's salvation in his Messiah including the marginal ones of Israel and adds weight to the angel's initial prophecy that Matthew's Jesus will "save his people from their sins" (1:21). Although Luke's narrative locates Jesus firmly within Israel's redemptive history, its canticles clearly move the reader beyond scripture's promise of a restored Israel (so Matt 1) to emphasize salvation's international reach that includes all the nations (so Luke 2:29-32). The shift from Matthew's "righteous" Joseph (1:19) to Luke's "servant" Mary (1:38, 48) as the pivotal character in the birth drama rounds out the profile of the Messiah's holy family, which is exemplary of faithful (or remnant) Israel. Powerfully imagined by the two infancy narratives, the importance of the holy family lends authority to the fourfold Gospel, especially by the mid-second century when the Gospel was first recognized as canonical within the church.[22]

---

[21] Childs, *New Testament as Canon*, 162.

[22] I would argue the harmony of the infancy narratives in the *Protevangelium of James* (mid-second century), although mostly dependent upon Luke's version to venerate Mary, also includes snapshots of Matthew's faithful Joseph in veneration of the entire holy family. Although the intention of doing so is unclear, one may reasonably suspect this is a practice of the canonizing community—that in some sense the holiness of Jesus rubs off on his entire family. For this reason, for example, the collection of Catholic Epistles is formed with James at its head and Jude as its other bookend. Bracketing the entire collection with letters attributed to the Lord's brothers, James and Jude, sounds a sacred note that underwrites the collection's canonicity when read as an integral whole.

Probe 3: Reading Canon and Creed Together

Irenaeus's programmatic statement of the apostolic Rule of Faith, which guided the early church's formation of both its biblical canon and ecumenical creed,[23] begins with the elemental confession that there is "one God, the Father Almighty, maker of heaven, and earth, and the sea, and all things that are in them" (*Adversus haereses* 3.4.1-2). In a church whose theology is typically ordered by its core beliefs about salvation, it is God's work in and through creation that tracks and interprets God's redemptive action in the world. The Exodus narrative that helps shape this text is replete with creational images (e.g., Ex 15).[24] Not only does God use non-human creatures to plague Egypt and force its release of captive Israel, but the narrator boldly claims that the prolongation of these horrific acts is to confirm "my name" throughout all creation, especially to the pagan Egyptians. In fact, the justice of such an act even upon the enemy of the elect people can only be understood by the prior claim that "all the earth is God's earth" (9:29; 19:5).

The Exodus typology that shapes the narrative of the holy family's great escape cues in turn the images of creation found in the biblical narrative of the Exodus. This highly textured reading of the set-text helps to illumine its analogical relationship to the Rule's confession of the church's Creator God. In particular, the odd presence of the star, which guides the guileless Gentiles to the world's ruler, is a theological prompt in this regard. While criticism's concern to test the historicity of the story's star, whether it is real or a redactor's trope, is legitimate, I think it is misplaced if the issue is apologetics rather than theology. The plain sense of the text is that the star is a celestial compass that serves as a heavenly agent of natural revelation for those who do not have scripture. What the text suggests, of course, is that the Maker of non-human creatures, such as stars, can use them all to achieve God's redemptive purpose for all things made.

In summary, this canonical approach to the canonical Gospel is ordered by theological rather than hermeneutical commitments. Rather than offering a distinctive interpretive strategy, its practices are of a piece with the church's core beliefs about scripture and the relationship of its canonization to the inspiring and sanctifying work of the Holy Spirit. A corresponding emphasis on the formation and final form of a canon of sacred texts does, however, underwrite a shift of interest from a biblical text's point of composition to its point of canonization, from how an authored text may have been understood by its first readers/auditors in light of their particular needs to how the church of every age continues to practice and parade this same text in ways that target holy ends: to make faithful readers wise for salvation and mature for every good work (2 Tim 3:15-17).

While a rigorous appraisal of the text's plain sense, the result of careful exegetical analysis, is the first step of any faithful interpretation, the applications of a sacred text are best protected from abusive, self-promoting interpreters by wrapping it in its various contexts (historical, linguistic, literary, rhetorical, compositional and canonical) in a way that coheres critically to the grammar of theological agreements articulated by

---

[23] For this historical and theological interaction between the formation the church's canon and creed, see Robert W. Jenson, *Canon and Creed* (Louisville: Westminster/John Knox, 2010).

[24] See Terrence E. Fretheim,*Exodus*, Interp (Louisville: Westminster/John Knox, 1991), pp. 12–14.

the apostolic Rule of Faith. Moreover, reading texts with a fellowship of believers that cultivates spiritual virtues necessary for faithful reading and hearing of God's word, such as love for God and neighbor, truth-seeking, humility, patience and forgiveness, is critical for using scripture in a way that targets holy ends.

Finally, the marks of the Christian church—one, holy, catholic, and apostolic—are analogous of the marks of its biblical canon. Accordingly, the practices of faithful interpretation must pay attention to the interpenetrating relationships of one text to other canonical texts (one), to the effect an interpretation has upon its recipients (holy), to the global scope of its influence in a diversity of social settings (catholic), and to the trustworthiness of its witness to God's truth (apostolic).

Part Two

The *Apostolos*: Acts and the Catholic Epistles Collection

2

A Canonical Approach to the Unity of Acts and Luke's Gospel (2010)

Introductory notes: This chapter was originally published in a collection that reconsidered the presumed unity of Luke-Acts from multiple angles; Rethinking the Reception and Unity of Luke-Acts, ed. A. Gregory and K. Rowe (Columbia, SC: University of South Carolina Press, 2010), pp. 172–91. My contribution to this collection seeks to secure a hermeneutical upgrade that results from shifting the focal point of critical exegesis from the moment of a text's composition (and its ancillary historical prolegomena) to the postbiblical moment of its canonization. I would add that this shift envisages a different set of orienting concerns regarding a text's "original" meaning. A canonical approach to theological interpretation earths a biblical composition in the deeply conflicted social world of early Christianity in which the idea of the church's two-testament biblical canon was introduced and then took its final shape. Not only does the canonization of a biblical text universalize the particular concerns that occasioned its composition, but also presumes a future role in forming the faith and witness of subsequent generations of faithful readers no matter their time-zone or social location within the church catholic.

In this regard, the division of Luke from Acts from the outset of the canonical process (there is no evidence of a canonical Luke-Acts) insinuates their different roles and canonical performances as scripture. No matter the circumstances of their composition, the identity of the unnamed story-teller(s), and whether they presumed a narrative unity between the two volumes, I consider the enduring effects of including the Gospel within this fourfold collection and placing Acts between this canonical narrative of Jesus and the two collections of apostolic letters in the NT canon generations later decisive when readers consider Luke <u>and</u> Acts (not Luke-Acts) as two discrete witnesses for a NT theology.

A brief footnote: this shift of interpretive focus to rework the postbiblical canonization of Luke as a member of the NT's fourfold Gospel and of Acts eventually to introduce the two collections of apostolic letters in no way mitigates against the findings of others who investigate the literary, socio-historical, or theological coherence of Luke-Acts as a single narrative of Christian origins, whether or not written by the same story-teller in response to the same or unfolding socio-historical circumstances. What I try to press for in this chapter is a different but hardly exclusive conception of unity cued by the textual residue evinced by the final redaction of the NT canon in which there is no such thing as a Luke-Acts.

Introduction

The purpose of the present study is to commend a different approach to the question of the unity of Luke and Acts: namely, an approach that seeks to retrieve its primary cues for defining the nature of unity from the location of their initial reception and use as scripture, and from the phenomena of a canonical process that divided Acts from Luke's gospel to perform different roles within the final (i.e., canonical) redaction of the NT.

Let me begin with an extended observation to frame this canonical approach. While the critical analysis of a narrative's literary texture and historical setting is an extraordinarily complex project, the epistemic demands we typically insinuate upon this hard work can complicate matters. In particular, modernity's mythology of originality has shaped the standard approach to a biblical text that seeks after "the" meaning most likely intended by its author and apprehended as such by his audience. This "original" meaning, then, serves as the regulatory norm to measure the validity of any subsequent meaning, especially to protect the text's author from his self-serving interpreters.[1]

The powerful impress of this interpretive axiom, along with the methodological interests that facilitate it, has monitored most academic readers of the Lukan original. Cadbury's invention of a "Luke-Acts" is the historian's observation of a single story-teller's production of a continuous narrative shaped by his particular theological grammar and historical circumstance. But once this observation is upgraded by the epistemic importance now given to an author's original, Cadbury's Luke-Acts is transformed into a powerful exegetical imperative: the very question of the "truth" of Luke and Acts demands that one study them together according to the reconstructed intentions of the story's presumptive author.[2] Tricky business, that, with so little evidence in hand!

Of course, the unity of Luke and Acts conceived by the intentions of a single story-teller has been challenged from the sidelines all along. Richard Pervo, for example, has famously argued against their literary unity, linking Acts with the novel genre of

---

[1] The same reasoning, of course, could be used to justify the use of *any* particular point in the pre-history or history of a biblical text as the plumb-line to measure future readings. Rarely does one find a more robust defense of originalism that includes theological or epistemological justifications; the reasons given are mostly practical and concern the preservation of critical orthodoxy. At least the fundamentalist (and hopelessly muddled) doctrine of "verbal plenary inspiration," according to which biblical authors were selected and inspired by God to produce a propositional medium of divine revelation—albeit in their own voice, does attempt to underwrite modernity's originalism with a theological warrant. Perhaps the best one can do is follow Andrew F. Gregory's lead in admitting to different readers with different interests in a text; so the scholar's approach to a biblical text and her attention to historical and literary matters will not be the approach of the ordinary believer whose reading may serve theological purposes and for theological reasons.

[2] This point is succinctly made by John Barton who writes, "The concern (of the historical-critical method) was always to place texts in their historical context, and to argue that we misunderstand them if we take them to mean something they could not have meant for their first readers ... The original meaning was the true meaning, and the main task of biblical scholars was to get back to this meaning, and to eliminate the false meanings that unhistorical readers thought they had found in the text." ("Historical-critical Approaches," in *The Cambridge Companion to Biblical Interpretation*, ed. John Barton [Cambridge: Cambridge University Press, 1998], pp. 10–11.)

antiquity—very different in form and function from a gospel genre. But his study is exceptional; and recent literary and historical studies have only confirmed a unified Lukan narrative, theological program, and social location; and a range of studies have even extended Cadbury's preliminary conclusion to understand better the interconnections between Luke and Acts and between Luke-Acts and contemporary Jewish and Hellenistic traditions.

What must be said, if only for the sake of clarification, is that a canonical approach to the study of Luke and Acts need not deny this rigorous historical criticism, with all its ancillary implications. The confirmation of a "Luke-Acts," however, envisages only one kind of literary unity that depends upon certain agreements about the nature of the text itself—that is, the ancient production of a single story-teller for Theophilus. Even an historical reconstruction of this Lukan original that posits considerable distance of time and circumstance between the two volumes, although subverting any sense of their chronological unity, need not problematize the more essential claim of a narrative unity intended by the author.

Nonetheless, the effect of the church's shaping of its authoritative writings into a single biblical canon creates another kind of literary aesthetic. In this case, different writings are placed together long after they are written to form a coherent and unified whole that facilitates a range of religious practices for different audiences unintended by their authors and unimagined by their first readers. Even though what I propose should not be considered a substitute for the critical constructions (or deconstructions) of a Luke-Acts, I would argue that the origins of a canonical Luke within the bounds of a fourfold Gospel (rather than as Luke-Acts) and of a canonical Acts that entered the NT in the company of a collection of Catholic Epistles (rather than as Acts-Luke) compels the biblical interpreter to exploit the importance of this later moment when books were received by new and different audiences in their canonical form to unify the faith of "one holy catholic and apostolic church."[3]

In fact, one may responsibly argue that any reconstruction of Luke's intentions in producing Luke-Acts for Theophilus may actually be less relevant to the contemporary reader than those ecclesial intentions and interpretive practices at work during the formation of the NT canon—which is, after all, the principal setting in which present

---

[3] The principal subtext of the present study is the proposal of a second "point of origins" (or "original meaning") that studies an authored text when it is first received and used as scripture (or "canonical" if this carries a different sense than "scripture"). The structure of my defense in granting elevated importance to the canonical origins of a text, with its ancillary claims of canonical (rather than authorial) intent or meaning, is similar to modernity's defense of a text's "original meaning." That is, Barton's definition of a critical orthodoxy (see fn 3 above) can be re-appropriated for defining the interpretive constraints given a text's canonization, except now the first readers of a canonical text are located differently both in relationship to their social worlds and in relationship to the literary text. The church now replaces Luke, Irenaeus replaces Theophilus, the late second century church requiring instruments to facilitate its catholic unity to counter its own splinter groups replaces Luke's church and its problems with supersessionism, and so on. In fact, we may know more about this second point of origins than the first, making it an even more effective critical measure than the reconstruction of an authorial original in protecting the sanctity of the text against abuse. But my primary justification project is meta-theological and not prudential or an ethics of reading. That is, by indexing a text's "original meaning" or intent to its initial reception as scripture, the interpreter receives and renders the text within its current and I would argue its most relevant context—the biblical canon.

readers receive Luke and Acts. What this reception history narrates is a kind of metamorphosis during which an authored text intended for a particular audience in the past is "transformed" into a canonical text for future audiences of readers. L. T. Johnson's dismissal of evidence from the second and third century reception of a canonical Acts as irrelevant to the present discussion because it "does not answer the question of how the first readers might have read and understood Luke's writing"[4] exemplifies the reductionism of modern criticism that freezes a Lukan original in its past without admitting that it underwent substantive post-production changes, not so much of plotline or material content but of readerly performances that cohere to the church's intentions for its biblical rule of faith. The dynamic textual history of Acts during the second century, climaxed by its posthumous publication, not only makes it difficult if not impossible to recover the Lukan original, it makes it equally difficult to dismiss the second century of Acts (and also of Luke) as unimportant.

This is especially so if Acts did not reach its final literary form until late in the second century and in an edited version more suitable for an ongoing role within the emergent Christian biblical canon to help secure the apostolic legacy of "authentic" Christianity against a variety of external and internal threats.[5] The most important early manuscripts (e.g., majuscules 01-04, 1739 ms. family) not only confirm that Acts is detached from Luke from the very beginning but that it combined with a collection of Catholic Epistles to form the so-called *Apostolos* (or *Praxapostolos*) for circulation within the Eastern church to help correct a misguided use of the extant Pauline canon in support of a *sola fideism*.[6] The placement of the *Apostolos* prior to the Pauline canon in many early canon lists did not intend to displace Paul's priority within the church— the extensive use of Pauline writings within earliest Christianity make this very clear— but rather seeks to frame the church's appropriation of the Pauline witness in a manner that coheres to the apostolic Rule of Faith.[7] In fact, one may reasonably infer from the suggestive title given to this new literary creation, *Apostolos,* that a secondary purpose of its circulation was to correct an overly determined Paulinism instantiated in some second century communities, not only by placing Jerusalem at the epicenter of its narrative world but then by placing the Paul of Acts outside the bounds of the church's Apostolate (cf. Acts 1:21-22).[8]

---

[4] Luke Timothy Johnson, "Literary Criticism of Luke-Acts: Is Reception-History Pertinent?," *JSNT* 28 (2005): 160.

[5] See W. A. Strange, *The Problem of the Text of Acts*, SNTSMS 71 (Cambridge: Cambridge University Press, 1992).

[6] See David R. Nienhuis, *Not by Paul Alone* (Waco: Baylor University Press, 2007), esp. pp. 85–90.

[7] See K.-W. Niebuhr and Robert W. Wall, *The Catholic Epistles and Apostolic Tradition: The New Perspective on James and Other Studies* (Waco: Baylor University Press, 2009).

[8] No explanation is given in the Patristic sources for the eventual dissolution of this *Apostolos* and for the role of a canonical Acts to bridge the fourfold Gospel with the Pauline canon. Nienhuis argues that the most likely explanation is the dominance of the West (and its Vulgate) and its claim of Pauline priority; *Not by Paul Alone*, 87. But the phenomenology of the canonical process itself includes the normal settling process that fixed a final literary form over time according to the practices of a biblical canon forge a religious (rather than a purely theological) aesthetic. In any case, the evidence of the early reception of Acts as the frontispiece of this *Apostolos* sounds a cautionary note to contemporary scholars against their standard presumption that the canonical Acts (and probably a Luke-Acts) intends from the outset a proprietary connection with the Pauline canon. The mss. and early canon lists suggest a closer connection existed closer to the point of the origins

In this sense, perhaps the phenomenology of the canonical process may be thought of as a type of evolutionary mechanism. That is, new external threats present by the mid-second century and on the horizon, a change of audiences, new responsibilities that come on line to meet the internal pressures of an expanding religious movement all forge a different ecclesial environment than Luke's to which Luke-Acts must be adapted in order for its story to survive. Put positively, subsequent readers of Acts, such as Irenaeus and Tertullian, found its narrative readily adaptable to this new environment. Again, my argument is that the church's preservation, canonization (even if in edited form) and continuing use of Acts, whether in its preaching or catechesis, is predicated on the adaptability of its narrative plotline to the social and religious exigencies facing the "one holy catholic and apostolic church."

The definition of a canonical unity, different than an authorial unity, regards a different set of textual relationships created by the formation of the NT canon. Acts is separated from Luke but remains related to the fourfold Gospel in which Luke is one member; and Acts is placed before two different collections of apostolic letters, Pauline and Pillars, to sound their introductory note within the biblical canon (see below). But this expansive textual unity forged by the canonical process aims at the enduring unity of the church catholic. Toward this religious end, surely the particular roles Luke intended Luke-Acts to perform for Theophilus, hinted at in Luke 1:4, are still in play for a canonical Acts if now on a more global stage. But the church's intentions for its scripture are different than the author's intentions for his narrative. The purpose of the present chapter is to suggest what these "canonical intentions" for Acts are and how they guide the interpreter's approach into its narrative world.

The Reception of Acts as Scripture

Recent studies of the pre-canonical reception history of Acts by C. Mount and A. Gregory are invaluable for recalibrating the relationship of Acts to Luke.[9] The

---

of a canonical Acts with the letters of the Jerusalem Pillars. My intuition is that the creation of this collection was to help the church battle the heretics and antinomianism dependent upon the Pauline canon, which may have been settled or replaced by other battles by the end of the canonical process.

[9] See especially, Andrew F. Gregory, "The Reception of Luke and Acts and the Unity of Luke-Acts," *JSNT* 29/4 (2007): 459–72. The reception history of Acts during the Patristic period is an obvious interest of Henry J. Cadbury's *The Book of Acts in History* (London: A&C Black, 1955) given that his hypothesis of a unified Luke-Acts may be challenged by the history of their canonization, which suggests a disunified Luke and Acts (see my brief comment below). Cadbury does confirm the ancient observation of the strategic role that Acts subsequently performs in giving shape and structure to a Gospel-Letters canon as a literary bridge between them—an observation that is contextualized and expanded by David Trobisch in his important study, *The First Edition of the New Testament* (Oxford: Oxford University Press, 2000). In any case, their studies along with others has been evaluated (and on occasion corrected) by Gregory, *The Reception of Luke and Acts in the Period before Irenaeus*, WUNT 2/169 (Tübingen: Mohr Siebeck, 2003), pp. 299–351, who concludes (against C. K. Barrett's optimism) that Irenaeus is the first to show the "influence" of Acts—I would rather observe that Irenaeus is the first to use Acts as "scripture"—in his *Adversus haereses*, even though not alone in his knowledge of Acts (350–1). In this regard, I would only mention in passing—even though with keen interest—that several of the clearest allusions to traditions used in Acts are found in the writings of groups linked to James and other Jerusalem pillars. Again, this implicit use of Acts within the Jacobean community may well anticipate a future role of Acts in the

central character in this historical narrative is Irenaeus who uses Acts in his polemics against so-called "heresies" to formulate a normative account of Christian origins. This initial use of Acts as scripture more than any other single episode in its early *Wirkungsgeschichte* defines its subsequent role within the biblical canon; in fact, "the canonical status of Acts is the result of (his) late second-century apologetic for a certain form of Christianity."[10]

Mount understands Irenaeus's reception of Acts in relationship to the origins of Pauline Christianity, and this well suits modernity's (and especially Protestantism's) disposition to read Acts with the Pauline letters. But this move is contrary to the reception of Acts immediately following Irenaeus, which read Acts with the Catholic Epistles (= CE) corpus. Whilst Irenaeus gives no indication that he knew of the *Apostolos*, which belongs to a later stage of the canonical process in any case, he does pay considerable attention to the traditions of the Jerusalem Pillars in his commentary on Acts. Of course, he is mostly interested to underwrite the theological unity between the three gospels associated with the Jerusalem apostles (and by implication their "letters"[11]) and the one marginal gospel linked by tradition to Paul (Luke's gospel). The unity of a fourfold Gospel tradition is not only against those who use Paul/Luke for heretical ends but against any who privilege a single gospel over its fourfold articulation; a myopia that privileges only a single apostolic tradition tends toward unprofitable ends. The central feature of his apologia is for the unity of a diverse fourfold whole. Acts plots a narrative of apostolic succession from a common christological fount to defend the theological unity and religious authority of a fourfold "gospels of the apostles."

The Rhetorical Design of Irenaeus' Adversus haereses. The design of Irenaeus's commentary on Acts in Book Three of *Adv. haer* develops two important themes. First, his commentary on the plotline of Acts is shaped by the passing exigencies of his social world and is *polemical* against the perceived "heresies" of particular people or groups—for example, Marcion, Valentinius, the Ebionites, and other second-century Gnostic movements within the church. While his reading of Acts provides us with an excellent example of Patristic exegesis, his commentary hardly has normative value for the church's future. In fact, we might judge his reading of Acts deficient and that other readings of Acts, especially related to James's role at the so-called "Jerusalem Council" (Acts 15:13-29, cf. 21:21-26), should be substituted for his. But then, secondly, Irenaeus's commentary is also *typological* of a way of thinking about the church's

---

formation and canonization of a "pillars collection" with James as its frontispiece. In my opinion, two other monographs, by David E. Smith, *The Canonical Function of Acts: A Comparative Analysis* (Collegeville, MN: Liturgical Press, 2002) and to a lesser degree by Christopher N. Mount, *Pauline Christianity: Luke-Acts and the Legacy of Paul*, NovTSup 104 (Leiden: Brill, 2002), are more useful for the purposes of this study since each seeks to understand Irenaeus's theological motive and hermeneutics in using Acts as a piece with the very idea of a biblical canon. In this sense, the use of Acts in Irenaeus's polemics defines its prospective canonical role—that is, the *raison d'etre* for its admission into the biblical canon and its use by scripture's faithful readers.

[10] Mount, *Pauline Christianity*, 57.
[11] Irenaeus does not seem alert to contemporary tensions between tradents of the Jerusalem apostles evinced in the Nag Hammadi tractates, between those loyal to the memories (and secrets) of the "Beloved Disciple" and those communicants attached to the catholic church that idealized Peter, or between Pauline Christians and those who lionized the spiritual authority of James and considered Paul an opponent.

different apostolic traditions (esp. Pauline and Jerusalem "Pillars") in a manner that unifies them by agreement with the apostolic Rule of Faith (= RF), by common succession from the same christological fount, and in service of a common missionary purpose by virtue of a common spiritual authority derived from God. This typological appropriation of Acts had continuing influence during the canonical process and has come even to us as a means to clarify the discrete role of Acts within the NT canon.

Irenaeus's reading of Acts as typological of the unity between epistolary corpora. When read as typological of a book's continuing authority, Irenaeus's use of Acts stipulates two interrelated criteria and proffers a reading strategy that insures the book's religious profit margin that shaped the hermeneutics of the canonical process.[12] In particular, it is Irenaeus's typological use of Acts (rather than his exegesis) that illumines the motive for placing Acts with the CE collection during the canonical process to regulate its formation and underwrite its inclusion in the NT canon.

The first criterion is that the substance of a book/person/tradition's teaching must cohere to the church's RF. The second criterion, related logically to the first by Irenaeus, is that a book/person/tradition to which an appeal is made must be linked to an apostle—since the RF comes to the catholic church from Jesus through his apostolic successors. For example, Luke's gospel has authority despite its marginal status and use by heretic groups because of his connection with Paul. Acts upholds the religious importance of Paul for the future of the church, not only because of his Damascus Road visitation from the risen Jesus but because of his unity in purpose and proclamation with the apostolic successors to Jesus. That is, Luke is Paul's successor who is successor to the apostles who are successors to Jesus—a succession authorized by God and imbued with the Spirit's presence. What is interesting here is that "apostolicity" is defined differently than in Acts 1:21-22, since spiritual authority is granted even to those early Christian leaders outside the Apostolate, such as James and Paul—clearly a contested point even into the third century. In any case, the "succession" of a Christian leader from the risen Christ underwrites the continuity of both purpose and unity of proclamation of the tradition he founded. Orthodoxy and apostolicity—so far, so good.

But herein lies the great deceit (or conceit) of heresy-making: "heresies" are clothed in ecclesial respectability, if not a presumptive theological superiority (!) by appeal to a *particular* apostle. Using his definition of Christian unity constructed by his reading of Acts, Irenaeus points out that the content and performance of any book linked to a particular apostolic tradition will be necessarily distorted because of its inherent theological myopia. The issue at stake is not so much whether a teacher appeals to an authorized "apostolic" tradition—to the memory of early Christian leaders or to their collected writings. All "heretics" did. The problem as Irenaeus understands it is that no one tradition must be used to the exclusion of all others. I would submit that this issues in a definition of canonicity predicated on notions of apostolic succession and Christian unity that assume all apostolic traditions work together in forming a

---

[12] Mount argues that Ireaenus's use of Acts "invents" a version of Christian unity for use in early catholic polemics that subverts the intentions of both story-tellers and the historical record of Christianity's origins. My point is rather that it is precisely this more poetic use of Acts that affords it canonical status and that defines its canonical role—not Luke's motive for writing Acts, whatever that is, nor the historical record of the church's beginnings, however that is reconstructed.

completed whole greater than the sum of its particular parts. Stated in negative terms, the use of a single tradition is more easily distorted for lack of balance and incomplete revelation. Thus, Marcion's use of a "mutilated" version of Luke's gospel (even though it may have only been an earlier recension to the one used in Irenaeus's church—see Gregory) is not so much what he has edited out but that he does not use it as part of a fourfold Gospel whole—the number "four" symbolizing holism to make this very point. Likewise, Marcion's appropriation of an incomplete Pauline canon is not so much that it is incomplete (without Pastorals, Philemon) but that in drawing upon only Luke and Paul he has rejected the completed "gospels of the apostles." It is the particularity of an appeal to use for universal ends to which Irenaeus finally objects.

Whilst we should leave open the real possibility that such theological myopia is not intentional (the result of a conscious editing of tradition) but rather a reflection of an inchoate canon, Irenaeus also claims that the appeal to a single tradition is often set in adversarial relation with others, thus subverting Christian unity. By quick survey of *Adversus haereses*, Marcionists appealed to Paul against the Jerusalem Pillars, the Montanists to John rather than to Matthew, various Gnostic/Libertine groups to Paul and John, the so-called "Ebionites" and other Jewish groups to St. James the Just (i.e., to the memory of his renowned piety but not yet to Jas which is never cited in the pseudo-writings of these Jacobean groups) against Paul, and so forth.[13] This observation in turn infers an interpretive practice that resists the myopia that attaches itself to one particular apostolic tradition to the exclusion of other authorized apostolic traditions. The roots of heresy are not found in the attenuation of the per se apostolic tradition in teaching and worship; rather, it is the privileging of one tradition above all others. The use of a pluriform collection (e.g., fourfold gospel), all parts of which cohere to RF and are linked to apostolic tradition, protects the church against theological myopia and thus heresy.

What is forged by Irenaeus's polemics is a positive *typos* of theological unity according to which every single biblical tradition is united by a common regard for the RF. No matter to what religious tradition an appeal is made, if that tradition is apostolic, then what is expected is essential coherence with the received teachings of Jesus. But also forged is a negative definition of unity so that a departure from the Truth is not only the per se rejection of the RF; it is also the result of considering only a single apostolic tradition to the exclusion of the full complement of apostolic traditions. In this sense, then, ecclesial unity is defined by a plurality that forges, in J. A. Sander's phrase, a "self-correcting, mutually-informing apparatus."[14] Thus, the unity of the apostolic traditions is another way of speaking of its completeness, of the complementarity of its different strands (not of the harmonizing *Tendenz* of Patristic

---

[13] Similarly, the Pauline canon consisting only of nine or ten letters rather than thirteen, the Petrine tradition remembered by only 1 Peter without 2 Peter, or 1 John without 2-3 John, or Jude without James (since Jude 1:1 mentions James), is incomplete of a robust apostolicity.

[14] I have heard Professor Sanders use this phrase in public lectures and private conversations. His elaboration of what it means is found in James A. Sanders, "The Issue of Closure in the Canonical Process," in *The Canon Debate*, ed. Lee M. McDonald and James A. Sanders (Peabody, MA: Hendrickson, 2002), pp. 252–63.

hermeneutics that François Bovon claims[15]). The value of Acts is that it allowed Irenaeus to speak of the incompleteness of any single apostolic tradition that is used without benefit of all the others that draw from a common Christological source and bear witness to a single RF. By the end of the canonical process, then, the placement of Acts to bridge the four "gospels of the apostles" and their various epistolary writings envisages a dynamic and pluriform catholicity that subverts any attempt to single out one particular text or one particular teaching as normative for the whole church. All scripture is analogical of the RF, and it is that apostolic canon and not any one apostolic tradition that plumbs the meaning made of any biblical text.

The Performance of Acts *as* Scripture

One of the most important questions raised by a canonical approach to Acts is this: what do Luke's reasons for producing a sequel for Theophilus have to do with the church's reasons for publishing Acts as scripture? Not only does a response to this question help envisage more clearly the "added-value" dimension of canonical readings, the interpreter who does not deny what is already learned about Luke's Acts will still need to calibrate an approach to the canonical Acts that seeks to bridge these two interpretive horizons.[16] What follows is a series of reflections that illustrate what I have in mind.

1. Reading Acts as scripture recognizes the importance of different literary relationships within the New Testament. The intracanonical relationships between Acts and the fourfold Gospel and between Acts and the following two collections of Letters (especially Pauline) are elevated in importance within canonical context. The "canon-logic" envisaged by the arrangement of the different parts within the New Testament whole, and sometimes even of individual writings within these canonical parts, stipulates important markers in guiding the reader's approach to the NT. According to this arrangement, then, the fourfold gospel (and not just the third) is perceived as prerequisite reading for the study of Acts, and the study of Acts under the gospel's light is then prerequisite reading for the study of the letters that follow. The implications of this "canon-logic" will be teased out below.
2. These new intracanonical relationships forged by the canonical process are also of importance when assessing the distinctive importance of the theology of Acts within the NT. No longer does the biblical theologian consider the thematic interests of Acts only in terms of their congruence with those found in Luke's gospel; rather, the theological contribution that Acts makes to *biblical* theology is now measured as an indispensable part of an integral whole. Put in different words, upon consideration of the various theologies that make up the NT's entire theological conception, the interpreter is now pressed to imagine what a fully

---

[15] See François Bovon, "The Synoptic Gospels and the Non-Canonical Acts of the Apostles," in *Studies in Early Christianity* (Grand Rapids: Baker Academic, 2003), pp. 209–25.
[16] This is an orienting concern of my commentary on Acts in volume 10 of *The New Interpreter's Bible*, ed. Leander E. Keck (Nashville: Abingdon, 2002), pp. 3–370.

biblical witness to God might actually lack if not inclusive of Acts. Even more specifically, what distorted idea of the church's faith, its religious or social identity or of its vocation in the world might result from a conversation with a body of sacred writings that did not include this book? What thin reading of the Pauline letters would result if the interpreter failed to prep herself by first reading the story of the canonical Paul of Acts? Simply put, reading Acts within its biblical setting reminds us that any theological understanding lacking the witness of Acts will distort Christian faith and life.

3. The Paul of Acts is valued more keenly from this canonical perspective than when his role is reduced to a cameo appearance in the modern quest of the historical Paul. At stake in following the story of the Paul of Acts is not so much the historical accuracy of Luke's portrait—even though this is currently being retouched—or even the important questions about his credibility within earliest Christianity. The most important issues from a canonical angle of vision are theological ones: that is, what does the Paul of Acts have to say about the future of the church and how does his story in Acts orient its readers to the implied author of the Pauline letters that follow and the Pauline witness they enshrine?

4. The church's conflict with the synagogue at the end of the canonical process was no doubt different than Luke's assessment when he wrote Acts. What began as an intramural "Jewish problem" had become a "Judaism problem" by the end of the second century. Keen competition had developed between two "world religions," made all the more prickly by their common history and theological conception. The scribal emendations to the Western version of Acts, with a more negative characterization of unrepentant Israel, may well reflect the canonizing community's heightened sensitivity to its relationship with Judaism and its sense of the biblical canon's function to delineate the church's identity as clearly as possible (see above, "Acts as Composition"). In a different sense, the portrait of Israel found in Acts clarifies the real difference between Christianity and Judaism in christological rather than in nationalistic or ethnocentric terms. Thus, Acts subverts any "Christian" prejudice against Jews either on ethnic grounds (= antisemitism) or on the mistaken presumption that God has reneged on promises made to historic Israel according to the scriptures or that God has replaced Jews with Christians in the economy of salvation. God's faithfulness to Israel remains inviolate; therefore, today's church must become more Jewish, not less so, in order to be fully Christian in its worship and witness.

5. The "primitivism" of Acts simply reflects the ecclesial experience of the earliest church, which fashioned itself after the Diaspora synagogues and other voluntary organizations of the Roman world. Worship consisted of prayer meetings and teaching, with Christian fellowship centered in the homes of middleclass believers. The sociology of the church dramatically changed during the canonical process; these loosely confederated house-congregations became in time participants of an emerging church catholic. For this reason, the ongoing interest in the images and ideas of "church" in Acts should be posited more squarely on its missionary vocation and prophetic message, its resurrection practices, and the nature of spiritual leadership—important claims on any congregation in every age—rather

than replicating outward forms of governance and worship or other time-conditioned practices.
6. In this regard, reading Acts as scripture seeks to insinuate its narrative world upon the changing "real" worlds of current readers. New layers of meaning hitherto hidden are discovered whenever sacred texts are allowed to penetrate and interpret the world of its interpreters. For example, contemporary readers will more easily discern the relevance of the Ethiopian Eunuch's story (see 8:26-40) for reflecting upon the relationship between the church and its homosexual membership; or the example of Priscilla in Acts 18, along with other women of Acts, as role models for prophetic ministry in congregations that once were reluctant to encourage women in ministry. The vivid snapshots of the community of goods or repeated episodes that depict Paul's relations with Rome may challenge today's congregations away from civil religion or prosperity gospels and toward a more prophetic understanding of church as counterculture. By inclining its readers in this direction, Acts provides an important element of a wider "canonical context" in which the faithful community gathers to reflect on those issues that either undermine or underwrite God's presence in today's world.
7. Finally, reading Acts as scripture cultivates a fresh sense of sacred time and space. The church continues to live in "the last days," betwixt Pentecost and *Parousia*, when the Spirit of God empowers Christ's disciples to bear witness to the resurrection throughout the world in anticipation of God's coming triumph and creation's final restoration (see 3:20-21). The continuing authority of the Book of Acts is to form a church that proclaims God's word and embodies a witness to its Truth to herald that coming day.

The Performance of Acts *within* Scripture

When the NT Acts is received and studied within the context of the entire biblical canon (rather than as the sequel to Luke's gospel), the reader will more naturally reflect upon the narrative as continuing scripture's plotline of Israel's OT story and Jesus's Gospel story. Within its present canonical setting, the sense of Acts 1:1's evocation "all that Jesus began to do and teach," is made plain by the amplified and enriched story of Jesus in the fourfold (rather than just the third) Gospel. Besides being made more alert to the importance of Israel's scripture that Acts constantly quotes or echoes, this approach also fills in the profile of key characters that populate the narrative world of Acts. For example, the reader is better prepared to acknowledge the role performed by the Spirit-filled Peter in the opening of Acts as successor to the now departed Jesus as leader of his messianic community—a role for which the third gospel does not adequately prepare the reader of Acts. The fourth gospel provides the better seam by its concluding story of Peter's spiritual rehabilitation and the Lord's farewell injunction to him to "feed the flock" (John 21:15-17). Moreover, the reception of the Spirit promised in Jesus's farewell discourse (John 14-16) shapes the reader's anticipation of the Pentecostal community of Acts.

The relationship between the canonical Acts and the two collections of NT letters, while considerably more strategic in the history of interpretation, is more difficult for the interpreter to arrange. Not only does the preface to Acts cue its story's continuity with the Gospel, the conventions of epistolary literature are different from those of narrative literature. For these reasons the differences between Acts and the following letters may seem more apparent to the reader. For example, the Paul of Acts is sometimes at odds with Paul's own self-understanding or missionary agenda evinced in the Pauline letters; nor does Luke characterize Paul as a letter-writer or quote extensively from any of Paul's letters.[17] Reading Acts by the church's intentions for its biblical canon, however, would seem to compel a less adversarial relationship between the Paul of Acts and the epistolary Paul.

The potential gains of this approach to Paul may be illustrated when considering the textual "seam" that weaves together the final snapshot in Acts of Paul in Rome (see 28:17-31) and the opening words of Paul to the Romans, which taken together introduce biblical readers to a missionary-minded apostle who is "eager to proclaim the gospel to you also who are in Rome" (Rom 1:15).[18] The interplay between the ending of Acts and Romans underwrites the orienting concern of a *canonical* Paul, who is not found in a secluded study writing dense Christian theology but on the city streets or in the living rooms of rented apartments relating the Christian gospel to life in practical and persuasive ways.

In this regard, among the most important roles a canonical Acts performs is to introduce the Bible's readers to the implied authors of the NT letters. While the historical reliability of these portraits is contested, their portraits convey a sense of their moral and religious authority that cultivates a high regard for the truth and importance of their letters for the future formation of their faithful readers. After all, these readers are the intended audience of canonical texts. In any case, the salient issue that shapes Acts' narrative of Christianity's expansion into pagan territory, which is narrated with great optimism, is not its use as an historical resource but as a theological source that contributes to the church's ongoing understanding of its vocation and identity in the "real" world.

Acts also cultivates a sense of their personal relationships and in doing so provides a distinctive angle into the nature of the literary relationships between the Pauline and Pillars letters. Similarities and dissimilarities in emphasis and theological conception found when comparing the two letter collections may actually correspond to the manner by which Acts narrates the negotiations between the reports from different missions, and of the theological convictions and social conventions required by each (e.g., Acts 2:42-47; 9:15-16; 11:1-18; 12:17; 15:1-29; 21:17-26). The relations between

---

[17] But see Steve Walton, *Leadership and Lifestyle: The Portrait of Paul in the Miletus Speech and 1 Thessalonians*, SNTSMS 108 (Cambridge: Cambridge University Press, 2000) who challenges this consensus by noting several allusions to a likely proto-Pauline canon. For a comprehensive listing and analysis of the intertextual echoes of Pauline letters in Acts, see David Wenham, "Acts and the Pauline Corpus," in *The Book of Acts in Its Ancient Literary Setting*, ed. Bruce Winter and A. Clarke (Grand Rapids: Eerdmans, 1993), pp. 215-58.

[18] See Robert W. Wall, "Romans 1:1-15: An Introduction to the Pauline Corpus of the New Testament," in *The New Testament as Canon*, LNTS 76 (Sheffield: JSOT Press, 1992), pp. 142-60.

James and Paul or between Peter and James as depicted at strategic moments on the plotline of Acts are generally collaborative rather than adversarial, and frame the interpreter's approach to their biblical writings as essentially complementary (even though certainly not uniform and sometimes in conflict) in both meaning and function. If the critical consensus for a late first-century date of Acts is accepted, which is roughly contemporaneous with the earliest, pre-canonical stage in the formation of the NT,[19] then it is likely that its collection of portraitures of early Christian leaders provides an important explanatory model for assessing the relationship between (and even within) the two emergent collections of canonical letters: The form and function of these Christian writings and their relationship to each other display another articulation of the early church's "sense" of the more collaborative relationship between their individual people and interpretative traditions, which is reflected then in the Book of Acts. So that, for example, if Peter and John are enjoined as partners in Acts, then we should expect to find their written traditions conjoined in an emergent Christian Bible; and that their intracanonical relations envisages the church's perception of their theological coherence. Likewise, the more difficult although finally collegial relationship between James and Paul as narrated in Acts 15 and (especially) 21 may well envisage their partnership in ecclesial formation in a manner that Protestant interpretation has sometimes subverted.

Because both the narrative world and its central characters are the literary constructions of the story-teller, and are shaped by his theological commitments, the interpreter should not expect a more precise connection between, for example, the kerygma of the Peter of Acts and a Petrine theology envisaged by 1-2 Peter. Nevertheless, there is evidence that Luke did indeed draw upon important traditions common to the Petrine letters when composing his narrative of the person and work of Peter. In particular, 1 Peter's interpretation of Jesus as Isaiah's "Servant of God" (1 Pet 2:21-25; cf. 1:10-12), the evident core of Petrine christology, is anticipated by four references to Jesus as "servant" in Acts (and only there in the NT), the first two in speeches by Peter (Acts 3:13, 26) and the last two in a prayer by the apostles led by him (4:27, 30).[20] Moreover, the God of the Petrine epistles, who is known primarily through Jesus's resurrection (1 Pet 1:3, 21; 3:21; cf. Acts 2:22-36) and as a "faithful Creator" (1 Pet 4:19; cf. Acts 4:24), agrees generally with Luke's traditions of a Petrine kerygma. Even Peter's claim that the central mark of Gentile conversion is a "purity of heart" (Acts 15:9) is strikingly similar to 1 Peter 1:22. Finally, the most robust eschatology found in Acts, famous for its sparseness of eschatological thought, is placed on Peter's lips (Acts 3:20-23), thereby anticipating the keen stress posited on salvation's apocalypse in 1-2 Peter (cf. 2 Pet 3:1-13).[21] A second example may be the far thinner portrait of John in Acts,

---

[19] Trobisch, *First Edition*. But now see the more recent studies of Richard Pervo, *Dating Acts: Between the Evangelists and the Apologists* (Santa Rosa, CA: Polebridge Press, 2006) and Joseph B. Tyson, *Marcion and Luke-Acts: A Defining Struggle* (Columbia: University of South Carolina Press, 2006), who date the earliest version of Acts to the early second century; and W. A. Strange who follows Cadbury and Kirsopp Lake in dating the canonical version of Acts to the late second century. But none of these reconstructions, even if accurate, undermines my essential claim.

[20] Cf. Oscar Cullmann, *Peter: Apostle-Disciple-Martyr. A Historical and Theological Essay* (London: SCM, 1953), pp. 63–9.

[21] See Robert W. Wall, "The Canonical Function of 2 Peter," BibInt 9/1 (2001): 77–9.

who although depicted as Peter's silent partner uses his one speaking role in Acts 4:19-20 to sound a key note of the Johannine epistles: "... for we cannot but speak of what we have seen and heard" (cf. 1 John 1:1-3).[22]

When these thematic connections are rooted in the narrative world of Acts—a world in which these characters have enormous religious authority and purchase for the church's future—the epistolary expression and development of these core themes are underwritten as also important for the church's future and formation. Moreover, the certain impression of kerymatic continuity between the Lord's apostolic successors (Peter/John) and Paul, cultivated by Acts, would seem to commend a more constructive relationship between their writings. Acts performs an interpretive role, not so much to temper the diversity envisaged by the two different collections of letters but to prompt impressions of their rhetorical relationship within the NT. According to Acts, the church that claims its continuity with the first apostles tolerates a rich pluralism even as the apostles do within Luke's narrative world, although not without controversy and confusion.[23]

Acts 15: A Test Case in Canonical Criticism[24]

Although perhaps not the watershed event of Acts that some commentators insist it is, Acts 15 performs a strategic role within the biblical canon. In particular, it plots a unity that is typological of how the biblical interpreter might relate together the NT's

---

[22] See Paul N. Anderson, *The Christology of the Fourth Gospel* (Valley Forge, PA: Trinity Press International, 1996), pp. 274-7, who suggests that at the one point in Acts where Peter and John speak with one voice (4:19-20)—Peter alone speaks when they are teamed elsewhere in this narrative world—the narrator has constituted a saying that combines Petrine (4:19) with Johannine (4:20) traditions. Their pairing in Acts in both work and speech may well envisage an emerging consensus within the ancient church that their traditions, both personal and theological, are complement parts of an integral whole.

[23] Brevard Childs explores some of these same issues in the final book of a brilliant career, *The Church's Guide for Reading Paul: The Canonical Shaping of the Pauline Corpus* (Grand Rapids: Eerdmans, 2008). While grateful that Childs engaged my efforts to develop a "critical methodology when interpreting Acts that is shaped by attention to canonical form and function" (222), his criticism of my interpretation of the relationship between Acts and Luke's gospel and with the Pauline letters in their canonical context is mistaken; his response actually suggests that we are closer than he supposes, which I trust is made clearer by this present essay. For example, he claims that I approach Acts "as Luke's intentional commentary on the Gospel" (233), when what I actually argue is that the canonical Acts provides NT readers with a new (i.e., canonical) context within which the *fourfold* Gospel of the NT canon is thickened and extended—whether in the kerymatic portions of the speeches or more allusively in the Christological shaping of several key episodes in Acts. Earlier Childs claimed that I use Acts "to bind Paul and the Gospels together" (225-6), which he then links with Adolf von Harnack's misguided analysis of the canonization of Acts as a political bid to unify a fractured early church. I actually pay scant attention to this idea in my work and never as an interpretive cue for reading Acts. In fact I take it that the principal role of the biblical Acts is to introduce and frame the two canonical collections of letters that follow—a point surely unintended by its narrator.

[24] This section revises the concluding portion of my "The Jerusalem Council (Acts 15:1-21) in Canonical Context," in *From Biblical Criticism to Biblical Faith: Essays in Honor of Le Martin McDonald*, ed. William H. Brackney and Craig E. Evans (Atlanta: Mercer University Press, 2007), pp. 93-101.

two letter collections. The construction of this interpretive typology depends upon distinguishing more adequately between two narrative pairs that shape the story's plotline in Acts: namely, the two questions that frame the Council's proceedings and its two key witnesses, Peter and James, whose respective testimonies forge a normative definition of purity for the church's mission in the Diaspora.

The pair of questions, the first raised in Antioch (15:1) and the second in Jerusalem (15:5), are typically collapsed as if they are different articulations of the same theological problem regarding the salvation of repentant pagans.[25] Simply on internal grounds this seems unlikely. First, the two questions are in fact stated differently and would appear to frame different responses to Paul's mission in the Diaspora. While both concern the circumcision of repentant pagans, the Antiochene question of 15:1 expressly concerns soteriology, whether circumcision is a necessary condition of salvation. The Jerusalem question of 15:5 concerns ecclesiology, whether circumcision is a necessary condition for Christian fellowship in a congregation whose membership also includes repentant Jews.

The two questions are precisely located in notably different congregations within Acts. Syrian Antioch is the center of the church's liberalizing circumcision-free mission to the nations, while the Jerusalem church under James remains the gatekeeper of the church's Jewish legacy and its mission to the Jews (cf. Acts 21:17-26). The worry of the traditionalists, consistent with the memory of the Maccabean rebellion that asserted circumcision as a national priority (1 Macc 2:46), is the attenuation of the church's Jewish roots—what Craig Hill has called the "gentilizing" of the church, a fear provoked by the successes of Paul's mission but now intensified by the prospect that Jesus's prediction of a mission at "the end of the earth" (1:8) would move the church farther and farther from the Holy City.[26]

But the agitators in Antioch are unauthorized by Jerusalem according to 15:24, and their lack of support casts suspicion on the per se question they provoke. Of course, Luke's opening phrase, οὐ δύνασθε σωθῆναι (Acts 15:1), cues the reader to his earlier uses of the σῴζω word-family in Acts, specifically at the first Jerusalem Council following Cornelius's conversion when their question had already been answered. That is, the agitators are unauthorized precisely because their question has become irrelevant.

Second, there is nothing in Acts that would lead us to believe that the question provoked by the Jerusalem Pharisees is either unauthorized or uncivil. In fact, their question occasions a Council's compromise rather than a congregation's conflict. By the time the deeply Jewish fear registered in Antioch travels down the interstate to Jerusalem the perceived worry about Paul's mission has been moderated—at least from

---

[25] See, e.g., John Painter, *Just James: The Brother of Jesus in History and Tradition*, 2nd ed. (Columbia, SC: University of South Carolina Press, 2004). Painter argues the narrative in Acts is plotted in such a way, especially when glossed by Gal. 2:11-14, that Antioch's conflict becomes Jerusalem's question. As such the issue of full membership in the covenant community is never resolved in Acts whose readers are left with the mediating position of James who does not require circumcision as a covenant marker—a position that Painter does not think historically accurate.

[26] So Craig C. Hill, *Hellenists and Hebrews: Reappraising Division within the Earliest Church* (Minneapolis: Fortress Press, 1992), pp. 103-47.

the perspective of the Jerusalem church, which warmly welcomes Paul and Barnabas (15:4). The question of 15:5, which mentions circumcision but not as a condition of salvation, anticipates a middle ground brokered by James on ecclesiological rather than on soteriological grounds—that is, on *being* a member of the covenant community rather than on *becoming* a member. Indeed, whilst the Antiochene response envisages a conservative overreaction to a perceived gentilizing tendency, Jerusalem Council convenes under the presumption of the earlier verdict hammered out in Acts 11 and is rather more concerned about *halakhah*: how will the Jewish church welcome repentant pagans into its fellowship in the same manner that it welcomed Paul and Barnabas upon their return to Jerusalem.

Toward this end the Acts narrative fashions a dialogue between a second narrative pair: the Peter and the James of Acts. Again, most commentators collapse the two, supposing that James confirms and then extends Peter's witness. But, again, this overlooks evident differences in their testimonies. For example, in response to the question of purity appropriately raised by the Pharisees, the Peter of Acts famously makes Paul's case by defining purity as a matter of the heart cleansed by faith (15:9). The James of Acts responds by alerting the council to what Simeon first related about God's visitation of the nations. While most take "Simeon" as a likely reference and so confirmation of *Simon* Peter's earlier testimony could this "Simeon" rather be a reference to the Jewish prophet whose Nunc Dimittis prophecy in Luke 2:29-32 first heralded the visitation of God's salvation to the nations at the Messiah's birth? If so, then James is not confirming either Barnabas or Paul's testimony, which he does not mention, nor Peter's but rather the fulfillment of Simeon's prophecy of Gentile inclusion.[27]

More significantly, the purity code he insists upon (15:20, 29), which is confirmed by the Spirit, hardly affirms uncritically the "purity of the heart by faith" formula. Almost certainly James thinks Peter's response to the Pharisees' question concedes too much to Antioch's more liberal position. While circumcision is no longer required of repentant pagans, whether for salvation or Christian fellowship, James believes that a code of public practices must be enforced to delineate a covenant community's purity before God in a pagan world. In this regard, the prohibitions against idolatry and sexual immorality, addressed subsequently by Paul in 1 Corinthians, are probably more apropos of the Diaspora mission than is Gentile circumcision. In any case, the point is that Peter's "purity of the heart by faith" is a necessary but insufficient condition of a repentant pagan's identification with the restored Israel scripted by Amos's prophecy. What James seeks is a compromise, not a concession, which will insure a more robust definition of Jewish purity for the future mission to the Gentile converts of the Diaspora. The code of purity practices insists on an embodied faith for all to see beyond Jerusalem.

And, indeed, beyond Jerusalem the Paul of Acts is exemplary of a more Jewish definition of purity (cf. 24:16-21). For example, he is arrested in Philippi for being a Jew

---

[27] Stephen Fowl first alerted me of this possibility in his unpublished paper presented at Princeton Theological Seminary; see also Rainer Riesner, "James' Speech (Acts 15:13-21), Simeon's Hymn (Luke 2:29-32), and Luke's Sources," in *Jesus of Nazareth: Lord and Christ*, ed. Joel B. Green and Max Turner (Grand Rapids: Eerdmans, 1994), pp. 263–78.

(16:20-21) and earlier circumcises Timothy (16:3; cf. Gal 2:3), not only to testify to his personal loyalty to the ancestral religion (cf. 21:23-26) but more critically to symbolize the importance of James's concern to preserve it in consecrated form. Consider, for example, the role Timothy performs in Acts in contrast to Titus in Galatians. Timothy is of mixed parentage, Jewish and Gentile; and in prospect of the Diaspora church, Paul circumcises him in order to preserve his mother's Jewish inheritance.[28] He stands as a symbol of Paul's missiological intent in Acts, which is to found Christian congregations in the diaspora with a mixture of Jewish and Gentile converts but whose faith and practices are deeply rooted in the church's Jewish legacy.

It should be pointed out that the repetition of familiar Pauline themes in the Pillars letter collection, even though perhaps idealized for rhetorical purposes, acquires a thickened meaning when read in light of a prior reading of Acts. The reader will be put on the alert that an increasingly gentilized church, which might seek to build a covenant-keeping community even though opting out of purity practices, must consider the nature of religious observance according to the norms of Jerusalem's canonical heritage. As such their public profession of faith must be embodied in the community's public practices.[29] The full experience of God's righteousness is by performance of works and not by *sola fide*.

There is a sense in which the role a canonical Acts best performs is to explain rather than to temper the very diversity envisaged by the two collections of biblical letters. According to Acts, the church that claims its continuity with the first apostles tolerates a rich pluralism even as the apostles did, not without controversy and confusion. What is achieved at the Jerusalem Council may be more a theological understanding rather than a theological consensus. The divine revelation given to the apostles according to Acts forms a pluralizing monotheism which in turn informs two discrete missions and appropriate proclamations, Jewish *and* Gentile (cf. Gal 2:7-10). Sharply put, Acts supplies the Bible's reader with a narrative that helps to contextualize the instruction of *both* collections of letters, Pauline and Pillars: on the one hand, the Pauline canon reflects the gospel of a Gentile mission while the Pillars collection reflects the gospel of a Jewish mission. However, rather than causing division within the church, such a theological diversity is now perceived as normative and necessary for the work of a God who calls both Jews and gentiles to be the people of God. As a context for theological reflection, Acts forces us to interpret the letters in the light of two guiding principles: first, we should expect to find kerygmatic diversity as we move from Pauline to Catholic letters; and second, we should expect such a diversity to be useful in forming a single people for God. Against a critical hermeneutics which tends to select a "canon within the Canon" from among the various possibilities, the Bible's

---

[28] The Jewish cast of Paul's story in Acts is thematic of my commentary on Acts.

[29] Of course, the Pauline letters would not disagree with this conclusion. I would argue, however, that for the Pauline tradition these social, moral and religious practices, which mark out a people as "Christian," are the natural yield of "being in Christ" and that "being in Christ" is the result of profession that "Jesus is Lord." A Pauline redemptive calculus, whether understood politically or personally, is concentrated by the beliefs of the Pauline gospel rather than by the practices of the Pauline churches. It is this essential difference of logic that fashions—I think from the early church—a different spirituality, which is centered by orthodox confession, than found in the congregations of the CE traditions.

own recommendation is for an interpretive strategy characterized by a mutually illuminating and self-correcting conversation between biblical theologies.

How then does this kind of "catholicity" deepen our understanding of God's people? The canonical approach to Acts (and by analogy to Luke's gospel set now within a fourfold canon) presumes a series of literary relationships that envisage a more complementary than adversarial whole. In this case, the Pauline church, which may be inclined to accommodate itself to the mainstream of the world system in order to more effectively spread the gospel (cf. 1 Cor 9:12b-23), is reminded by the witness of the Jerusalem Pillars that it must take care not to be corrupted by the values and behaviors of the world outside of Christ (cf. Jas 1:27).[30] That is, the synergism affected by the orienting concern suggests that the diverse theologies that make up the whole biblical canon compose a dynamic self-correcting apparatus, which prevents the reader from theological distortion. In fact, the verdict of the James of Acts that a purity of the heart by faith in Christ is a necessary but insufficient condition for maintaining membership within a covenant-keeping community sounds the very cautionary note that illumines the reason the Pillars collection is added to the biblical canon to join a conversation that already includes the Pauline witness. It should not surprise us, then, to note that it is the Diaspora Letter of James that embraces the James of Acts most warmly when stipulating that a pure and undefiled religion is not characterized by professions of an orthodox faith apart from works, but only when faith is publicly embodied in the performance of God's "perfect law of liberty" (Jas 2:14-26).

---

[30] This point is developed more fully in "Toward a Unifying Theology of the Catholic Epistles: A Canonical Approach," in *Catholic Epistles and the Tradition*, ed. Jacques Schlosser, BETL 176 (Leuven: Peeters, 2004), pp. 43–71; it also is a principal interest of a "new perspective on James" introduced in the collection, *The Catholic Epistles and Apostolic Tradition*, ed. K.-W. Niebuhr and Robert W. Wall (Waco: Baylor University Press, 2009).

3

The Unifying Theology of the Catholic Epistles (2003–13)

Introductory notes: This study combines revised excerpts from a decade-long series of three articles. Part one of the present chapter reissues the earliest version of my proposal of the Catholic Epistles (CE) collection's "unifying theology," first as a contribution to the Colloquium Biblicum Lovaniense (2003) and subsequently published in The Catholic Epistles and the Tradition, *ed. Jacques Schlosser, BETL 176 (Leuven: Peeters, 2004). A week after the colloquium in Leuven, I presented this same paper to the SNTS seminar on the Catholic Epistles meeting in Bonn, which was published in slightly revised form in a collection of the seminar's main papers,* The Catholic Epistles and Apostolic Tradition, *ed. K.-W. Niebuhr and R. W. Wall (Waco, TX: Baylor University Press, 2009), pp. 13–41.*

The problem of claiming a "unifying theology" for the Catholic Epistles collection is the evident disparity of every sort among them.[1] In response, this seminar paper proposed a rubric of coherence consisting of a narrative of theological agreements mined from the Letter of James, presuming its placement and priority within the collection, and then applied to the collection's other six letters. Later revisions of my proposal have shifted from that CE-centric rubric introduced by James to employ a more ecumenical, external criterion of theological agreements first proposed by Irenaeus as an apostolic "rule of faith." This criterion of coherence has the advantage of facilitating an intracanonical discourse between the CE collection and all other canonical collections within the Christian two-testament canon, presuming all have this same theological referent.

---

[1] Francis Young extends this problem beyond the CE to include all "non-Pauline letters" in her essay, "The Non-Pauline Letters," *The Cambridge Companion to Biblical Interpretation*, ed. John Barton (Cambridge: Cambridge University Press, 1998), pp. 276–304. The criterion she uses to distinguish "Pauline letters" from "non-Pauline letters" presumes theological coherence is possible only when a minimalist (and arbitrary) criterion is met: criticism's corpus of "genuine letters" written (in some fashion) by the historical Paul in comparison to which all other canonical letters are "non-Pauline." These letters, including Pauline pseudepigrapha, form a second corpus or "non-Pauline letters in which no sense of theological coherence should be presumed. Of course, hers are not the church's canonical collections; they are criticism's collections of canonical letters. But Young's study does stipulate a theological definition of coherence, even if based upon common authorship and theological vision. My understanding of theological coherence stipulates a different interpretive rubric based upon a grammar of theological agreements. By this criterion, both the thirteen-letter Pauline collection as well as the seven-letter Catholic collection are theologically coherent as fixed by the final form of the NT canon.

Part two of this chapter explores more fully the working relationship between "the James of Acts and the Letter of James" in a way that seeks to underwrite the prospect of a so-called Apostolos—*a discrete volume from an early stage of the canonical process consisting of Acts and the CE collection.*[2] *The sequence suggests that the narrative world of Acts introduces and contextualizes the church's ongoing reception of the CE collection.*[3] *This material is excerpted from a second SNTS seminar paper I presented in 2004 at the Barcelona meeting that is also included in* The Catholic Epistles and Apostolic Tradition, *127-51. I am grateful beyond words for the international community of scholars who participated in this SNTS seminar whose suggestions and corrections helped me develop this way of thinking about scripture as a purposefully arranged collection of canonical collections.*

In this regard, part three proposes a way of ordering the implicit "canon-logic" within this discrete canonical collection and so understand better the working relationships between individual CE, which modern criticism typically treats as self-standing compositions. It revises a chapter I contributed to the book co-authored with my colleague, David R. Nienhuis, Reading the Epistles of James, Peter, John & Jude as Scripture *(Grand Rapids: Eerdmans, 2013). This particular chapter (40–69) discusses the final "shape" or theological aesthetic of the CE collection and is paired with Professor Nienhuis's historical work that traces the "shaping" of this same collection. Together these two chapters of our book, one more rhetorical and other more historical, form the methodological and intellectual basis for a canonical approach to a theological reading of the sevenfold CE collection as an interpenetrating whole. Readers will note that this study recalls and revises ideas introduced in the 2003 "Unifying Theology" paper and then in a series of other published works thereafter that seek to elaborate the hermeneutical importance of the sequences and seams within the biblical canon. I take it that the importance of these intracanonical relationships and connections for theological interpretation have been an interest of canonical criticism from its beginning.*

---

[2] I note that Tyndale House's recent edition of the *Greek New Testament*, ed. Dirk Jongkind (Cambridge: Cambridge University Press, 2017), is ordered by tendencies evinced in early manuscripts that "reflect the strong tendency to place the Catholic Epistles immediately after Acts" (p. 512). The editors, however, provide no epistemic or theological reason why a "strong tendency" from this particular moment in the history of manuscripts should order the final arrangement of their version of the Greek New Testament. In effect, this essay trades on that finding as the residue of a canonical process that produced the church's scripture and in doing so produced new working relationships between selected writings that had a track record of effective performances in forming the church's apostolic faith and Christian discipleship. The placement of Acts with the collection of CE is hardly an arbitrary decision but purposeful for realizing the epistemic and theological ends intended by the church for its biblical canon. Did Luke have prior knowledge of the Catholic Epistles or an intuition of a mutually glossing relationship with them in mind when he wrote the Book of Acts? There is no evidence that he did. *If the form or aesthetic of scripture accords with ecclesial (rather than authorial) intent, consideration of these new working relationships—e.g., between Acts and the CE collection—should help regulate the manner in which it is rightly interpreted and used.*

[3] John Painter, *Just James* (Columbia: University South Carolina Press, 1997); see also the collection, *James the Just and Christian Origins*, ed. Bruce Chilton and Craig Evans, NovTSup 98 (Leiden: Brill, 2014).

"The Unifying Theology of the Catholic Epistles" (2003)

This theological chapter proposes an interpretive strategy by which the CE are read together as a collection whose seven books are integral parts of a coherent theological whole. The perceived theological coherence of the CE is at odds with the modern critical assessment that underscores their literary, rhetorical, and theological diversity, and therefore their independence from each other no matter what interpretive strategy is employed. Those who chase down the sources of theological beliefs submit theological definitions retrieved from different points of origin where different authors respond to the spiritual crises of their different recipients who are shaped within different social and religious worlds. On the exegetical landscape of modern biblical criticism, then, the theological diversity found within the catholic corpus has been explained as the byproduct of differing moments/places of origin and their respective trajectories/tradition histories.

Those who treat the CE as literary media do not disagree with this conclusion. Their own explanatory constructions, however, explicate the same theological diversity as the byproduct of different genre, textual structures or rhetorical patterns—regardless of who wrote these texts, for whom, when, or where. In this light, then, the critical consensus is that the CE is no real "collection" at all, but is an arbitrary grouping of literary miscellanea gathered together and arranged during the canonical process at a non-Pauline address, without any thought of their theological coherence or canonical function *as a per se collection*. In fact, the theological incoherence of the CE, and their independence from each other, has become a matter of critical dogma.[4]

The present chapter will incline the angle of approach toward the CE collection differently, thereby admitting into evidence new findings from the "canonical period" when these seven books were formed into a second collection of letters "to provide a broader and more balanced literary representation of the apostolic witness than the letters of Paul furnished by themselves."[5] In doing so, I intend to challenge the critical consensus regarding the theological incoherence of the CE collection; in fact, my thesis is that when this epistolary collection is rendered by the hermeneutics of the canonical process both its theological coherence and its canonical role will be more clearly discerned.

At the center of this study are two related observations about the final redaction of the CE collection that are laden with hermeneutical promise: First, when the CE became a collection, the Letter of James became its frontispiece to introduce the deep logic—or what I call the "grammar"—of the collection's unifying theology and its anticipated role within the biblical canon. Second, when the CE became a collection,

---

[4] I should note in passing how different the status of this question is when compared to the scholar's scruples regarding the Pauline corpus of letters. Biblical theologians typically approach the Pauline collection, even inclusive of its disputed membership, with the presumption of its essential theological unity. Whoever their real authors or implied readers are and no matter in what literary shape they have arrived at our canonical doorstep, the Pauline collection extends the thought of a particular person and the theological conception of each Pauline letter is measured by the theological dispositions of that particular person.

[5] Gamble, "*Status Quaestionis*," in *The Canon Debate*, 288.

it did so with Acts which supplied a narrative context that not only vested the entire collection with religious authority but cued the priority of James within it. At that "canonical moment" when the final redaction of this collection evoked a recognition of its theological wholeness, the one (James as its surprising frontispiece) was made explicable by the other (Acts as its narrative context).

A Canonical Approach to the CE as a Collection

The question is reasonably asked whether interpreters should elevate the importance of the canonizing community's intentions when mining these texts for their theological material, especially when the modern bias is to define the theological goods of a biblical writing by those meanings retrieved from original locations or as envisaged by a composition's rhetorical design and literary genre. I think so. In fact, if the angle of one's approach to the theology of the CE is inclined by the relevant properties of the canonical process, then what should be assumed about these books is in fact their theological coherence as a canonical collection and the importance of their collective role whenever the interpreter seeks to render a fully biblical witness to the word of God. In this portion of the chapter, let me simply catalogue those findings that are suggestive of a unifying theology and role of the CE collection.

1. I begin with the most basic of observations: the final redaction of the CE collection *stabilizes a fluid movement within the bounds of the canonical process*. This may be deduced from Eusebius's initial statements about the CE in *Ecclesiastical History*, by what he did and did not observe about received traditions at the outset of the fourth century. He notes, for example, the widespread acceptance and use of 1 Peter and 1 John in the ancient church—at least as early as Polycarp's use of 1 Peter in the early second century (*HE* 3.14)—but observes that other CE are disputed, mainly because of their lack of widespread use by the Fathers of the church.[6]

The most important data in consideration of this phenomenon are the variety of canon lists preserved from both the East and the West, and the literature generated by the various theological debates and conciliar gatherings in these regions of the church.[7]

---

[6] Eusebius clearly does not think the authority of these "disputed" CE, and especially James, was challenged because of theological error but rather because of their lack of use. It may well be that his observation of their "catholicity" (if *not* canonicity) is a way of underwriting the theological and functional unity of the collection. Moreover, it should be said that the canonical redaction of the CE collection was contested through the Reformation and Luther's famous concerns about James, and the other four letters remain disputed by the Antiochene communion within the Orthodox Church to this day. Before Luther, however, were still others, such as Isho'dad of Merv who in the ninth century considered only James, 1 Peter and 1 John—the three "pillars"—as canonical. He claimed that other CE lacked religious authority because of their literary "style" (by which he surely means their subject matter—apocalyptical, mystical) and their lack of use in the teaching ministry of the ancient church, which is hardly different from Luther's criticisms of James! Only 1 Peter and to a lesser extent 1 John escaped the disputations of ancient Bible scholars.

[7] For a record of these various canon lists see Bruce M. Metzger, *The Canon of the New Testament* (Oxford: Clarendon Press, 1987), pp. 299-300, 305-15. Indices of quotations and allusions are found in many sources as well; but now consider also the variety of data (and relevant indices) included in *The Canon Debate*.

Depending upon one's account of the chronology of the canonical process, these data are retrieved from the second through the fourth century. To these data are added the quotations and allusions of the CE found in early Christian writings—or their stunning silence in some cases—which also spans the canonical stage of scripture's formation.[8] Naturally, the sociology and hermeneutics of the canonical process, by which these data are contextualized and analyzed, could compel a different account of the performance and meaning of these texts than when they were first received by their original readers/auditors. But my principal observation is this: the CE collection did not stabilize until quite late in the canonical process and the various internal changes that took place along its way to canonization, especially the placement of James as its frontispiece and its initial circulation with Acts as the collection's narrative (= biographical) introduction, provides important clues to its theological contribution and continuing role within the biblical canon.

Insofar as the formation of the CE collection occurs within the catholicizing milieu of the canonical process, its final redaction also reflects the general commitments of the canonical process itself. For example, the hermeneutics of the canonical process were not those of conflict but of consolidation, by which common ground rather than irreconcilable differences was sought. The theological perspicuity of every part of the whole was measured by an ecumenical *regula fidei* to insure the unity of the canonical whole by this common theological referent.[9] While critical exegesis of the seven-letter Catholic collection articulates the profound theological diversity across the biblical canon—a diversity that aptly reflects what might be found within the church catholic, ancient and modern—the inclusion of each writing within the "catholic" collection of non-Pauline epistles and this collection's inclusion within the NT assumes a general theological coherence to all other parts of the canonical whole, including the Pauline collection. I suspect this is exactly what Eusebius meant by the rubric "catholic"— *allgemeingültig* rather than *allgemein*—which would then be apropos of any other collection of biblical literature, not just this one.

2. At the same time, the final redaction of the CE collection was the byproduct of an *intentional movement*. That is, its sevenfold shape does not appear to follow a mechanistic pattern of arrangement—for example, according to length,[10] perceived date of composition,[11] or as a matter largely determined by the print technology of a

---

[8] What is clear from even a cursory reading of Eusebius's observations about "the traditional Scriptures" is this functional criterion of biblical authority, whether or not "any church writer made use of (a book's) testimony" (*HE* 3.3). Thus, for example, even though the authority of 2 Peter is rejected by some, Eusebius admits that "many have thought it valuable and have honored it with a place among the other Scriptures."

[9] For the idea that the biblical canon as a whole and each part within are judged as roughly analogous to an ecclesial (and ecumenical) *regula fidei*, see my, "Rule of Faith in Theological Hermeneutics," in *Between Two Horizons: Spanning New Testament Studies and Systematic Theology*, ed. J. Green and M. Turner (Grand Rapids: Eerdmans, 2000), pp. 88–107.

[10] James has 1749 words/247 stichoi; 1 Peter has 1678 words/237 stichoi; 1 John has 2137 words/269 stichoi. Adding 2 John (245 words/32 stichoi) and 3 John (219/31 stichoi) to 1 John and 2 Peter (166 stichoi) to 1 Peter does not alter this arrangement, especially when throwing Jude (71 stichoi) into the mix.

[11] Although dating biblical compositions is tricky business, the early use of both 1 Peter and 1 John would commend an early date of composition, probably sometime during the first century in their

canonical edition in codex format.¹² In fact, I am aware of no scholar who denies that the production of the NT served mostly religious aims, whether epistemic or sacramental. Thus, the different canon lists extant from different regions of the church catholic at the time of the canonical process reflect differing theological judgments made by ecclesial traditions that resulted in different groupings of writings, which were then "ranked" according to their importance when performing a variety of religious tasks (liturgical, educational, missional, etc.). The arrangement of these different collections, and even of individual writings within them, envisages ecclesial value judgments that reference scripture's *canonical* role in forming a community's theological understanding of God, and its practical witness based upon those beliefs.

In this same manner, the emergent NT was edited over time into a final canonical edition by particular arrangement of its discrete collections, set in theologically suggestive relationships with each other, rather than by recognition of the importance of individual writings, one at a time. Individual writings did not circulate as such; rather, during the canonical process individual writings were preserved, edited and then reproduced, circulated, read and then canonized in combination with other individual writings *as canonical collections*.¹³ Indeed, the earliest history of the two epistolary collections would seem to indicate that they were placed side-by-side within the biblical canon to facilitate a constructive ("self-correcting and mutually-informing") conversation between them.¹⁴

3. In my recent study of the formation of the Pauline canon, I argue that the theological conception of the canonical Paul, articulated initially in a nine- or ten-letter corpus, was brought to its completion and "fixed" by the late addition of a small and marginal collection of three so-called "Pastoral Epistles," probably toward the end of the second century. The methodological rubric I use in drafting this idea is "*the aesthetic principle*" by which I mean that the final redaction of the Pauline (and any biblical) collection became "canonical" precisely at the moment the faith community recognized the theological integrity or wholeness of a particular literary "shape"—in this case the final grouping of thirteen Pauline letters inclusive of the Pastoral Epistles. In this sense, the formation of a biblical collection might be studied as a phenomenon of the canonical process, which appears to follow a general pattern by which a fluid body of writings is finally stabilized, completed, and arranged by the addition (or subtraction) of certain writings. Moreover, the recognition of a collection's canonical shape cannot somehow be abstracted from its performance in the formation and practice of Christian faith.¹⁵

---

final form. By the same token, 2 Peter and James are probably later pseudepigraphy—perhaps even concurrent with and intended to complete the CE collection; see Nienhuis, *Not by Paul Alone*.

12 Trobisch, for example, seems to posit a great deal of importance in the production of codices in the "final redaction" of the NT canon. See also Eldon J. Epp, "Issues in the Interrelation of New Testament Textual Criticism and Canon," in *The Canon Debate*, 503–5.

13 Trobisch, *First Edition*, 40–3.

14 For a fuller description of this project, and illustrations of it, see Wall and Lemcio, *NT as Canon*.

15 Robert W. Wall, "The Function of the Pastoral Epistles within the Pauline Canon of the New Testament: A Canonical Approach," in *The Pauline Canon*, ed. S. E. Porter (Leiden: Brill, 2004). I find no compelling objection to David Trobisch's thesis that Paul himself may have placed a collection of his "major" letters into circulation, which were then added to and recognized as "scripture" (if not also as "canonical") shortly after his death by important Pauline tradents; see

By this same principle, then, the final shape of the CE collection, symbolized perhaps by its sevenfold membership (seven = wholeness), may satisfy an implicit aesthetic criterion by which this particular grouping of seven CE is stabilized, completed, and arranged as *canonical* upon the community's recognition and religious experience of its theological wholeness. *There are at least five properties inherent to the canonical redaction of the CE collection that would seem to envisage a motive to meet such a criterion, however implicit:*

James 2:22. Without proposing a theory of the book's composition as pseudepigraphy, I suggest that the eventual canonization of James accords with a theological judgment made about the canonical function of the CE collection as a whole (see below). Unlike the case for 2 Peter, which was added (and perhaps even composed) to extend the theological conception of 1 Peter, James was added to an emergent *collection* much later, probably toward the end of the third century, to help delimit its working relationship with a Pauline collection, which was already a fixed property within an otherwise still fluid biblical canon.

The catholic tendencies of the canonical redaction, by which an aesthetic of theological wholeness is pursued, are reflected by what is arguably the controlling text of the book's famous essay on "faith and works," James 2:22.[16] Read canonically, this verse stipulates that "faith alone" (i.e., professed faith without works)—what had become the somewhat troubling hallmark of the Pauline tradition—cannot stand alone but is rather "brought to completion by the works" (ἐκ τῶν ἔργων ἡ πίστις ἐτελειώθη)—a phrase that both captures the moral inclination of the entire CE collection and sounds a cautionary note that any reductionistic reading of the Pauline corpus may well degenerate into a *sola fideism*.[17]

---

his *Paul's Letter Collection: Tracing the Origins* (Minneapolis: Fortress Press, 1994). Marcion did *not* create a Pauline canon, then, but simply valorized one already in circulation. What is more important than the early fact of a Pauline canon is the church's realization early on that his teaching also supplied biblical warrants to "heretical" teaching, especially for various second century Gnostic movements including the one founded by the teachings of Marcion. Given this internal threat to the church, need for a second collection of letters to bring balance and constraint to the letters of the canonical Paul was readily apparent—perhaps a collection similar in emphasis to the concerns voiced by James to the Paul of Acts according to Acts 21:20-21 (see below). In any case, I take it that Marcion is an important symbol of a canonical process that forms or edits collections of writings as necessary correctives in order to function more effectively analogically to the church's *regula fidei*.

[16] For this argument, see Robert W. Wall, *Community of the Wise: The Letter of James*, NTC (Valley Forge, PA: Trinity Press International, 1997), pp. 148–52. Most of my subsequent comments about the meaning of James are found in expanded form in this book.

[17] Even though, as many contemporary scholars have opined, James 2:14-26 does not carry the same hefty weight for its author that it has during its (esp. Protestant) *Wirkungsgeschichte*, it is probably this one text more than any other—precisely *because* of its "anti-Pauline" correction and not in spite of it—that attracted the canonizing community to it: James 2:14-26 captures well the intent of the canonical process if not then of its authorial motive. Indeed, many understand Pauline tradition (rather than the traditions of a first or second century Judaism which are rarely mentioned in any case) as the book's primary conversation partner. In any case, from a perspective *within* a NT setting, James now responds to what Paul might become or how Pauline traditions might be used if as a canon within the Canon. It is from its profoundly Jewish ethos that canonical James corrects canonical Paul. But to focus attention on 2:22 (rather than 2:21) reminds the reader that the canonical motive is not adversarial but complementary of a closer analogy to the church's *regula fidei*.

2 Peter 3:1-2. At a relatively early and more fluid stage in the formation of the CE collection, 2 Peter was added to 1 Peter in order to complete a Petrine theological conception.[18] Again without proposing a theory of 2 Peter's composition as pseudepigraphy, whether as 2 Jude (as critical orthodoxy would have it) or as 2 Peter (as the canonical redaction would have it), I contend that 2 Peter is added to the CE collection in light of its relationship to 1 Peter (rather than to Jude). The importance of this composition within scripture, then, is as a "second letter" written "that you should remember the words spoken in the past …" (3:1-2) in order to complete a more robust Petrine witness to better form the theological understanding of subsequent generations of believers.[19]

Coherence of the three John epistles and the church's recognition by the fourth century that the three form a discrete unit.[20] The intertextuality of the three Johannine letters is clear from even a cursory reading. My point again is that 2 John and 3 John bring to completion the theological conception introduced by 1 John. Painter's recent commentary is helpful in this regard, not only by reading the three epistles together but then by locating them within the CE collection and by resisting the tendency of reading them either as three bits of a NT Johannine corpus—an exegetical practice as early as Origen—or as a written response to problems created by the Fourth Gospel in a dialectical fashion that decidedly is not prompted by the final form of the NT canon itself.

Jude's addition to the CE collection. Painter's reading strategy agrees with the motive of the canonical redaction that places Jude between, thus separating the three John letters from The Apocalypse. That is, as a canonical metaphor, the inference is that John's letters are to be read together and within context of the CE collection and not as members of a NT Johannine corpus.

It should be noted that the memorable benedictory that concludes Jude (Jude 24-25), which some contend is reason alone for its preservation and canonization, is also a suitable ending to the entire collection, not because of its doxological argot but because of its practical interest in safeguarding those who might "stumble" into false teaching or immoral lifestyle (cf. Jude 4). Significantly, James concludes with a similar exhortation that to rescue believers who "stray from the truth" is to save their "souls from death" (Jas 5:19-20); and, in fact, this orientation to the congregation's internal spiritual welfare will become an organizing thematic of the entire collection. Accordingly, then,

---

[18] See Wall, "2 Peter," 64-81.

[19] I recognize the nature of a pseudepigrapher's motive is an important feature of the critical discussion of the literary genre. My own view is that reducing the discussion of motive to a psychological level, whether in writing pseudepigraphy the author intends (or not) to commit a fraud, is misguided because such a motive is irrelevant to its canonical status. Canonicity is a more *functional* consideration, having mostly to do with the religious utility of a book's performance. The canonical motive, which may also have occasioned its production (rather than more particular historical exigencies) and certainly determined whether to include 2 Peter in the CE collection, has to do with its theologically constructive relationship to 1 Peter—as indicated by 2 Pet 3:1-2.

[20] For this point, see John Painter, *1, 2, and 3 John*, SP (Collegeville, MN: Liturgical Press, 2002), pp. 51–8 whose interpretive strategy is to read the three letters together; also C. Clifton Black, "The First, Second, and Third Letters of John," in *New Interpreter's Bible* 12, ed. Leander E. Keck (Nashville: Abingdon Press, 1998), pp. 365–78, 366.

Jude's benediction, when reconsidered in the context of the final redaction of the CE, is apropos to the collection's motive and role within the biblical canon.

Jude along with James—books named after brothers of the Lord—form the literary brackets of the entire collection, thereby guaranteeing their religious authority and importance for the future of the church catholic. What must be said, however, is that the authority of this collection is due not only to its connection with the Jerusalem pillars, made famous by the Book of Acts, but by its connection to the Holy Family.[21] The importance of this relationship in the sociology of the canonical process has less to do with the hagiography of persons and more to do with the authoritative traditions linked to their names.

Each of these various "properties" of a final redaction evinces historical moves that in some sense "complete" and make more effective (with respect to the church's intentions for its scripture) an earlier form of the collection. At different moments along the way and in different regions of the church catholic, 2 Peter, 2-3 John and Jude are added as constitutive elements of a more theologically robust whole—an historical phenomenon that may reasonably be explained as evidence of the church's recognition of the importance of this second collection of letters within its biblical canon. Such an "aesthetic principle" is similar to that which measures the integrity of other biblical collections as well; in this sense, religious authority is a property of canonical *collections* rather than of individual writings. For example, the authority of 2 Peter is recognized in relationship to 1 Peter or of James in relationship to the CE collection. Or a roughly parallel case is the fourfold Gospel, which Irenaeus said has an inherent integrity much like the "four corners of the earth" and which according to most canon lists of antiquity is placed first within the NT to recommend its formative value, with Matthew's gospel typically given priority among the four as the most relevant continuation of *Tanakh*'s narrative of God's salvation.[22] That is, the theological integrity of the final redaction of a biblical collection, its placement with the NT, or even of an individual composition within the collection "signs" a role apropos to the motives of a biblical canon.

4. The question, "*When did the sevenfold CE collection become scripture?*," appears related to the broad recognition that the Letter of James was necessary in completing the pages of a Peter-John epistolary catalogue.[23] Perhaps the most decisive observation from a canonical perspective, then, is to discern the motive for this late inclusion of James, which may be properly assessed by its placement as—in my words—the

---

[21] Richard Bauckham's study of members of Jesus's family, in particular James and Jude, makes a compelling case for their lasting influence within the Jewish church in Palestine; *Jude and the Relatives of Jesus in the Early Church* (Edinburgh: T&T Clark, 1990). In particular, they sought to preserve the Jewish legacy of the church and in particular the importance of a Jewish way of salvation that elevates the church's moral obligations as conditional of life with God against a "Paulinism" (but not necessarily Paul's idea) that "faith alone" liberated believers not only from sin's consequence but from any moral responsibility to flee from sin. In my mind, the final redaction of the CE, which encloses them by James and Jude, reifies this point within the canon and in self-correcting conversation with the Pauline corpus.

[22] See D. Moody Smith, "When Did the Gospels First Become Scripture?," *JBL* 119 (2000): 3–20.

[23] My exposition presumes only a formal canon. We all recognize that informal "canons with within the Canon" delimit which books have "real" authority by their actual use—or lack of use—by their different readers. For this reason, it might be argued that the "1 Peter-1 John" canon survives to this day, since other CE are typically neglected in worship and instruction.

frontispiece of the collection's final redaction.[24] While the fourfold Gospel and the thirteen-letter Pauline canon were almost certainly fixed by then, and probably Acts had emerged in its two different versions to perform a strategic role within the emergent NT canon,[25] the same cannot be said of the CE collection (or either Hebrews or John's Apocalypse).

That a grouping of non-Pauline letters from the two leading apostolic successors of Jesus, especially when read by the first half of Acts where the story of their triumphant succession from the Lord is narrated, and his two brothers (see above) is formed to add to the biblical canon makes good sense, especially within a community that confesses its identity as a "holy apostolic church" and venerates the memory of the Holy Family. Moreover, according to Acts it is Peter who defends Paul's mission—even using Pauline terms in doing so (Acts 15:6-12)—before the leaders of the Jerusalem church led by James (cf. Acts 15:13-29; 21:19-26). It would seem reasonable, then, that the canonical process would delimit an epistolary collection to reflect their close working relationship, especially within a community in which the legacy of Paul had evidently triumphed and within the canonical process, then, for which the relevant question had become what literature should be read alongside of Paul to enable the church to hear Paul's word more precisely to prevent its distortion. And the Book of James had become the critical means to that end; but why?

Given the importance of James whose résumé includes founding and pastoring of the Jerusalem church, the brother of Jesus, and an important leadership role in the missions of both Paul and Peter (cf. Gal 2:1-15; Acts 15:4-29; 21:17-25), the addition of a book in his name to the CE collection makes good sense.[26] This very logic is evinced by Eusebius who recalls the narrative of Hegesippus (*HE* 2.23.3-18) regarding the martyrdom of "James the Just (or 'Righteous One')" as testimony to his courageous fidelity and Jewish piety and as the apparent reason why his "disputed" book should be included in the so-called "catholic" collection (*HE* 2.23.25). While the connection between these traditions about the Jewish piety of James and his "catholic" letter

---

[24] This is a principal thematic developed in my unpublished seminar paper on "Acts and James," presented at the 2002 Durham meeting of the SNTS, although my interest is largely rhetorical (the role of a "frontispiece" within a canonical collection) rather than historical. Without doubt the Fathers from Eusebius forward vested theological value in the proper ordering of the letters.

[25] I find, however, no hard evident to prove Bruce M. Metzger's unsubstantiated assertion that "the Acts of the Apostles was added chiefly to prove Paul's apostolic character and to vindicate the right of his Epistles to stand alongside the Gospels"; *The Canon of the New Testament*, 257–8. This more likely is an anachronistic construction of modern Protestant scholars to support a variety of claims about the canonical Paul, his Gentile mission and his message. In any case, if this were true such a move will be grounded on a misreading of the Book of Acts.

[26] In this regard, we should note the debates over the apostolicity of James and his "biological" relationship to Jesus, given the church's belief of Mary's perpetual virginity; the subtext of both debates was the ongoing authority of the Jacobean legacy within the broader church. In fact, the Book of Acts would seem to legitimize the continuing importance of James on different grounds than his apostolicity or his relationship to Jesus: namely, as the leader of the Jerusalem church. In this regard, I note in the preface to his early commentary "On the Seven Catholic Epistles" (c. 700), Bede the Venerable writes, "Although in the list of the apostles Peter and John are accustomed to be ranked as more important, the Letter of James is placed first among these for the reason that he received the government of the church of Jerusalem, from where the source and beginning of the preaching of the Gospel took place and spread throughout the entire world" (trans. David Hurst, O.S.B., CSS 82 Kalamazoo, MI: Cistercian Publications, 1985), p. 3.

appears to underwrite the authority of his "disputed" letter, my suspicion is that the "canonical" portrait of James found in the Book of Acts (rather than those found in other non-canonical Jewish and Gnostic writings) is more decisive for understanding the origins and ultimate canonization of the letter of James.[27]

It therefore remains a puzzlement for most scholars, especially given the evident importance of personal traditions about James reflected in canonical Acts, that no second- or third-century canon list mentions a letter from James, nor does any Christian writer quote from or clearly allude to it.[28] While Origen is the first to mention the letter (*ComMatt.* 19.61),[29] neither he nor then Eusebius seems familiar with its teaching; and Athanasius is the first to list it a generation later as "canonical" in his famous Easter letter of 367 CE, a verdict then confirmed by the Councils of Rome (382) and Carthage (397). Moreover, traditions about the legacy of James are pivotal to several writings outside the mainstream (Jewish Christian, Gnostic), in which he is depicted as the pious pastor of the Jewish church and key strategist of the church's universal mission, in particular as the sometimes opponent of Paul's law-free mission to the nations. These same writings, however, do not refer to a letter, nor does their portrait of James explain the thematics found in the letter of James.[30]

Most explain this silence of an epistolary James by the sociology of a mainstream church where the negative response to the anti-Pauline bashing by the second-century

---

[27] Note for example the close linguistic and conceptual relationship between Acts 15:13-29; 21:17-26 and the letter of James. I should mention that the addition of the dominical "do unto others" saying to the all-important 15:20, 29 (but strangely not to 21:25) in Codex Bezae may well intend to draw linguistically the close connection between the teaching of Jesus and of James to underwrite his religious authority for the future of the church. This is an important datum as the motive of this second version of Acts is primarily canonical as I have suggested in "Acts," *New Interpreter's Bible*, 17–18.

[28] Some scholars continue to argue that Clement of Alexandria who wrote an interlinear commentary on 1 Peter and 1 John (*Adumbrations*) and included James in this work as well. Since his commentary survives only in a much later and highly edited Latin "translation" from Cassiodorus, the inclusion of James may reasonably be doubted given the silence of a "Letter of James" from this same period and region. The first important interpreter of the CE as a collection, including James, appears to be Didymus from the mid-fourth century, who is noteworthy as a pioneer of the "commentary" genre. It should be noted that Augustine mentions in passing a commentary on James (*Ret.* 58) but unfortunately we no longer possess a copy of it. In any case, the authority and importance of a *letter* of James is almost certainly a fourth century phenomenon.

[29] Origen claims that James is "scripture" but evidently this is not then to claim that James is also "canon." Recently, several scholars have demonstrated the differences between the two from both historical and systematic perspectives.

[30] Esp. the Pseudo-Clementines, Gospel of the Hebrews, Gospel of Thomas, Apocryphon of James and the two Apocalypses of James, Eusebius's recollection of Hegesippus in *Historia Ecclesiastica*, Clement of Alexandria's *Hypotyposes* portray his personal piety, his reception of special revelation from God, his political importance in Jerusalem, and his martyrdom; however, whether or not fictitious, these personal characteristics do not carry over directly to the letter of James whose thematics are more "practical" and its Jewish ethos and beliefs are not cast in overtly personal terms. I do find the repeated references to a priestly James—as the Aaron to Jesus's Moses—fascinating, given the letter's emphasis on purity; cf. Scot McKnight, "A Parting within the Way: Jesus and James on Israel and Purity," in *James the Just and Christian Origins*, ed. Bruce Chilton and Craig A. Evans (Leiden: Brill, 1999), pp. 83–129. In this same collection, Chilton offers the suggestive hypothesis that the practice of Nazirite vow-keeping within primitive Christianity "has been underestimated, and that James' deep influence is perhaps best measured by the extent to which other prominent (Christian) teachers fell in with his program (of Nazirite purity); 252.

tradents of James and to their more "conservative" Jewish convictions and practices (and in some cases heretical inclinations) led to the letter's suppression. Only later is this letter from James reclaimed, perhaps in edited form, and put back into circulation as suitable reading for the mainstream apostolic church. Yet the same could be said of the Pauline canon, which was also used by marginal and even heretical movements within the church but which was already fixed by the end of the second century. The suppression of a letter from James also fails to explain why a similar silence is found among more marginal Jewish and Gnostic writings of the second century for whom the legacy of James was valorized.[31] Again, the present paper offers no alternative theory of the origins and transmission of James in earliest Christianity; my thesis about the performance of James as the frontispiece of a canonical collection of CE does not depend upon a particular theory of its production.[32]

5. If we can assume that the "canonical" redaction of the CE as an epistolary collection occurred in the fourth century when a thirteen-letter Pauline canon was already in wide circulation and use, then its primary motive would likely have been to forge a more viable reading of the extant Pauline canon to which this non-Pauline letter corpus was now added. In this sense, any new reading of the Pauline corpus would have been regulated by the teaching of the CE collection, thereby promising to prevent a distorted reading of the Pauline gospel within the church. Given the history of heretical currents emanating from Pauline traditions in the early church, one should not be surprised that a substantial Pauline criticism, an important hallmark of the James tradition within the early church (e.g., the Pseudo-Clementines, Gospel of the

---

[31] I have argued, with others, that the Ebionites followed such a "canon," which included Jesus traditions found in Matthew's gospel; in *NT as Canon*, 250-71. A more precise articulation of this same point would have distinguished between the legacy of James the Christian leader and the *Letter of James*. In absence of a quotation or clear allusion to a textual tradition—a "Letter of James"—in their writings, one must assume that these various Jewish Christian groups were tradents of a Jacobean legacy rather than students of a Jacobean Letter, even though the legacy is doubtless the principal source of the letter.

[32] Most modern constructions of the authorship of James fail to distinguish a theory of composition from its canonization in any case. But to argue that James is second century pseudepigraphy simply avoids the vexing silence of this letter into the third century, even among those groups who remembered James as the church's exemplary apostle. Given its apparent Palestinian sources, which seem to reflect a first century *Sitz im Leben* and its literary genre as a diaspora letter from the same period, if James is pseudepigraphy, its motive must include the preservation of the memory of James even if to underwrite its important role in the final redaction of the NT. These issues have recently been reconsidered in a highly suggestive essay by Matthias Konradt in which he offers a tradition historical theory of the composition; "Der Jakobusbrief als Brief des Jakobus," in *Der Jakobusbrief. Beiträge zur Aufwertung der "strohernen Epistel,"* ed. Petra von Gemünden, Matthias Konradt, and Gerd Theißen (Münster: Lit. verlag, 2003), 16–53. His study compares the use of traditions James holds in common with 1 Peter, which form a discrete trajectory of earlier Pauline and Jesus traditions. His reconstruction of the "Antioch incident" in Galatians 2 (rather than Acts 15, which would have greater purchase for a canonical construction than Gal 2) leads him to conjecture that the provenance of James is Antioch in which the pseudepigrapher edits the James legacy to produce a revised version of Christian existence for a congregation in which trials occasion a spiritual (rather than sociological) testing of the internal quality of its life with God. In a sense, the different handling of common traditions about Christian existence reflect the different legacies of a missionary Peter (hence greater concern with the church's relations with pagan surrounding) and a pastor James (hence greater concern with believers' relations with other believers), which are already reflected in the Book of Acts. Konradt's study, among its other accomplishments, links together James and 1 Peter that may well have "canonical" implications of the sort I am trying to cash out in this chapter.

Hebrews), is largely retained in the letter of James, especially (but not exclusively) in 1:22–2:26. Moreover, the Jewish roots of these traditions are hardly obscured in the letter.[33] The viability of such an intracanonical conversation between Pauline and Catholic, then, would not rest on the prospect of conceptual harmony but on a mutual criticism that does not subvert the purchase of the Pauline canon but rather insures that its use by the church coheres to its own *regula fidei*.[34]

By the same token, the internal calculus of the catholic collection, consisting early on of letters from Peter and John which when viewed through the lens of Acts merely supplemented (rather than corrected) the extant Pauline canon, now is transformed by the inclusion of James: the Peter-John grouping is recalibrated as a more functional Pauline criticism. The relations between the "Pillars" and Paul recalled from Galatians 2:1-15, and hinted at elsewhere in his letters and also in Acts, are transferred differently to gauge the relations between the two epistolary corpora that are regulated by the canonical motives of the catholicizing church and by the theological grammar of the *regula fidei*—as textual representatives of partners engaged in a self-correcting and mutually informing conversation. The first element of a unifying theology of the CE is thus conceived in more functional terms. The reception of James cues the church's critical concern about a reductionistic use of Pauline tradition that edits out the church's Jewish legacy, especially an ethos that resists any attempt to divorce a profession of orthodox beliefs from an active obedience to God's law in a pattern of salvation (see below).[35]

6. David Trobisch's observation that the Book of Acts played a strategic hermeneutical role in the canonical process is certainly correct.[36] But the application of a reading of Acts as an "early catholic" narrative, written to moderate the conflict between Paul and the "Jerusalem Pillars" articulated in Galatians 2:1-15, to the canon project is mistaken

---

[33] The Jewish background of James has been constructed by modern criticism; however, this background has more to do with maintaining a distinctively Jewish "ethos" than with the ongoing performance of particular elements of a Judaic religion, whether from the Second Temple or the Diaspora. In this sense, James's rejection of supersessionism is neither formalistic nor legalistic but adheres in a principled way to a Jewish way of life—a way of life that James contends is threatened in part by certain tendencies of the Pauline tradition. I would add that the addition of the catholic collection to the NT canon serves this "canonical" function of delineating the boundary between Christianity and Judaism, not by doing so sharply but rather by underwriting the continuity between them.

[34] Ironically, Luther's negative appraisal of James—that it fails a Pauline test of orthodoxy—illustrates this same methodological interest in reading James and Paul together; yet Luther fails to engage the two according to the hermeneutics of the canonical process. To do so would have led him to recognize that the CE collection as a whole might actually render a Pauline "justification by faith" gospel more faithful to the church's *regula fidei* and for the very reasons he rejected James!

[35] My formulation of the relationship between the Pauline and Catholic witnesses draws on an insight of James A. Sanders who long ago commented that the Pauline witness concentrates upon the "mythos"—or unifying narrative—of God's salvation as articulated/promised in the Torah and fully articulated/fulfilled in Christ; cf. James A. Sanders, "Torah and Paul," in *God's Christ and His People: Studies in Honour of Niles Alstrup Dahl*, ed. Jacob Jervel and Wayne A. Meeks (Oslo: Universitetsforlaget, n.d.). In my opinion, it is the *ethos* of the Torah—obedience as loving response to God's saving mercies—that the CE collection concentrates upon. The result of reading *both* corpora together, then, is a fuller presentation of God's gospel. See Wall and Lemcio, *NT as Canon*, 232–43.

[36] Trobisch, *First Edition*, 80–5.

in my view. I remain unconvinced that Acts is "early catholic" in either its theological or sociological sensibility; but my primary concern is that this perspective undermines the special relationship between Acts and the CE collection evinced during the fourth century when they circulated together and appear together in the canon lists. Moreover, such a harmonistic reading of Acts fails to recognize the substantial role the James of Acts plays within the narrative world of Acts in moving the plotline of Paul's mission to the nations. In fact, my growing conviction is that the Acts narrative (rather than Galatians 2) best explains the importance of a final redaction of the CE collection that posits the Letter of James as its frontispiece and therefore as central for its theological definition and canonical responsibility—especially if Acts and James arrived together at this same canonical moment.

For this reason, the relevant question for my project is not the historian's, "Is the letter of James a letter from James?", but rather is, "What does the James of Acts have to do with the letter of James?" My suspicion is that the portrait of James in Acts not only underwrites the authority of a letter of James but gives reason why it should function as frontispiece to a second corpus of letters when read as elements of a "self-correcting and mutually-informing" conversation within the biblical canon.

The Role of Acts in the Final Redaction of the CE Collection

The Acts of the Apostles narrates a story whose central characters are the same authors (e.g., Peter, Paul, James) and audiences/sources (e.g., Jerusalem, Timothy, Corinth, Ephesus, Rome) referenced or alluded to in the subsequent NT letters.[37] NT readers naturally make associations between these common elements, noting as well a common concern for important topics of Christian existence (e.g., sharing goods, purity, suffering, the performance of the word of God, congregational unity). Literary intertexts of this sort suggest a logical relationship as members of the same conceptual universe; from a perspective within the NT, Acts supplies the "authorized" narrative behind its most important epistolary texts.

Considered from this angle of vision, then, the critical orthodoxy of reading only the Pauline collection (Knox, Goodspeed, Bruce, A. Delatte, and many others) by Acts seems misplaced—even though the rehabilitation of Acts (perhaps even in a "new and improved" version) during the second half of the second century and then a renewed interest in Acts criticism during the second half of the twentieth century may well have been prompted by the evidently strategic relationship between the Paul of Acts and certain Pauline letters (e.g., Romans, Ephesians, Galatians).[38] During the canonical

---

[37] While the logical relationship between Acts and the NT letters is reflected by the canonical process (see below), the narrator's own claim (Acts 1:1) is that Acts is better related to the preceding gospel probably for christological rather than literary reasons.

[38] As an exercise in a recent "Acts" class, I had my students reflect upon the importance of studying a particular Pauline text (e.g., Ephesians, 2 Timothy) in light of their prior study of related pericopae in Acts (e.g., Acts 18:24–19:41, Acts 20:17-38). The purpose of their project was more than identifying common Pauline traditions; it was to explore the meanings of a Pauline text that were brought to clearer light by its intracanonical relationship with Acts.

process, Acts came to supply a narrative introduction for the entire epistolary canon, Pauline *and* Catholic; in fact, from a canonical perspective, the relationship between Acts and CE is elevated in importance because they "came into life" together during the canonical process. In any case, the interpreter approaches the NT letters with the orienting concerns of Acts in mind, and in light of its story more wakeful when negotiating between the NT's two different epistolary corpora as theological complements.

Given the reemergence of Acts as a text of strategic importance for underwriting the hermeneutics of the canonical process, I consider it highly likely that its narrative portraits of the church's earliest leaders (i.e., of Peter and John, Paul and James)—drawn as they are from early traditions of their teaching and ministry concurrent to the earliest stage of the canonical process—envisage a particular account of their religious authority,[39] the nature of their ministry (e.g., prophetic, pastoral, missionary), and the subject matter of their kerygmata. This supplied the canonizing community with both an explanatory context and religious warrant why then these NT writings were considered together as formative of Christian theological understanding.[40] I especially think Acts provides the impetus for the circulation (and perhaps even composition) of James which led to the formation of a "pillars" collection.

In particular, the manner by which Acts narrates the personae of Christian leaders and their relations with each other as characters of this authorized story of emergent Christianity frames a particular account of how "intracanonical conversations" between the canonical writings linked to these same leaders might be negotiated. Similarities and dissimilarities in emphasis and theological conception found when comparing the Catholic and Pauline letters may actually correspond to the manner by which Acts narrates the negotiations between the reports from different missions, and of the theological convictions and social conventions required by each (e.g., Acts 2:42-47; 9:15-16; 11:1-18; 12:17; 15:1-29; 21:17-26). The relations between Peter and Paul, Paul and James, James and Peter or even Peter and John as depicted within the narrative world of Acts are generally collaborative rather than adversarial, and frame the interpreter's approach to their biblical writings as essentially complementary (even though certainly not uniform and sometimes in conflict) in both meaning and function. In fact, if the critical consensus for a late first-century date of Acts is accepted, which is roughly contemporaneous with the earliest moment of the canonical process, then it is likely that this collection of portraitures of early Christian leaders provides an important explanatory model for assessing the relationship between (and even within) the two emergent collections of canonical letters: The form and function of these Christian writings and their relationship to each other is another articulation of the

---

[39] For an argument that the church's title for this composition, "Acts of the Apostles," cues its interest in the religious authority of the church's "apostles" (including Paul and James); see "The Acts of the Apostles in the Context of the New Testament Canon," *Biblical Theology Bulletin*, 18 (1988): 15–23.

[40] I am mindful of Heikki Räisänen's probing historicist response to his entitled question, *Neutestamentliche Theologie?* (SB 186, Stuttgart, 2000), which distinguishes more precisely between first and subsequent readers, within faith and academic communities. The canonical approach presumes that biblical theology is a theological rather than historical enterprise, whose aims are determined by the church's (rather than the per se academy's) intentions and so religiously formative more than intellectually informative.

early church's "sense" of the more collaborative relationship between their individual people and interpretative traditions, which is reflected then in the Book of Acts. So that, for example, if Peter and John are enjoined as partners in Acts, then we should expect to find their written traditions conjoined in an emergent Christian Bible; and that their intracanonical relations envisage the church's perception of their theological coherence. Likewise, the more difficult although finally collegial relationship between the James and Paul as narrated in Acts 15 and (especially) 21 may well envisage their partnership in ecclesial formation in a manner that Protestant interpretation has sometimes subverted.

Because both the narrative world and its central characters are the literary constructions of the story-teller, and are shaped by his theological commitments, the interpreter should not expect a more precise connection between, for example, the kerygma of the Peter of Acts and a Petrine theology envisaged by 1-2 Peter. Nevertheless, there is evidence that Luke did indeed draw upon important traditions common to the Petrine letters when composing his narrative of the person and work of Peter. In particular, 1 Peter's interpretation of Jesus as Isaiah's "Servant of God" (1 Pet 2:21-25; cf. 1:10-12), the evident core of Petrine christology, is anticipated by four references to Jesus as "servant" in Acts (and only there in the NT), the first two in speeches by Peter (Acts (3:13, 26) and the last two in a prayer by the apostles led by him (4:27, 30).[41] Moreover, the God of the Petrine epistles, who is known primarily through Jesus's resurrection (1 Pet 1:3, 21; 3:21; cf. Acts 2:22-36) and as a "faithful Creator" (1 Pet 4:19; cf. Acts 4:24), agrees generally with Luke's traditions of a Petrine kerygma. Even Peter's claim that the central mark of Gentile conversion is a "purity of heart" (Acts 15:9) is strikingly similar to 1 Peter 1:22. Finally, the most robust eschatology found in Acts, famous for its sparseness of eschatological thought, is placed on Peter's lips (Acts 3:20-23), thereby anticipating the keen stress posited on salvation's apocalypse in 1-2 Peter (cf. 2 Pet 3:1-13).[42] A second example may be the far thinner portrait of John in Acts, who although depicted as Peter's silent partner uses his one speaking role in Acts 4:19-20 to sound a key note of the Johannine epistles: "... for we cannot but speak of what we have seen and heard" (cf. 1 John 1:1-3).[43]

When these thematic connections are rooted in the narrative world of Acts—a world in which these characters have enormous religious authority for the church's future—the epistolary expression and development of these core themes is underwritten as also important for the church's future and formation. Moreover, the certain impression of kerygmatic continuity between the Lord's apostolic successors (Peter/John) and Paul, cultivated by Acts, would seem to commend a more constructive relationship between their writings. Acts performs an interpretive role, not so much to temper

---

[41] Cf. Cullmann, *Peter: Apostle-Disciple-Martyr*, 63–9.
[42] See Wall, "2 Peter," 77–9.
[43] See Anderson, *The Christology of the Fourth Gospel*, 274–7, who suggests that at the one point in Acts where Peter and John speak with one voice (4:19-20)—Peter alone speaks when they are teamed elsewhere in this narrative world—the narrator has constituted a saying that combines Petrine (4:19) with Johannine (4:20) traditions. Their pairing in Acts in both work and speech may well envisage an emerging consensus within the ancient church that their traditions, both personal and theological, are complement parts of an integral whole.

the diversity envisaged by the two different collections of letters but to prompt impressions of their rhetorical relationship within the NT. According to Acts, the church that claims its continuity with the first apostles tolerates a rich pluralism even as the apostles do within Luke's narrative world, although not without controversy. What is achieved at the pivotal Jerusalem Council (Acts 15) is confirmation of a kind of theological understanding rather than a more political theological consensus. The divine revelation given to the apostles according to Acts forms a "pluralizing monotheism" (= James A. Sanders) which in turn contextualizes Paul's idiom of two discrete missions and appropriate proclamations, Jewish and Gentile, in Galatians 2:7-10. The variety of theological controversies Paul responds to in his letters, with whatever rhetoric he employs in doing so, is roughly analogous to the "Cornelius problem" in Acts.

Of course, Acts portrays Peter (rather than Paul) as first initiating and then explaining the admission of uncircumcised (= unclean) Gentiles into the church; and the Peter of Acts finally defends Paul's mission and its spiritual results in a speech that is remarkably Pauline in theological sensibility (15:7-11)—perhaps reflective of Luke's familiarity with and perceived unity of the Petrine and Pauline traditions used in Pauline/Petrine letters, as many modern interpreters have noted.[44] More remarkably, however, the question of whether or not to "Judaize" repentant Gentiles is settled *before* Paul comes back into the narrative to begin his mission to the nations in Acts 11:1-18. In fact, Peter's second rehearsal of Cornelius's repentance at this "second" Jerusalem Council responds to a different problem altogether, posed by the church's Pharisaic contingent that is concerned (as evidently is James) about a normative *halakhah* for mixed Christian congregations (15:4-5). Peter's response concentrates—presumably agreeing with Paul's initial proclamation (cf. 13:38-39)—on an internal "purity of the heart" (15:9).

James, however, expands this Pharisaic concern for religious purity to include socio-religious *practices* (15:20); in fact, his *halakhah* reflects the more "traditional" worry of Jewish religion regarding syncretism—the "gentilizing" of repentant Israel (15:20; see also 21:17-26)—and in particular the possible attenuation of the church's Jewish legacy in the Diaspora as Paul's mission to the nations takes the word of God farther from Jerusalem, the epicenter of the sacred universe (15:21). It is in response to James's Jewish concerns that the narrative of Paul's mission to the nations is shaped in Acts; and, therefore, he provokes and responds to a different set of theological controversies than does the epistolary Paul who responds to internal opponents who want "to judaize" repentant Gentiles. According to Acts, this issue is settled by Peter at the earlier Jerusalem council (11:1-18), and even though this issue resurfaces in Antioch (15:1-2) those who raise the question again are summarily dismissed by James as "unauthorized" teachers who do not represent the position of the Judean church (so 15:24). In fact, the *entire* narrative of Paul's European mission in Acts (Philippian, Thessalonian-Athenian, Corinthian, Ephesian) is simply not shaped by the same

---

[44] Although I think this critical conclusion is typically overstated, since there are fundamental differences between scripture's Petrine witness and the Pauline kerygma.

theological controversies that Paul stakes out in his letters as provoked by his Gentile mission.

In general, the Paul of Acts is exemplary of a more Jewish definition of purity (cf. 24:16-21). Thus, he is arrested in Philippi for being a Jew (16:20-21) and earlier circumcises Timothy (16:3; cf. Gal 2:3), not only to testify to his personal loyalty to the ancestral religion (cf. 21:23-26) but more critically to symbolize the importance of James's concern to preserve it in consecrated form. Consider, for example, the role Timothy performs in Acts in contrast to Titus in Galatians. Timothy is of mixed parentage, Jewish and Gentile; in prospect of the Diaspora church, Paul circumcises him in order to preserve his mother's Jewish inheritance.[45] He stands as a symbol of Paul's missiological intent in Acts, which is to found Christian congregations in the Diaspora with a mixture of Jewish and Gentile converts but whose faith and practices are deeply rooted in the church's Jewish legacy.

From this canonical perspective, then, it may well be argued that a principal concern of the *second* collection of epistles is to bring balance to a *Tendenz* toward religious syncretism by which the pressures of the surrounding pagan culture may distort if not then subvert the church's substantially Jewish theological and cultural legacy. The repetition of familiar Pauline themes in the CE, then to problematize them, acquires a thickened meaning when read in context of the antecedent Acts narrative: that is, a prior reading of Acts alerts the reader of CE that an increasingly Gentile church (= Pauline) must consider its religious and public purity as God's people according to the redemptive calculus of their Jewish canonical heritage (scriptures, practices, prophetic exemplars, etc.). As such a Christian congregation's profession of faith must be embodied in its public and internal practices in keeping with the ethos of its Jewish legacy.[46] The full experience of God's righteousness is by performance of works pleasing to God and neighbor, and not merely by *sola fide*—no matter how orthodox or sincerely confessed.

II. "The James of Acts and the Letter of James" (2004)

I have argued that within the bounds of the NT, Acts provides a canonical narrative that contextualizes the church's reading of the apostolic letters than follow. In particular, the characterization of James in Acts orients the interpretation of the Letter of James as scripture. The functional priority of James within CE, raised already by the Bede in the preface to his commentary on the CE, may well be a canonical reflection of the

---

[45] The Jewish cast of Paul's story in Acts is a principal exegetical interest of my commentary on Acts; see 213-15 for an introduction to this narrative thematic.

[46] Of course, the Pauline letters would not disagree with this conclusion. I would argue, however, that for the Pauline tradition these social, moral and religious practices, which mark out a people as "Christian," are the natural yield of "being in Christ" and that "being in Christ" is the result of profession that "Jesus is Lord." A Pauline redemptive calculus, whether understood politically or personally, is concentrated by the beliefs of the Pauline gospel rather than by the practices of the Pauline churches. It is this essential difference of logic that fashions—I think from the early church—a different spirituality, which is centered by orthodox confession, than found in the congregations of the CE traditions.

important role performed by James at the "second" (15:4-21) and "third" (21:18-25) Jerusalem synods narrated in Acts. Perhaps Paul already recognized the importance of James for the church's future in his somewhat ironical ranking of the reputed "pillars" of the Jewish church[47] in which James is placed before Peter and John (Gal 2:9).[48] In any case, this privileging of James in the NT canon—at least according to Acts—is not based upon the principle of apostolic succession or even upon his per se religious authority, which by either criterion would have privileged the Petrine or Johannine epistles. Even the familial relationship between James and Jesus, which later church leaders appealed to in explaining the canonicity of the letters from James and Jude, is given no currency whatsoever in the NT itself. *From a canonical perspective, however, the importance of the Letter of James is clarified by the James of Acts who articulates the central theological crisis facing emergent Christianity at the end of the first century: namely, the loss of the church's Jewish legacy as the church's mission moves farther away from Jerusalem, the epicenter of God's sacred universe, toward pagan Rome, and becomes increasingly "uncircumcised" in constituency.*

The sheer distance between the church's spiritual resources, including the apostolic memories of Jesus preserved within the Jewish church, and the missiological frontier in places such as Philippi where the "house of prayer" exists outside of city limits or in other Roman cities where the synagogue is evidently a marginal institution within Acts' narrative world (e.g. Athens, Ephesus) or Malta where there is no Jewish presence, depicts the lack of Jewish presence but threatens to paganize the church. James reflects Jewish theology in its call for Torah observance and concern for social purity; that is, a Pauline concern for a purity of the believer's repentant heart (Acts 15:9) must then be embodied in the social practices of the entire faith community (Acts 15:20; Jas 1:27).

The portrait of the canonical James in Acts. Later traditions of various leaders within earliest Christianity are received in Acts to underwrite the religious authority of the implied authors of those letters that follow in the NT canon, and so also of their particular account of God's word.[49] In this regard, James is portrayed as the respected leader of the Jerusalem church. Unlike Peter, Paul and other leaders whose religious authority is predicated by their missionary vocation as prophets-like-Jesus, the religious authority of James is tied to his pastoral vocation and tasks (midrashist, strategist, power-broker, letter writer, pastor) within the church. This more ecclesial contour of his authority, placed within the repentant Jewish community, is reflected by the Letter of James whose tone and interests are more Jewish and pastoral—that is, its instruction

---

[47] Cf. Roger Aus, "Three Pillars and Three Patriarchs: A Proposal Concerning Gal 2:9," *ZNW* 70 (1979): 252-61.

[48] Writing a generation before Acts for readers struggling with a different theological concern, Paul's principal concern is with the "Judaizing" of his Gentile mission whose authorization is from the risen Christ rather than from the Jerusalem "pillars" (Gal 1:11-15; 2:3-5) and confirmed by God's effective power (Gal 2:6-8)—a spiritual reality that these same "pillars" evidently (but not surprisingly) have found difficult to embrace fully (Gal 2:11-14).

[49] Of course, the unwritten assumption about this James is that he is the Lord's brother and this relationship underwrites his authority in Jerusalem (see 1 Cor. 15:7). As is well known, Acts does not refer to any second generation leader of the church (e.g., James, Paul) as an "apostle;" this office is reserved only for the Twelve to whom Luke gives "special" authority in his preface to Acts (1:1-26; cf. Luke 22:28-30).

is concerned with the relational and religious well-being of a particular congregation of believers in accordance with the Jewish scriptures. Thus, Matthias Konradt argues that the different applications of common traditions in James and 1 Peter may be explained by the different profiles of James and Peter found in Acts: whereas Peter is a missionary and more interested in the reception of the gospel truth (and faith community) by pagan outsiders, James is a pastor and more interested in the internal adherence to the gospel imperatives by faithful insiders.[50]

Konradt's important traditional critical conclusion is slightly adjusted when viewed from a "canonical" angle of vision: these precious stories of James (and other leaders) in Acts contextualize a reading of their epistles that conform to these different vocations/conceptions of authority introduced by Acts. Within this canonical context, framed by their prior reading of Acts, the "implied" readers of the NT (= the faith community) are predisposed to approach the Letter of James as scripture proffering priestly advice about how they should resist their impure affections that may subvert their life together and rather pursue a way of divine wisdom. These same NT readers approach the Petrine epistles as instructive about how purified believers should live courageously in contretemps to the surrounding pagan (and hostile) society. And so forth.

The second and more important element of this intracanonical relationship between Acts and James is *thematic*. The theological interest of the James of Acts in purity suggests that his principal concern is not with the "Judaizing" of Gentile believers (as found earlier in the Pauline letters) but with the "gentilizing" of the church's Jewish legacy, which he evidently thinks threatened by the church's (= Paul's) mission to the nations. Indeed, rather than oppose the church's mission or seek to subvert God's redemptive purpose, the repentant Pharisees who raise the salient issue of table fellowship between *believers* (15:5) for deliberation (15:6) do so without contending that such purity practices are required for salvation (cf. 15:1). While Peter contends in Pauline voice that "purity of the heart" is sufficient, clearly this does not satisfy James.

The theological shaping of James's verdict (15:13-21, 22-29) within this narrative world no doubt reflects the situation of the narrator's own religious location toward the end of the first century/beginning of the second century (and so from the very earliest period of the canonical process). The salient issues at stake concern the right interpretation (and transmission) of Israel's scriptures and the purity of the church's practices (= "resurrection practices") whether they are contaminated by "the pollutions of idols, unchastity, from what is strangled and from blood" (Acts 15:20; cf. 15:29; 21:25)—that is, by the insinuation of pagan religious practices upon the Diaspora synagogues where Moses is taught (Acts 15:21) and Messiah is proclaimed. In his response to James/Jerusalem, the Paul of Acts takes considerable care to identify himself publicly as an observant Jew and to maintain a Jewish way of faith in the congregations he founds in the Diaspora: there is in Acts no parting of the ways, Jewish and Christian. Ironically, he is like James and other Jewish believers in Palestine, "zealous for the law" (Acts 21:20) as a mark of covenant loyalty to Israel's God.

---

[50] Konradt, "Der Jakobusbrief als Brief des Jakobus."

Acts, Paul and the "Pillars" of the Jewish Church. Besides the portrait of James in Acts, the only other relevant NT text that shapes the reader's impressions of the implied author of the Letter of James is Galatians 2:11-18, where Paul describes different responses to James—a so-called "pillar" of the Jewish church (2:9). On the one hand, he speaks of certain missional agreements made with James (2:7-10) but then in famously polemical terms implies that he has certain theological disagreements with those "who came from James" to subvert his ministry in Antioch (2:12). In context of his letter, Paul seems to identify the James tradition with a definition of the "Israel of God" (6:16; cf. 2:15) that posits the "works of the law" over the "faith of Jesus Christ" alone (2:16; cf. 6:12-16). In this case, Torah observance forms a Jewish identity that bears public witness to its covenant with God. While the Reformation may have been incorrect in defining "works of the law" as the "good works of self-achievement," to use Bultmann's famous phrase, or in understanding that in Galatians Paul describes two mutually exclusive kinds of justification, one by faith in Christ alone and the other by good works, surely the Reformation is right to suppose that the plain meaning of Paul's polemic is against the centrality of Torah observance as an identifying mark of Christian community. On this issue, the biblical Paul apparently disagrees with the biblical James.

Given my earlier comments, this conclusion must be qualified: whatever were the circumstances that provoked the famous conflict between the church's Jewish and Gentile missions reported by Paul in Galatians and however this conflict is then skewed by the rhetorical design of Paul's letter to the Galatians, it envisages a different controversy than found within the narrative world of Acts. Perhaps this difference is a simple matter of time: when Paul wrote Galatians, there evidently still was optimism surrounding the church's mission to the Jews (Gal 2:7; cf. Acts 21:21-26). This is no longer the case when Acts is written and the Paul of Acts begins his mission. Now the controversy obtains to Paul's mission to the Jews, whether their religious legacy and social identity will be attenuated (see above). In any case, Paul's ironical reference to his personal relations with the church's "pillars"—"James, Cephas and John" (an index that the ancient church may have used to arrange the CE as scripture)—may well suggest something about the literary relations between the two collections of NT letters, and in particular between Paul and James.

Within a canonical setting and following Acts, then, the cautionary note sounded by James in Acts 15:20-21 (cf. 21:25) regarding the possible attenuation of the Jewish practices (*hallakah*) and social identity of the church has its roots in the Jewish-Gentile tensions of the Antiochene church and perhaps also in widely circulated reports (= Jewish Christian traditions) concerning the Pauline mission to the nations (cf. 21:20-21).[51] The face of these tensions in the Jerusalem church (cf. 15:4-5) seems to have been more abstract and perhaps reflects an anti-Gentile bias that is native to observant Jews as reflected in several of their Second Temple writings. James, a Palestinian Jew, may be worried that Paul, a Diaspora Jew with more liberal attitudes toward all things

---

[51] These same tensions, mentioned directly in both Acts 15:1-2 and Galatians 2:11-14, are in the background of Matthew's gospel and certainly of the *Didache* whose distinctive traditions are possibly of Antiochene origin.

"Gentile," may be unwilling to maintain a more scrupulous separation from "the pollutions of idols" and other defiling activities pertaining to pagan moral and religious conventions (15:20, 29; 21:25). From his perspective, Paul may have been more inclined to accommodate some negotiable aspects of pagan culture into the practices of his congregations (cf. 1 Cor 9:19-23), which some leaders of Judean Christianity evidently feared might result in the disappearance of the church's distinctive Jewish identity.[52]

"Test case": Acts 15 and James 2:14-26. In my commentary on James, I argue that among its various roles within scripture James sounds a cautionary note that the church must become more "Jewish" in order to become more fully "Christian."[53] The same can be said of Acts. The traditional "Jewish" concerns registered by the James of Acts for repentant Gentiles to embody their "purity of heart" in religious practices separated from cultural idols and pagan practices have profound currency is shaping a theology that resists the facile separation of orthodoxy from orthopraxy.[54] Moreover, the role of James as an inspired midrashist for his community exemplifies the importance of Israel's scriptures in resolving the variety of intramural squabbles the emergent church must deal with to maintain its vocation and identity. Perhaps Luke is responding to a nascent Marcionism within his own church, fostered in large part by the failure of the church's mission to Israel and its successes among Gentiles and deepened by the pervasive anti-Semitism of Roman culture. Against a resulting tendency away from scripture as a medium of God's Spirit and from those religious practices that maintain the church's public identity within a pervasively pagan world, the James of Acts both interprets the relevant meaning of scripture for his congregation in practical terms (15:16-21), and then writes that his findings "seemed good to the Holy Spirit" (15:28; cf. 15:19). When James is read with Acts, these same concerns of the James of Acts frame and freight the contribution the Letter of James makes within the NT canon.

As an example of the performance of this interpretive strategy, what follows briefly considers the influence Acts may have—as the canonical narrative behind the text—upon an interpreter of James 2:14-26. It hardly needs noting that the recent history of this text within Protestantism has lifted it from its immediate rhetorical context to perform a role as principal foil to a particular reading of Pauline theology that accords with the terms of the Magisterial Reformation (see Appendix B). Within James, however, this passage is merely illustrative of the principle that God blesses those who are doers of the "royal law" of neighborly love (1:12, 25-27; 2:8-13).

Significantly, the density of purity language used in drafting this congregational principle in James (1:21, 27; 2:9-11), especially when coupled with quotations and loud echoes from Leviticus and other Jewish writings that touch on *halakhic* requirements,[55] resonates with the concern for social purity expressed by the James of Acts (15:20, 29; 21:25). In fact, the regulatory norms of corporate life given in the Book of James are cast in "insider-outsider" terms (e.g., 1:27; 2:2-3) in a way that continues the subtext

---

[52] See in particular the works of P. Esler, A. Cheung, E. P. Sanders for tensions between Palestinian and Diaspora Jews over purity issues.
[53] Wall, *The Letter of James*; cf. Richard Bauckham, *James* (Routledge, 1999), pp. 112–57.
[54] See in particular Stephen E. Fowl and Gregory Jones, *Reading in Communion* (Grand Rapids: Eerdmans, 1991).
[55] Cf. Luke Timothy Johnson, *James*, AB (Doubleday, 1995), pp. 34–46.

of James's *halakhic* midrash in Acts 15:20, supported by clear allusion to the Levitical injunctions regulating Israel's social relations with its unclean neighbors (Lev 17-18).[56] What seems also clear is that religious practices, whether to abstain from pagan conventions (15:20) and embrace a Jewish pattern of worship (15:21), are not viewed by James as a condition of salvation but rather as its social, public expression (cf. 15:19). Consistent, then, with the pattern of conversion found in Acts, being cleansed from sin (cf. 2:38; 3:19) in prospect of eternal life (cf. 13:46) is the experience of those who repent, whether Jew or Gentile; and the community's religious practices (cf. 2:42) mark out its common life as "graced" by God's presence (cf. 2:47; 4:33) as mediated through God's Spirit (cf. 2:38). A repentant response to the "word of God" about Jesus and purity/social practices are not causally related but represent deliberate and distinct properties of the community's religious life together.

Likewise, according to the epistolary James the community's faithful reception of the "word of truth" and "putting away of all filth" (1:21) are discrete, deliberate choices of the repentant "soul" that form a whole witness to the righteousness of God (2:22). In this symbolic world, then, "pure and undefiled religion," uncontaminated by the anti-God world order, is characterized by religious act (1:27; θρησκεία)— caring for the poor and powerless in obedience to God's law (1:27; cf. Acts 2:43-44; 4:32-5; 6:1-8)—while mere professions of faith are judged "vain" (1:26; 2:14-17, 18-20). There is no bifurcation of "heart" religion from the performance of public service, nor is one the logical cause of the other; each is the mutual complement or concrete evidence of the other (2:22, 26). While James has unmistakable eschatological commitments and concerns, so that divine judgment is rendered upon evidence (or lack) of obedience to God's law (2:8-13), his pastoral concern is equally unmistakable: there are impoverished believers who presently are unjustly treated (2:2-7) and lack material goods (2:15; cf. 1:27) whose very existence depends upon the faith community's obedience to God. That is, the social and spiritual well-being of the eschatological community depends upon the performance of those public practices that mark out its faith as the "faith of the Lord Jesus Christ, the Glorious One" (2:1).

While the intertextuality of Acts 15:13-21 and James 2:14-26 is illuminating in several ways, now especially in light of the *Wirkungsgeschichte* of James since Luther, let me draw attention to one conclusion of particular importance. The James of Acts does not underwrite the church's Jewish legacy, whether to abstain from idols (15:20, 29; cf. 21:25) or to maintain Mosaic definitions of purity (21:21-26; cf. 15:21), as a substitute for repentance—which remains in Acts the defining mark of Christian conversion (15:14, 19; cf. 2:38). For him, as for all the other Christian leaders who populate Luke's narrative world, "there is salvation in no one else, for there is no other name (= 'Jesus Christ of Nazareth whom God raised from the dead', 4:10) under heaven given among humankind by which we *must* "be saved" (4:12; ἐν ᾧ δεῖ σωθῆναι ἡμᾶς stipulates the so-called "δεῖ of divine necessity"). For this reason, he says that those who promote a different gospel in Antioch (cf. 15:1) are "without portfolio" (15:24)—they have no

---

[56] Richard Bauckham, "James and the Gentiles (Acts 15:13-21)," in *History, Literature, and Society in the Book of Acts*, ed. Ben Witherington (Cambridge: Cambridge University Press, 1996), pp. 154-84.

authority to do so. Rather, the preservation of this Jewish legacy protects the integrity of Christian mission, Christian fellowship, and the Christian gospel. I rather think this is precisely the relationship the epistolary James also asserts between faith and works in 2:14-26. The performance of works has not displaced the profession of faith as heaven's currency, nor is the "obedience of faith" viewed as the progenitor of the "obedience of works." The profession of an orthodox faith is presumed by James (2:14): he addresses believers, not sinners; communicants, not outsiders. Brought to sharper focus by Acts, James 2:14-26 advocates a variety of Christian existence that is characterized by the interpenetration of faith and works. When the performance of Moses is replaced by mere professions of orthodox faith (1:25-27; 2:2-3; 2:18-20), faith itself remains incomplete (2:22) and in any case is not the faith of the Lord Jesus Christ (2:1). Even though faith is central, "faith alone" without a complement of purity practices is ultimately ineffectual for building Christian community or for preserving Christian witness. If the Book of James introduces the CE to orient its readers to this collection's principal contribution to a fully biblical witness, then I would argue it is this concern for the practices of the faith community that should concentrate a theological reading of the CE as a whole.

III. "The Shape of the CE Collection" (2013)

Since critical orthodoxy assumes that the theological and literary diversity of the CE marks out their material independence from one other, even those rare interpreters who admit to common themes among them (e.g., Lockett, Karen Jobes) do so without any sense of their integral, interpenetrating wholeness. In this chapter I seek to illustrate this wholeness as a quality of the collection's "aesthetic excellence." My contention is that the sequence of compositions within this sevenfold collection is not arbitrary or mechanical; that is, it is not based upon a chronology of their compositions or canonization, nor are they arranged by some quantitative metric such as word count. Their dates of composition are indeterminate; and both 1 Peter and 1 John were received as scripture very early, perhaps already in the first century and long before either 2 Peter or James were recognized and received as scripture. Further, while 2 John was added to 1 John and put into circulation in the second century, 3 John was added to the first two much later. Nor, evidently, is this collection ordered by descending length as was, evidently, the Pauline collection. Finally, readers, ancient and modern, have surmised the sequence is a matter of convenience, simply following the biblical ordering of the Jerusalem Pillars in Gal 2:9, "James, Cephas and John." Even though I find this explanation appealing (and have even appealed to it on occasion), the "pillars" metaphor cannot be applied precisely to a collection that also includes Jude.

In any case, my contention all along is that the seven CE are bound together in a sequence that recommends an ordered reading of them for maximal benefit in forming theological understanding, whether in worship, catechesis, mission, or personal devotions. The precise placement of the individual writings within the sevenfold collection thereby secures a kind of internal "canon-logic" that relates the theological goods retrieved from each letter to the other letters in a way that facilitates their collected use.

The elevated importance I grant to the sequence of writings within a canonical collection does not envisage a linear progression of thought that only looks forward, one CE to the next. Rather a collection's witness to God's word unfolds in a more dynamic way, reading its witness both forward and backward. Not only do successive letters elaborate prior points (reading forward), but the reader will also be prompted by the repetition of these scored points to recall their antecedent iterations in ways that expand their meaning in earlier settings (reading backward).

I have hypothesized a crucial element of the church's decision that a collection of sacred writings was complete and fixed for canonization must have been recognition of the completed collection's aesthetic excellence—that its different parts were now properly placed, working well together when performing the roles given them. The consistency of a particular sequence of CE in both manuscripts and canon lists at the point of canonization in the East secures my point: it suggests the church recognized that each letter, while making its own distinctive contribution, is materially linked to the others in a precise and deliberate way. Themes introduced by James are next picked up by 1 Peter, which is then linked to 2 Peter even as 2 Peter is linked to 1 John, epitomized by 2 John, qualified by 3 John and concluded by Jude, apprehends a collection that is held together like links of a chain! *I commend an interpretive approach to these seven CE, therefore, that approaches the aesthetic of the whole collection as envisaging a working grammar or logic that aids the reader in bringing to full potential the contribution it makes to scripture's witness of God's word.* What follows is a provisional description of the collection's canon-logic.

From Paul to Pillars. In his programmatic study of scripture's Pauline canon, B. Childs contends the church's theological reflection should begin with a Pauline definition of apostleship.[57] His contention is first of all based upon his observation that a collection's apostolicity was an essential category of the early church's recognition of authority, designating the earliest witnesses of Jesus who were appointed to receive and transmit God's word disclosed in him. The apostolic origins of the church's authoritative tradition, then, is an encounter—a "witness"—of Jesus Christ, which was then applied to a variety of settings in a variety of ways, including epistolary.[58]

Childs readily observes the contested nature of Paul's claims to his apostolic office, evident in several of his letters (see Gal 1-2), and rightly argues that Paul's apologetic use of "apostle" intends to secure his calling to proclaim God's word about Jesus to the nations. But Childs makes nothing of this controversy that swirled around Paul's claim, which seems over the nature or phenomenology of his "witness" of Jesus. And yet this is a crucial subtext of the *Acts of the Apostles*, whose canonical performance supplies the narrative setting that frames a reading of the two corpora of letters that follow. Clearly the Paul of Acts, his message and mission, are important to the church's future; and yet, just as clearly, he does not have the résumé required for membership in the church's apostolate (see Acts 1:21-22). Paul's most robust defense of his apostolic

---

[57] Childs, *Reading Paul*, 81–3.
[58] Ibid., 21–2.

appointment, found in Galatians, is against those within the earliest community who apparently argued that his is a pseudo-apostleship, derived secondhand from the Jerusalem Pillars who schooled him in the gospel since they knew the historical Jesus and Paul did not (cf. Gal 1:1, 16b-24). He grounds his street cred in revelation (Gal 1:11-12) and prophetic ecstasy (Gal 1:15-16a) rather than in an eyewitness encounter of the historical Jesus.

This, then, is the epistemic nub of the issue: what is the real source of the church's apostolic tradition? The reader of Acts recognizes that the source of Paul's authority and by extension of his message is different than the Twelve, who were eyewitnesses of the historical Jesus. Paul's religious authority is rather grounded in his vision of the resurrected Jesus on the Damascus Road and, according to his canonical letters, a transformative experience of participation by faith in his messianic death. Whilst Luke's triadic formulation of this event is surely a trope of his narrative's emphasis on an experienced resurrection, it also suggests that Paul's message about Jesus is *ex post facto*. That is, the content of his gospel, its announcement of the apocalypse of God's salvation and its promise of a transforming experience with Christ, is logically contingent upon his death and resurrection. Every gospel claim, every pastoral exhortation, every missionary act, every appeal to scripture Paul makes in his letters— the epistemic substance of his theological grammar—is commentary on the effects that follow from Jesus's dying and rising. Everything prior to that messianic moment, even though he is certainly aware of Jesus's biography (cf. Gal 4:4), is not a contingency of the new creation; every promise God has made to Israel and now realizes in partnership with Jesus Christ follows from, *ex post facto*, his Cross and empty tomb.

The reason I have made so much of the importance of the CE collection's appeal to the apostolic tradition is to locate the origins of its theological conception in a different place than does Paul: its critical source is an encounter/eyewitness of the historical Jesus "from the beginning" (1 John 1:1). What logically shapes the epistemology of the CE theological (and especially Christological) conception, then, is an *ipso facto* experience of the historical Jesus rather than an *ex post facto* experience of the exalted Lord. The result is more than rhetorical—the "canonical" use of what was heard and seen in close proximity to the real Jesus to settle disputes or define orthodox faith—but lends material substance to how God's word is articulated, especially in relationship with the Pauline witness.

James: the Collection's Frontispiece. The Letter of James is especially well suited to function as the collection's frontispiece: it is a structurally important piece because it not only frames the pastoral tone of the entire collection but also introduces its core theological elements. These theological agreements target a community of believers whose covenant-keeping practices, following the example of Christ, maintain its loving relationship with God from whom it receives the "crown of (eternal) life" (James 1:12).

The priority of James is, to a significant extent, the semiosis of its placement at the front of the final edition of a canonical collection. It is the first CE read, if read in sequence, and so sets into play a range of orienting concerns that are glossed by a succession of CE. In fact, according to Nienhuis, James was composed for and added to a still inchoate CE collection to introduce a Pillars collection. The letter's strategic role is already cued by the James of Acts, who moderates the second Council (Acts 15) to stipulate the church's (and by analogy its scripture's) working relationship with Paul's mission to the nations (by analogy scripture's Pauline corpus) and Jerusalem's mission to Israel (by analogy scripture's "Pillars"/CE corpus).[59]

From James to 1 Peter. The Apostle Peter's pre-eminence in earliest Christianity is especially evident in the Western Church, which consistently ranked Peter alongside Paul as the two most glorious of all the apostles. But the final ordering of the CE, which emerged out of the Eastern Church, placed Peter's epistles *after* the letter of James, a sequence which is significant for a canonical reading of the collection.

James refers to himself as "the servant of God and the Lord Jesus Christ," a title which is deeply rooted in Jewish literature as a designation for the heroes of Israel's past who mediated between God and the people. This authoritative Jewish leader writes from a center (presumably Jerusalem) to readers cast abroad in the Jewish diaspora (James 1:1). Peter, by contrast, writes as an apostle ("*one sent*") to readers suffering a dispersion of which he is himself a participant (1 Pet 1:1; 5:13). He resides in "Babylon" (most likely a thinly veiled reference to Rome), but he is an elder among elders (5:1) and not the later monarchical bishop of church tradition. This symbolic world created by the literary association of James and 1 Peter provides a particular narrative context for reading their letters. Though later Western leaders would honor Peter as the first pope and Paul as the apostle par excellence (both martyred in Rome), the content and sequence of the CE remind readers that James and Peter shared an earlier connection through their relationship with earthly Jesus and their service in the mother church in Jerusalem. In that context, *James* was the bishop, and *Peter* was the one sent. The narrative world of the CE, therefore, is that of the two-sided apostolic mission described in Acts and Galatians.

Of course, that latter letter describes a conflict involving James, Peter, and Paul, one that has been interpreted to pit James *against* Paul with Peter caught in the middle (so Marcion in the ancient church, and F. C. Baur more recently). The close linking of James and 1 Peter helps to alleviate this potential misunderstanding. I note, first of all, that James and 1 Peter often "speak" in the same voice—especially in the opening sections of each letter. Each bears a prescript locating recipients in the diaspora (James 1:1; 1 Pet 1:1), and then immediately calls believers to rejoice in "various trials" (πειρασμοῖς περιπέσητε ποικίλοις) because of the role testing plays in producing genuine faith (τὸ δοκίμιον ὑμῶν τῆς πίστεως—James 1:2-3; 1 Pet 1:6-9). Soon thereafter James quotes, and 1 Peter alludes to, Isaiah 40 (James 1:10-11; 1 Pet 1:23-24), and then each speak of the believer's birth by a word from God (James 1:18; 1 Pet 1:23). Subsequent close parallels (compare James 4:6-10 with 1 Pet 5:5-9, and James 5:20 with 1 Pet 4:8) clearly indicate that James and Peter are in theological agreement.

1 Peter, in turn, ends by referring to the apostle's close association with Mark and Silvanus (1 Pet 5:12-13), figures presented in the Acts narrative as coworkers of Paul

---

[59] The thematic links between James and Romans noted by Nienhuis hold real promise for facilitating the intertextual study of the NT's two letter collections. Because both Romans and James function as theological gateways into their respective canonical collections, links between may well guide how we understand the relationship between the collections themselves; see David R. Nienhuis, "Reading James, Rereading Paul," in *The Early Reception of Paul, the Second Temple Jew*, ed. Lester L. Grabbe, LSTS 92 (London: T&T Clark, 2018), pp. 236–51.

(Acts 12 and 15-18). When 2 Peter then speaks glowingly of "my beloved brother Paul" and describes his letters as occasionally "hard to understand" (2 Pet 3:15-16), a bulwark is established against a reading of Galatians that might leave readers with a vision of apostles in conflict: I am not to follow "the ignorant and unstable" who understand James, Peter and Paul to be in conflict.

Clearly the opening designation of readers in a diaspora struggling under trials of faith should be taken to underscore the central orientation of the CE as a whole. Between them, James writes from Jerusalem to readers in the diaspora, warning them against the *external* threat of worldly seductions that enflame the passions that give birth to sin and death. James thus *afflicts the comfortable* with a call to repentance. 1 Peter is also written to believers in the diaspora, but now the external threat comes in the form of hostile neighbors whose harassment produces suffering and tests the patience of those called to love without retaliation. 1 Peter thus *comforts the afflicted* with a call to entrust their souls to a faithful Creator.

From 1 to 2 Peter. Despite the many substantial differences between them, the two letters of Peter are clearly marked by a series of intertextual linkages securing the intent that the letters be read together.[60] Each is addressed from Peter, and they share similar greetings (1 Pet 1:2; 2 Pet 1:2) and closing doxologies (1 Pet 4:11; 2 Pet 3:18). 1 Peter is written to readers designated "the elect" (1:1), and 2 Peter follows this up by exhorting readers to "confirm their call and election" (1:10). Both also seem to be linked by a shared purpose: in the first letter, Peter says, "I have written this short letter to encourage you and to testify that this is the true grace of God" (5:12); in the second, Peter says, "This is now, beloved, the second letter I have written to you; in them I am trying to arouse your sincere intention by reminding you" (3:1-2). Indeed, 2 Peter continues the "trials" thread established by James, reminding readers of OT stories that assure believers that "the Lord knows how to rescue the godly from trial" (2:9). Even more can be said: each letter bears a strikingly similar reference to the traditions of the disobedient angels (1 Pet 3:19-20; 2 Pet 2:4) and the flood (1 Pet 3:20; 2 Pet 2:5 and 3:6), and each speaks of prophecy in relation to scripture (1 Pet 1:10-12; 2 Pet 1:20-21 and 3:2).

Other conspicuous parallels help stake out the different orientations of the two letters. Where 1 Peter is written to marginalized Christians whose trial comes in the form of an *external* threat of social harassment, 2 Peter is written to middle-class Christians who suffer an *internal threat* coming from false believers. Accordingly, 1 Peter says, ὡς ἐλεύθεροι καὶ μὴ ὡς ἐπικάλυμμα ἔχοντες τῆς κακίας τὴν ἐλευθερίαν ἀλλ᾽ ὡς θεοῦ δοῦλοι (2:16). 2 Peter in turn condemns the false teachers because ἐλευθερίαν αὐτοῖς ἐπαγγελλόμενοι αὐτοὶ δοῦλοι ὑπάρχοντες τῆς φθορᾶς (2:19). Likewise, whereas 1 Peter calls readers to imitate the Christ who is ὡς ἀμνοῦ ἀμώμου καὶ ἀσπίλου (1:19), 2 Peter condemns the false teachers as σπίλοι καὶ μῶμοι (2:13) and reminds readers to hold fast so that they may be found by Christ without ἄσπιλοι καὶ ἀμώμητοι (3:14).

---

[60] For a full accounting of the lexical agreements between 1 and 2 Peter, see John Elliott, *1 Peter*, AB (New Haven, CT: Yale University Press, 2001), pp. 27, 141.

From 2 Peter to 1 John.[61] While it is a commonplace to extract the Johannine epistles from the collection by appeal to their dissimilarity to other CE (and similarity with the fourth Gospel), in fact there are clear verbal and thematic linkages between 1 John and 2 Peter. 1 Peter ended with a reference to Peter as a "witness to the sufferings of Christ" (5:1). 2 Peter makes this the centerpiece of its authoritative claims: the apostles "did not follow cleverly devised myths" when they proclaimed the *parousia* of the Lord, "for we were eyewitnesses of his majesty" (1:16) who "heard" (ἠκούσαμεν) the voice of God on the holy mountain (1:18). So also 1 John begins by grounding the declaration of the author in his eyewitness status, proclaiming "that which I have heard (ἀκηκόαμεν), which I have seen with my eyes, which I have looked upon and touched with my hands" (1:1).

Both letters also share a similar occasion for writing. 2 Peter was written to readers/auditors of 1 Peter (3:1) to warn against scoffers who will come saying, ποῦ ἐστιν ἡ ἐπαγγελία τῆς παρουσίας αὐτοῦ; ἀφ᾽ ἧς γὰρ οἱ πατέρες ἐκοιμήθησαν, πάντα οὕτως διαμένει ἀπ᾽ ἀρχῆς κτίσεως (3:4). 2 Peter's reply directs readers to the λόγος of God by which judgment will soon come (3:5-7). If read in sequence, soon thereafter 1 John opens another declaration (ἀπαγγέλλω; 1:3):῾Ὁ ἦν ἀπ᾽ ἀρχῆς...περὶ τοῦ λόγου τῆς ζωῆς (1:1). The opponents may think they know what is from the beginning, but Peter and John agree that only the apostles of Christ can speak to these things with authority.

Reading on, I find that 1 John describes opposing leaders or a rival Christianity using precisely the same language as 2 Peter. As in 2 Peter, so also in the Johannine communities the trial involves an internal threat from the presence of apostate Christians, though a progression of sorts is detected: in 2 Peter the apostates are still in church promoting moral laxity (2 Pet 2:13); in 1 John the apostates have left the community (1 John 2:19), leaving the church struggling with the reality of schism. Nevertheless, in both letters the opponents are accused of being false teachers (2 Pet 2:1) or prophets (1 John 4:1)—the same identity since false prophets are identified as teachers (2 Pet 2:1; 1 John 2:27) who "deny" (ἀρνέομαι) a key Christological claim (2 Pet 2:1; 1 John 2:22-23). They are deceivers who have strayed from the truth into error (repeated use of πλανάω-words in 2 Pet 2:15, 18; 3:17; 1 John 2:26; 3:7; 4:6; 2 John 7). They are associated with "the world" (2 Pet 2:18-20; 1 John 4:1-6) and are therefore corrupted by the desires of the flesh (2 Pet 2:9-10 and 3:3; 1 John 2:15-17).

From 1 John through 3 John. The prologue to 1 John picks up this same theme (and implied theological crisis) to frame its distinctive contribution to the CE collection. 2 John then "epitomizes" 1 John, not only to clarify the core themes but to elaborate them in practical ways.

---

[61] The strategic role of 2 Peter is the focus of David R. Nienhuis's ongoing work on the CE collection; see especially his "'From the beginning': The Formation of an Apostolic Identity in 2 Peter and 1-3 John," in *Muted Voices of the New Testament: Readings in the Catholic Epistles and Hebrews*, ed. Katherine M. Hockey, Madison N. Pierce, and Francis Watson, LNTS 565 (London: T&T Clark, 2017), pp. 71-86. The following few paragraphs that forge the link between 2 Peter and 1 John mostly trade on his work.

In particular, 3 John is read after 2 John to help readers better understand the practice and administration of hospitality as the principal instantiation of the command to love *other believers*, forcefully made and elaborated in 1 John (1 Jn. 4:16-21). It is this moral practice of loving other members of the community that ultimately tests its allegiance to the truth of the apostolic witness. 3 John also adds the haunting note that it is in the practice of the faith that the community's governance is also tested.

Jude: the Collection's Conclusion. The reader's ready recognition of the idiomatic similarity of Jude and 2 Peter, which is clearly linked to 1 John, should also lead one to recognize that Jude continues the interests and idiom of the Johannine letters. As in the Johannine letters, readers are addressed as "beloved in God" (Jude 1); emphasis is also placed on a threat within the community from those who oppose the apostolic message.

Among other things, the addition of Jude to the three Pillars in the final shape of the collection commends the reader's awareness that it is not only the analogy of Galatians 2 that glosses the sequence of the CE collection but the narrative of Acts as well, since the Lord's "brothers" (i.e., James and Jude) join the Pillars (i.e., Peter and John) to lead the community's witness to the risen Jesus in Jerusalem (so Acts 1:12-14). Read in the canonical setting of Acts and Galatians 2, Jerusalem thus becomes a kind of theological trope and not merely a geographical location. That is, even though sent as encyclicals to catholic addresses, the titles of the CE place the origins of each letter in an apostolic tradition shaped by the theological agreements of "the gospel for the circumcised" (Gal 2:7) as preached in Jerusalem.

Finally, the reader picks up Jude to continue a thread initiated by 2 Peter, especially the importance of "building yourselves up in your most holy (i.e., apostolic) faith" (Jude 20), while also recalling the message of James, especially the church's vocation to rescue its wandering membership (cf. James 5:19-20; Jude 22-23), to ensure the coherence of the collection as a whole. The reader hears the closing words of Jude's famous doxology as a reminder that God is a gracious covenant partner perhaps to moderate the collection's persistent call to holiness as a condition of their eternal life with God. This concluding note not only corrects a potentially legalistic reading of the CE collection but it also encourages a faithful discipleship that is predicated on a loving God's capacity "to protect (believers) from falling, and to present (believers) blameless and rejoicing before God's glorious presence" (Jud 24).

Conclusion: From Chaos to Coherence

The emphasis on the theological aesthetics of the CE as a discrete collection of scripture and its placement within the final form of the NT canon intends to move beyond the current discussion of these epistles, their canonization and reception history, as individual (and independent) compositions to the constructive proposal of reading them together as a coherent literary whole. Conventional interpretive strategies approach each CE to examine its distinctive literary form and theological perspective, including compositional prehistories and postbiblical histories. These studies have produced many important insights; nonetheless, this chapter seeks to reorient criticism's study of the CE as interpenetrating members of a single canonical collection. I take it that this final form is a deliberate and purposeful production of the church whose uses of scripture in worship, catechesis, mission, and personal devotions intend to bring to maturity its theological understanding and moral practice.

4

Probing 2 Peter: The Role of a "Neglected" Letter in the NT (2016)

Introductory notes: 2 Peter's role within the NT canon caught my interest because it was routinely dismissed by scholars (and in various critical Introductions to the NT) as somehow unfit for the church's consumption as scripture. Moreover, modern criticism almost always studied 2 Peter in relationship to the Letter of Jude because of their linguistic similarity: 2 Peter was in fact a 2 Jude. Yet without question its primary conversation partner during the canonical process was 1 Peter and most interpreters agree that 2 Peter even nods toward 1 Peter in 2 Peter 3:1. My first study of 2 Peter, then, attempted to read it in relationship with 1 Peter as its theological complement; "The Canonical Function of Second Peter," Biblical Interpretation 9/1 (2001) 64–81.

This chapter considers the interpretive implications of another property of 2 Peter's canonicity: it was received into the NT to perform supportive rather than a principal role in the community's worship and catechesis. 2 Peter is "neglected" only in a relative sense when compared to other canonical letters whose history of interpretation evinces their indispensable importance in the church's continuing theological education. No one would dispute, for example, the greater importance of 1 Peter in this regard, whose reception in both the church and academy testifies to its importance. It is precisely in its relationship with 1 Peter, however, that 2 Peter demonstrates its strategic even if secondary importance as a member of the CE collection. This chapter considers other dimensions of 2 Peter's "secondary" or supportive role for a fully NT theology.

A passing note is sounded regarding the formation and fixing of a biblical canon that included a book like 2 Peter, which strikes some as unworthy of continuing religious authority. In fact, 2 Peter may well challenge the enduring value of any fixed or closed canon that makes such a book required reading! In allowing for books of secondary (but enduring) importance, such as 2 Peter, to be included in a canonized collection of Catholic Epistles, I appeal to core theological conceptions of Christian faith to secure such a claim, such as divine providence and inspiration, rather than to a particular historical phenomenon of the canonical process that fixes the limits of a canonical collection once in time for all time.

While I agree that there is no historical confirmation for such a date, the lack of such is not a sufficient reason to demur from offering a theological, more functional explanation of what we do know: that the dynamic phenomenology of canon formation eventually did produce a stable collection of canonical collections for ongoing performances in the worship, catechesis, mission, and devotion life of the church catholic. Jonathan Z. Smith's well-known history of religions comparison of canon lists and their variegated "divinatory situations," while illuminating, proceeds from a very different conception of scripture's ontology and religious authority than does a canonical approach to biblical interpretation.[1] It is difficult to debate the relative merits of different beginning points; the purpose of the essays gathered in this collection is to clarify the interpretive implications that follow from a particular theology of scripture, grounded as it is in conceptions of divine revelation and providence, which underscore the importance of its postbiblical origins and enduring performances as the biblical canon in forming one holy catholic and apostolic church.

This chapter on 2 Peter combines revised excerpts from two recently published studies: its "Introduction" comes from the "Epilogue" in Muted Voices of the New Testament: Readings in the Catholic Epistles and Hebrews, LNTS 56, ed. K. Hockey, M. Pierce, F. Watson (London: T&T Clark, 2017), pp. 199–210, while the chapter's main body is excerpted from "What if no 2 Peter?" in Der zweite Petrusbrief und das Neue Testament, WUNT 397, ed. Wolfgang Grünstäudl, Uta Poplutz and Tobias Nicklas (Tübingen: Mohr-Siebeck, 2017), pp. 37–54. My primary intention is to help encourage a shift in criticism's focus on individual writings to include the theological importance mined from relationships between these same writings, in particular 2 Peter (rather than Jude) with 1 Peter (rather than Paul) as an artifact of the postbiblical canonical process that intended to guide the community's subsequent reading of scripture's normative Petrine witness.

Introduction

The academy's longstanding "neglect" of the NT's non-Pauline epistles and its trickle-down effect on the training of the church's clergy evinces in my mind a troubling effect of the academy's reception of the church's scripture. This inattentiveness subverts the otherwise noble attempt of Bible scholars to gain a responsible understanding of earliest Christianity. The resulting "neglect" of these ancient witnesses to the Christian faith envisages a serious theological problem as well, since it subverts the biblical canon's proper role within the church in forming a robust Christian faith and a vital life with God.[2]

The presumed triumph of Pauline Christianity, most evident today in the communions of the magisterial Reformation, has had the effect of either flattening the subject matter of certain non-Pauline letters for their uneasy compliance to a Pauline theological grammar (e.g., Hebrews, 1 Peter) or marginalizing others from serious attention for a fully NT theology (e.g., James, 2 Peter). The Johannine epistles are typically relocated to a subgroup of NT writings that includes the fourth Gospel

---

[1] Jonathan Z. Smith, *Imagining Religion: From Babylon to Jonestown* (Chicago: University of Chicago Press, 1982), pp. 36–52.

[2] I place "neglect" in quotes not because I disagree with this collection's orienting concern but because I will suggest below a different typology for the intracanonical relationship between the Pauline and non-Pauline NT collections that may revise how we understand this longstanding practice.

and sometimes the Apocalypse. This subgroup of epistles is studied, then, outside the canonical (Catholic Epistles) collection within which they were first received and read as scripture.

Anecdotal evidence suggests that this studied disregard of these "neglected" texts in the clergy's theological education has shaped a bias against their use in parish worship, catechesis, and mission. Even when the Lectionary, for example, includes NT lessons from non- (and deutero-) Pauline books, they are rarely the focus of the church's preaching or teaching ministry and are, in fact, typically ignored—at least in my experience—even when appointed for ecclesial use to thicken the canonical context for hearing God's word in the gospel of Christ. One may assume that this disregard is typically justified for critical reasons.[3] What also seems clear is that this disregard is instantiated from the very beginning during the canonical process. It is, I would argue, a *canonized* imbalance and so is normative of their reading and use.

Most recent historians who have attempted to reconstruct the formation of the NT canon–a project that began with the Reformation and always with sparse evidence in hand–admit to its dynamic nature that unfolded over an extended period of time. On the one hand, there were always in play two relatively stable collections, Gospel and Pauline, in wide circulation early on. No conciliar confirmation was needed. It would seem the church's steady and effective uses of this proto-canonical core through the second century, when it was perhaps more widely used than earliest Christianity's LXX (the OT of the NT), forged an ecclesial intuition of their catholic authority. Certainly the collected nature of the fourfold Gospel tradition and the Pauline letters collection produced a sustained and substantial effect among congregations of mostly converted non-Jews already in the first half of the second century.[4] The failure of the church's mission to Jews, both in Roman Palestine and the Diaspora, only exacerbated this effect—an effect that implicitly slowed the reception of the writings of the Jewish apostolate ("James, Cephas, and John," so Gal 2.7—a rubric contextualized by the narrative of the church's Jewish mission in Acts). In any case, this proto-canon of Gospel and Apostle, even if not in response to Marcion as Harnack imagined it, reified the overall aesthetic of the NT's final redaction.

What must be said, however, is that the church's earliest canon lists, which began to appear once this proto-canonical core stabilized during the second century, envisage a considerably more fluid "second stage" of the canonical process that extended at least into the fifth century when uncial manuscript collections reflect greater stability that roughly corresponds to our current 27-book New Testament. In light of this historical datum, it would seem a mistake for us to argue against the formation of a fixed and

---

[3] My co-author, Anthony Robinson, and I were told by publishers that our proposed book on the Pastoral Epistles, despite its relevance for our intended audience, would have difficulty attracting readers (especially among Robinson's mainline ministerial colleagues in America) whose seminary education has turned them against these biblical books. On the other hand, more conservative readers tend to look for agreement on a variety of critical issues (e.g., Pauline authorship), which are mostly indeterminate, as a criterion for the book's usefulness.

[4] My principal conversation partner in this regard is David Trobisch, both his published/presented work and in private conversations, regarding the manuscript evidence that sustains his reconstruction of the four canonical volumes that came to make up the "final edition of the New Testament," the *Gestalt* of each volume in place early on but then achieving its canonical form over time.

closed biblical canon that, with the ecumenical creeds from this same period, helped to regulate the continuing growth of "one holy catholic and apostolic church." Given the variety of studies in this collection that seek to reconstruct the "identities" of the implied Christian congregations addressed by the NT's non-Pauline books, I would suggest the global church's self-confession of these four marks constitutes its essential identity going forward.[5]

I find Albert Sundberg's contested distinction between "scripture" and "canon" nonetheless useful in understanding the fluid nature of this second stage of the canonical process. The relevant phenomena of the third and fourth centuries evinced the church's wide-ranging use of edifying texts useful in forming an apostolic faith, including non-canonical writings (*Hermes, Letters of Clement, Didache, Apocalypse of Peter*, et al.), which Sundberg refers to as "scripture." Among these texts the church found some had the unique or added capacity to function as a doctrinal and moral plumb-line in defining and defending the church's apostolic faith; these texts, Sundberg suggests, were selected for inclusion in the emergent NT canon. The relevant issue in this selection process was more than the frequency of a text's religious uses but the manner of its use, whether it is quoted or listed to distinguish its capacity for canonical performances in early Christian worship and catechesis.[6]

Moreover, the spotty inclusion of Acts and some Catholic Epistles in canon lists into the third century along with no mention of a discrete volume of CE at least until Eusebius (320–30 CE) may reflect the church's hesitancy to valorize any text outside of its proto-canonical core.[7] Based upon this datum, I would contend the early church engaged in this practice of privileging a proto-canon consisting of the four Gospels of the apostles and the Pauline letters collection, relegating those outside this core to a "second string" status—a pattern of reading that has continued to this day.[8] Indeed, the dialectic this collection envisages between scripture's privileged core and all others was present from the very beginning of scripture's formation and may even be hermeneutical in relating the different collections of the whole canon.

---

[5] See Robert W. Wall, *Why the Church?*, RNTT (Abingdon, 2015); also Daniel Castelo and R. W. Wall, "Scripture and the Church: A Précis for an Alternative Analogy," *JTI* 5/2 (2011): 197–210.

[6] John Barton calls attention to the work of Franz Stuhlhofer who counted the number of quoted or alluded Christian texts found in extant second- and third-century works. Barton uses this numerical analysis to present a more functional definition of canon. That is, the more frequently a text is used, the greater its importance or authority. Stuhlhofer is also able to index the expansion of the NT canon by the statistical increase in the uses (as recorded in ancient Christian postbiblical texts) of specific biblical books during the first several centuries of the CE; see Barton's summary of this idea in *Holy Writings, Sacred Text: The Canon in Early Christianity* (Louisville: Westminster/John Knox, 1997), pp. 14–24. A concern I share with Barton is the absence of agreed-upon criteria that would guide careful readers to distinguish between a writer's appeal to a text in a way that performs a genuinely "canonical" role (e.g., Irenaeus's use of Acts in Book Three of *Adversus haereses*) and other more mundane uses. Stuhlhofer's counting is a necessary first step but finally an insufficiently critical line of evidence in making this distinction.

[7] Edmon L. Gallagher and John D. Meade, *The Biblical Canon Lists from Early Christianity: Texts and Analysis* (Oxford: Oxford University Press, 2017).

[8] Note that the final order of the Gospels collection remained somewhat fluid as was also true of the Pauline collection, which added the three Pastorals toward the end of the second century to complete its canonical edition; Robert W. Wall, *1 and 2 Timothy & Titus*, THNTC (Grand Rapids: Eerdmans, 2012), pp. 15–27.

As a former athlete and now attentive fan, allow me this crude analogy from team sports. Every successful team is constituted by two groups of athletes. There is a core of star players who play the most minutes, who attract the most attention from the press, and who are paid the highest salary because the effectiveness of the entire team is predicated on the consistency of their performance. These are the players who are most intensely recruited because the team's owners and manager know that their success rises and falls on their performance. Yet, no team can compete successfully over an entire season without a group of role players each of whom offer special talents that a manager can call upon at a moment's notice to fill a needed gap—to substitute for an injured player at a moment's notice, for example, or to come off the bench in the final minutes to apply a particular skill that defends against a competitor's strength or exploits its weakness. Even though these role players do not receive the same attention or salary of the star players, they are essential to the team's success.

The two stages of the canonical process initially formed a proto-NT of star performers—the fourfold Gospel and Pauline letters collections—but then selected another collection of "role players" to complement this core in a way that made the entire NT canon more effective in accomplishing what the church intends its scripture to do: to teach and train its membership in the Christian faith and to refute and correct error that would distort the community's theological understanding or subvert its moral formation (cf. 2 Tim 3:16-17). This division of labor, so to speak, is characteristic of the canonical whole; it is what it is. Even though the Catholic Epistles collection, along with Hebrews whose orphaned status compromises its reception, do not receive the same press or "compensation" in either the church or academy as scripture's star performers, their complement role is critical to the effective reception of the whole canon. To mute the voices of their collective chorus will surely have a deleterious effect on the canonical performances of the whole.

What If No 2 Peter?

Whether we track the history of 2 Peter's reception within the church or more recently within the modern academy, we find that its primary role has been as an illustrator of important matters, whether of church doctrine (e.g., scripture's inspiration, apostolic tradition, apocalyptic eschatology), or the early existence of a Pauline canon (cf. 3:14-15), or the relevant features of earliest Christianity's post-apostolic trajectory. The letter, when it is consulted at all, has always been ancillary to other, seemingly more important interests. My response to this consensus does not seek to reassess 2 Peter's origins as a composition; frankly, I have no interest in challenging criticism's settled conclusions about the letter's authorship, its linguistic or stylistic oddities, its literary dependence on Jude, its post-Petrine social location or theological conception shaped by it, and the like. Rather my more theological interest in 2 Peter's status as scripture is cued by its postbiblical reception, especially with 1 Peter, as an integral part of a second canonical collection of apostolic letters that completed a still inchoate biblical canon sometime in the fourth or fifth century.

The church would probably not have selected 2 Peter for inclusion in its biblical canon had canonization unfolded on an individual, case-by-case basis. Surely by the end of the second century other potential candidates for canonization had emerged—texts put in wide circulation and recognized as apostolic in content and practically effective—that were by-passed for canonization whereas 2 Peter was not. I would note in passing that scholars routinely admit that 2 Peter is no more special in effect than other scripture that the church by-passed; this phenomenon infers that canonical texts were not selected on the basis of their *individual* merit. Rather the church's appointment of selected books was cued by their fit and performance as integral parts of whole collections and received as such into the church's biblical canon.[9] Against the currents of modern biblical criticism, the essential phenomenology of canonization is the formation of collections, which over time were arranged into a particular sequence of collections that not only facilitated dialog between them but also articulated the apostolic proclamation of the gospel in its most useful (i.e., canonical) form for subsequent generations of Christians.

This leads me to suppose that 2 Peter would not have been included in the biblical canon without a CE collection to wrap around it. Moreover, there would be no CE collection without 2 Peter to function as its pivot point[10]—a hunch secured by its sevenfold shape, symbolic of its final shape as a canonical collection.[11] The various projects of modern criticism that might challenge the current consensus of its fictive authorship or explain away the lack of its external attestation or hunt down early allusions to 2 Peter in antiquity or correct the current anachronisms about stylistic elements or implied opponents or seek to harmonize perceived theological disagreements with other NT witnesses, tend to isolate its theological goods from other CE and no matter how diverse these letters are[12] this intellectual practice works against any effort to understand 2 Peter's contribution to NT theology. *I simply do not think 2 Peter can survive modern criticism by pressing for its merit as an individual writing.*

---

[9] See Wolfgang Grünstäudl and Tobias Nicklas, "Searching for Evidence: The History of Reception of the Epistles of Jude and 2 Peter," in *Reading 1-2 Peter and Jude: A Resource for Students*, ed. Eric Mason and Troy Martin, SBLRBS 77 (Atlanta: SBL, 2014), pp. 215–28. The manuscript tradition suggests that both letter collections, Pauline and Catholic, were never transmitted as single letters but as parts of unfolding collections of letters from the very beginning. Moreover, the two collections were kept separate in their reception and canonization (however, see P^{72}!).

[10] David R. Nienhuis and Robert W. Wall, *Reading the Epistles of James, Peter, John and Jude as Scripture: The Shaping and Shape of a Canonical Collection* (Grand Rapids: Eerdmans, 2013).

[11] At least from Eusebius forward, the church (both East and West) has recognized the sevenfold shape of the CE collection although sometimes in a different internal order and in a different placement within the NT (East = with Acts after fourfold Gospel [to form the so-called "*Apostolos*"] and in West after Pauline corpus). Prior to the fourth century, there is awareness of a second collection of "catholic" letters but not always as a fixed sevenfold tradition; for this see Nienhuis, *Not by Paul Alone*.

[12] Origen is a good case in point. His early mention of 2 Peter is always in combination with and predicated by its relationship with 1 Peter. Eusebius's comment on 2 Peter or reference to the past of 2 Peter (Clement's supposed commentary) is always in connection with other CE. The Bodmer (P^{72}) is the earliest ms of 2 Peter, in which it is combined with 1 Peter. There is no evidence from the manuscript tradition that the church received 2 Peter detached from 1 Peter (although there are mss that include 1 Peter without 2 Peter); cf. John K. Elliott, "The Early Text of the Catholic Epistles," in *The Early Text of the New Testament*, ed. Charles Hill and Michael Kruger (Oxford: Oxford University Press, 2012), pp. 204–24.

The rehabilitation of a canonical 2 Peter must do its work within the bounds of the canonical collection to which it belongs. This work begins with an analysis of its early reception to amplify 1 Peter's theological deposit as integral to the canonical performances of the CE collection as a whole.[13] I recognize that this claim opposes modern criticism's tendency to throw its spotlight on individual books, to track their history of reception as individual writings in a way that isolates them from their textual and ecclesial surroundings—a tendency that has effectively marginalized 2 Peter's status within the NT.[14] Bible scholars tend to work on isolated bits and pieces of text, distinguishing each from the other to explain and rank them in importance. Yes, we are now able to see and explain more clearly the differences between biblical books; but it strikes me that modern criticism subverts what we find at the moment of canonization, when the Bible became the Bible precisely because textual differences were arranged to facilitate their dialog with the other texts to form mutually glossing wholes greater than the sum of their individual and diverse parts.

The church's recognition of 2 Peter's status as a canonical writing, then, whilst perhaps surprising when considered on its own merit, is made more intelligible when read with 1 Peter within the bounds of the CE collection (and also Acts with which it entered the biblical canon). Even allowing that 2 Peter may indeed make distinctive theological contributions to NT theology (e.g., Bauckham and T. Fornberg), those contributions are recorded differently than from a canonical perspective, not as those of an individual writing but as complementary of a Petrine witness and of an entire canonical collection that vocalizes a much more robust contribution to NT theology than any single writing ever could on its own.

With these three orienting observations in mind, then, let me clear away some brush to get at a response to this chapter's subtext: <u>what would NT theology lack without a canonical 2 Peter?</u>

1) *Aesthetics*. Some might say that 2 Peter's brevity or its literary dependence on Jude must count against its potential theological contribution. It just doesn't have the exclusive look of canonical literature—it's too brief, too redundant, too oddly angled, too peculiar in tone and content for a catholic audience. One should add that the linguistic differences between 1 Peter and 2 Peter prompted some to doubt 2 Peter's usefulness as an apostolic letter already in antiquity. We might sharply respond to this criticism that the canonicity of 2 Peter regards a different aesthetic, one that studies the form of the sevenfold collection to which it belongs.[15] From a canonical perspective, such a collection studied in absence of any of its members would form in its readers a distorted, imbalanced, and ineffective performance. (The church's recognition of this

---

[13] By analogy, think of Acts 1's succession story of Matthias's replacement of Judas. If a twelvefold apostolate is necessary for the movement of God's plan of salvation, Matthias's selection is necessary to complete the apostolic circle in preparation for Pentecost and beyond.

[14] This point is brilliantly developed by Michael Legaspi, *The Death of Scripture and the Rise of Biblical Studies*, OSHT (Oxford: Oxford University Press, 2011).

[15] I have formulated an idea of a canonical collection's "aesthetic excellence" in several earlier studies, following Nicholas Wolterstorff's idea of the functional aesthetic of public art, the effect of which enhances a whole community's life; cf. Nicholas Wolterstorff, *Art in Action: Toward a Christian Aesthetic* (Grand Rapids: Eerdmans, 1980). Moreover, in that scripture is a revelatory text and the God it reveals and that its readers experience is transcendent Beauty, I argue that the final shape of

excellent is not materially but spiritually discerned, and from its public use, not its per se linguistic appearance.)

2) *Authorship*. Whether the letter is judged a forgery or more recently as pseudepigraphy, skepticism about the "genuineness" of 2 Peter contaminates its theological goods in the eyes of biblical scholars. Although the question of a forgery also raises moral issues, the dispute over the letter's authorship is really a theological matter[16]: authorship always in some sense has been equated with a book's apostolicity—a formula that Andrew Lincoln now calls an "authorial fallacy."[17] If the letter's apostolic provenance is a criterion of its canonicity, as it surely was for the Reformers, then the conclusion of the non-Petrine authorship of 2 Peter would subvert both its usefulness for a genuinely "NT theology" or even of its *de facto* canonicity. One might allow that the current tendency to detach 2 Peter from 1 Peter, while contrary to the letter's own perspective, is justified by the evident differences between the letter writers and their implied readers. Quite apart from the question of real authors, if 1 Peter is accepted as apostolic testimony as it was from the first century, then its theological and linguistic dissimilarity from 2 Peter dooms the latter as an apostolic writing.[18]

But we are reminded that the very idea of a NT canon, first presented by Marcion, then Irenaeus and finally during its formation into the fourth century unfolded from its beginning in close connection with the apostolic tradition. Certainly for the church's great Apologists, the theological agreements between the genuine apostles, even if differently articulated, regulated the formation of different ecclesial rules to help form liturgical and catechetical materials for the rapidly developing church. The forces or impulses that shaped this forward process, whether political, sociological, practical, or aesthetical, have this more theological idea of apostleship in mind. It strikes me that this reality remains more relevant for our constructions of a NT theology than those alternatives proposed by modern criticism.

In this regard, there is a kind of circularity often noted in modern criticism, typical of those who follow W. Wrede's skepticism, that if a book like 2 Peter is judged to have had little real influence on NT theology, it must be unimportant and deserves to be neglected—a kind of evolutionary mechanism in which only the fittest survive canonization. 2 Peter's neglect in contemporary NT theologies only confirms history's judgment of its unimportance. I would argue that such a judgment mistakes the

---

canonical collections produces its most effective performance in the church's intended roles for a "catholic" canon—to define and form a unified (but not uniform) theological understanding.

[16] I include here Richard Bauckham's speculation that 2 Peter is a purposeful fiction, not written nor received as a genuine Petrine letter but as a vehicle that translates the apostolic tradition for a new day; cf. Bauckham, *Jude-2 Peter*, WBD 50 (Waco: Word Books, 1983), pp. 158–62. I have no idea, however, how the reader would actually be able to detect this from the letter itself.

[17] Andrew T. Lincoln, *Ephesians*, WBC 42 (Dallas: Word Books, 1990), lxxii–lxxiii.

[18] Robert E. Picirilli has cataloged the precanonical allusions to 2 Peter as early as 1 Clement and the *Apocalypse of Peter* in "Allusions to 2 Peter in the Apostolic Fathers," *JSNT* 33 (1988): 57–83. Even when compositional and canonical considerations are collapsed (see Michael Kruger, "The Authenticity of 2 Peter," *JETS* 42 [1999]: 645–71) the value of this allusive material, which dates to the early second century, is questionable since nowhere is 2 Peter cited as its source. Origen is the first to do so in the third century. Indeed, Bauckham argues that these early contacts between 2 Peter and Christian writings do not suggest literary dependence but shared sources; *2 Peter-Jude*, 149–51.

criterion of usefulness on which the materials for constructing NT theology are weighed and measured.

3) *Theological coherence*. A final reductionism of modern criticism maintains that a text's real canonicity is determined not by the church but by its theological coherence to an interpreter's "canon within the canon." This criterion, of course, is typified by Käsemann; the result is his now famous apologia that 2 Peter "is perhaps the most dubious writing in the canon"[19] (169). The theological goods of 2 Peter, contaminated by the postbiblical impress of the so-called "early catholicism's" response to a Gnostic threat,[20] places it on the other side of Käsemann's kerygmatic canon of Pauline Christianity. One suspects that Käsemann's theological criterion, which is binding in a way the church's biblical canon is evidently not, follows others who suppose the NT canon is provisional and even replaced by their own "biblical" narratives or theological formulae.

The irony, of course, is that Käsemann's reading of 2 Peter is explanatory of why the letter works well in its canonical context! In particular, the elevation of the apostolic tradition to serve the postbiblical community as its norm to police its contested theological and moral borders for an ever changing cultural setting is precisely the situation confronting the church's ongoing use of its biblical canon. 2 Peter's adaptation of apostolic traditions, whether of the historical Jesus or of Jewish apocalyptic theology, is exemplary of canonical hermeneutics; and I would argue that this is featured in 2 Peter's pivotal role within the CE collection.

Especially read as a rejoinder to Käsemann, there is a great deal I appreciate about Jens Schröter's (JS) stimulating monograph on canonization as an historical phenomenon, *Von Jesus zum Neuen Testament*. I am less satisfied with the shape of his NT theology, which I think needs revision. At the very least JS recognizes, as did Brevard Childs before him, the importance of moving the work of historical criticism from the moment of composition, which has and largely still shapes the NT theology project, to the postbiblical moment of the earliest reception history and canonization of the church's variegated apostolic tradition. The hermeneutical pivot point of a biblical book or collection is no longer left to reconstructions of the author or editor's communicative intent but now also the church's intentions for using that book or collection as theologically binding. My disagreement does not lie with JS's historical critical conclusions about canonization but with his theological insistence that "inspiration" (a trope for God's involvement in the formation of the church's Bible) has nothing to do with it.

How can historical criticism reconstruct the *mechanism* of canonization, which applies "the criterion of usefulness for the building up of the community" in a way that distinguishes canonical from non-canonical writings? For example, JS's conclusion that the NT was produced amidst contention and turmoil—an epistemic crisis—as

---

[19] Ernst Käsemann, "An Apologia for Primitive Christian Eschatology," in *Essays on New Testament Themes*, SBT 41 (London: SCM Press, 1964), pp. 149-68, 156.

[20] The result is the institutionalization of divine inspiration, a retributive view of apocalyptic eschatology, an ascetic moralism (more secular Hellenistic than prophetic Jewish), a reified apostolic tradition that replaces "faith in" Christ as the identifying mark of real Christianity, and so on, in absence of a robust Christology characteristic of the church's earliest mission under the direction of Christ's apostles.

the criterion of usefulness for the building up of the faith community.²¹ But nowhere does he suggest what *mechanism* of canonization could produce such a book. There is no explanation for the church's decision to choose one book over another book as better suited for this work when the book not selected is also apostolic in content and effectively used by diverse congregations of different regions of the church catholic. Why 2 Peter and not Shepherd of Hermes or *Didache* or letters from Clement or Ignatius? When set side-by-side JS allows that each is more theologically substantial than 2 Peter—although I think this is a mistake. What explains the choice between those received into the canon and those worthy applicants that were not? Not a council or some other political process.

And what about the church's discernment that a canonical collection had reached its final form and no further editing was needed; it was ready for admission into the biblical canon. Are we to accept the claim that the final form of the NT canon as binding for Christian faith and practice had a "taken for granted validity"? Nowhere does historical criticism explain on what theological basis or by what practical means did the church recognize the moment the NT's final redaction was complete and received as canonical. JS firmly and repeatedly rejects the doctrine of inspiration as a mechanism of canonization.²² Whilst certain conceptions of inspiration must be ruled out, in my view a robust theology of divine providence remains an elegant way of explaining the church's formation of a book that binds it to a particular way of life and faith. Whilst we might also admit Schleiermacher's point that the church was attracted to scripture as an artistic achievement—what I have called scripture's "aesthetic excellence"—historical criticism cannot adequately explain those undocumented final moments that produced the final redaction of the NT canon and a hermeneutic apropos to practicing a fixed form of scripture. At day's end, we need theological confession in addition to historical criticism to explain the church's recognition and reception of the CE collection's precise sevenfold form, inclusive of 2 Peter, as integral of a process that preserved a particular form of apostolic testimony binding upon one holy catholic apostolic church for the long haul.²³

A Theological Reading of 2 Peter within Canonical Context

My essential contention to this point is that we get closer to the church's communicative intention for canonical 2 Peter, which has more purchase than the author's for its

---

[21] Jens Schröter, *From Jesus to the New Testament (ET)* (Waco, TX: Baylor University Press, 2013), p. 325.

[22] Inspiration is, I take it, historical criticism's trope for a wide range of ecclesial beliefs and practices of the Bible that are determinative in its formation and reception as the church's biblical canon (see Barton's *Biblical Criticism*); contra Stulmacher, Wilkens, Childs, et al. For inspiration as a comprehensive belief in God's role in the production of scripture, see Robert W. Jenson, *On the Inspiration of Scripture* (Delhi, NY: American Lutheran Publicity Bureau, 2012); William J. Abraham, *The Divine Inspiration of Holy Scripture* (Oxford: Oxford University Press, 1981).

[23] See, in particular, John Webster (following Calvin and K. Barth), *Holy Scripture: A Dogmatic Sketch*, CIT (Cambridge: Cambridge University Press, 2003), pp. 58–67.

ongoing performance as scripture, by considering its canonization rather than its composition. From the evidence gleaned there, we conclude that 2 Peter was added to a still inchoate second collection of apostolic letters that already included 1 Peter to complete the church's extant Petrine witness for worship and catechesis. Conversely, the imagined result of not doing so—if 2 Peter were not added to gloss 1 Peter—would have been to render scripture's Petrine witness less effective in performing the appointed roles of the church's biblical canon, including its contribution to a biblical theology.[24]

I argue this in the face of a modern criticism that has not succeeded in producing a consensual NT theology with or without 2 Peter. This observation after taking a quick survey of those NT theologies sponsored by SBL and SNTS, which either propose a center by ceding to a particular theological canon within the Canon or more simply retreat to a catalogue of the NT's diverse theologies as a reasonably accurate picture of earliest Christianity. Neither reductionism has achieved a consensus because neither is very convincing.

In responding to the second half of my paper's title, which seeks to propose 2 Peter's contribution to NT theology, let me suggest that we try another model for doing NT theology cued by 2 Peter itself. Thematic of 2 Peter is a grammar of Christian faith founded on the apostolic eyewitness of the historical Jesus. The social world that shaped the canonical process was unsettled precisely because of an epistemic conflict over competing visions of genuine Christianity.[25] For this reason, 2 Peter presses a canonical Peter into service, introduced by the Peter of Acts, who is received as an eyewitness of Jesus's transfiguration (1:17), including God's audition of his divine majesty. As a result, it is this apostolic Peter who knows full well the Christological foundation that secures the Christian faith and lifestyle (1:12). And it is this apostolic Peter who definitively announces the apocalypse of God's salvation at the end of history and so corrects those scoffers of this truth (3:1-14). And so it is this canonical Peter who makes clear the enduring importance of Israel's inspired prophets (1:19-21; cf. 1 Pet 1:10-12) and even of the sometimes confusing letters of Paul (3:15-16).

2 Peter's appeal to this apostolic testimony aims readers to an epistemic criterion *external* to the community's scriptures (cf. 2 Pet 3:16). We might assume, for example, that Peter's witness clarifies the Pauline canon because its effectiveness for doing so is grounded in an eyewitness's "knowledge of our Lord Jesus Christ" (1:8)—something, of course, the Pauline tradition cannot claim.[26] 2 Peter's admission into the biblical

---

[24] The positive work that demonstrates 2 Peter's theological contribution is found in Robert W. Wall, "The Canonical Function of Second Peter," *Biblical Interpretation* 9/1 (2001): 64-81.

[25] In this regard, one notes the similarities between 2 Peter and the Pastoral Epistles (esp. 2 Timothy), not only in terms of their testimonial genre but also in terms of their canonical function. Both perform similar roles within their respective canonical collections—a point I seek to develop in my recent commentary on the Pauline Pastorals; Wall, *1 and 2 Timothy & Titus*, 32-6; cf. Childs, *NT as Canon*, 472. In particular, the portrait of a canonical Paul drawn by these letters, complemented by the Paul of Acts, underwrites not only the church's reception of Pauline tradition Titus presents the revelation of Paul's gospel as a decisive event of salvation's history (Titus 1:3; cf. 1 Tim 1:11-17) to secure the imperative of its transmission into the next generation and beyond (cf. 2 Tim 1:12-13; 2:1-2). On this basis, the Pastorals' Paul is *the* exemplary apostle, the personification of spiritual authority for the church's future whose instruction of God's word is canonical for the nations (so 1 Tim 2:3-7).

[26] It is striking to me that various recent efforts to survey the theological goods of the CE collection (e.g., Lockett, Steve Moyise, P. Davids, Karen Jobes) either omit the Johannine Epistles altogether

canon stipulates with Acts a complementary way of reading the extant Pauline canon *with* the Jerusalem Pillars, monitored by the theological agreements of the apostolic witness.

That is, if we allow that 2 Peter functions typologically of the manner NT theology negotiates diverse apostolic traditions, we might then also allow a rubric that includes Petrine and Pauline accounts of the gospel. 2 Peter's benedictory emphasis on the full apostolic heritage as complement of Israel's scripture is especially crucial at those moments of intramural conflict when the church's confessed faith appears confusing, contested, or even no longer viable to a growing number of disaffected Christians.

I conclude this chapter, then, with three theological reflections that seek to illustrate 2 Peter's intracanonical dialog with 1 Peter in producing a more robust Petrine witness of Jesus. Each dialog is regulated by theological agreements that align with an apostolic grammar of faith that was in all probability current during the canonical process when 2 Peter was added to the CE collection for this end.[27]

1) *Theology*: *2 Peter 3 appeals to apostolic tradition in responding to disputations over the timing and manner of a patient Creator's realization of the promised new creation.* Much of the debate over the canonicity of 2 Peter since Käsemann has concentrated on theodicy, and in particular on 2 Peter's Hellenized depiction of an eschatological theodicy. At its most basic level, 2 Peter's narrative of the apocalypse continues 1 Peter's conception of theodicy in which the innocent suffer as resident aliens of a hostile social world that ridicules their faith in Israel's God. By submitting to the example and destiny of Jesus (1 Pet 2:21-25; 3:18-22), the faithful anticipate God's coming victory over the very social evils responsible for their suffering.

The focus of 1 Peter is on the present age in which the suffering of God's elect people, purified from sin to be a holy people, tests their covenant relations with God: an *existential* theodicy, then, in which the spiritual and moral performances of God's people passes the testing of their faith and assures their participation in kingdom come. The paraenetic cast of 1 Peter underwrites this overall sensibility. The unjust suffer justly, while saints resolve the problem of suffering by their obedience—evil will

---

or treat them as independent from the other CE, often in relationship with the fourth Gospel and sometimes John's Apocalypse. (Note: Lockett has since revised his initial work to include the Johannine Epistles, but in my view awkwardly so.) The typical substitution of "General" for "Catholic" to title these writings sometimes carries with it the connotation of "miscellanea"—that is, a catalog of independent, non-Pauline letters without connection to one another, sometimes even including the so-called "deutero-Paulines" and Hebrews. Perhaps the variety of links between 2 Peter and 1 John (see Nienhuis, "'From the beginning': The Formation of an Apostolic Identity in 2 Peter and 1-3 John") has the effect of adhering the Johannine Epistles to the CE collection as a whole, thereby preventing this kind of reductionism.

[27] Nienhuis and I have argued that a principal contribution of the CE to NT theology is to check-and-balance the church's sometimes misguided appropriation of the Pauline witness, whether to advance sola fideism or supersession, to name two well-known examples. The implicit effect of 2 Peter within the bounds of the collection, then, is not only to complete the canonization of the Petrine witness but also to safeguard the church's reception of the Pauline heritage; see Tobias Nicklas, "'Der geliebte Bruder': Zur Paulusrezeption im zweiten Petrusbrief," *in Der zweite Petrusbrief und das Neue Testament*, ed. Wolfgang Grünstäudl, Uta Poplutz, and Tobias Nicklas, WUNT 397 (Tübingen: Mohr-Siebeck, 2017), pp. 133–50.

not have its due in them. While the demise of evil is signaled already by the risen Messiah whose suffering fulfills God's prophetic promise of salvation (1 Pet 1:10-12), 1 Peter reminds readers that God's end-time judgment is based on why people suffer whether or not according to God's will (1:17; 3:13-17).

But the images of God's future in 1 Peter are faint and abstract. There is no expression of worry about its delay, even if the resurrection intimates that creation's salvation has a future. This lack of attention may fall trap to the dangerous tendency Paul corrects in 1 Thess. in which an abstract eschatology has led to moral laxity. A people without a keen sense of God's future judgment, Neyrey allows, allows people who feel at home in this fallen world.[28]

One imagines this same tendency may be the effect of reading 1 Peter without 2 Peter. Käsemann's complaint over the retributive sense of 2 Peter's eschatological theodicy is precisely the point: 2 Peter's shift from the past inauguration of God's promised salvation (1 Peter) to a vivid narrative of the future apocalypse of new creation rounds out a Petrine response to theodicy and makes the promise of new creation decisive and concrete. Moreover, the blatant ridicule of an unrealized *parousia* to which 2 Peter responds may reflect the negative effect of reading 1 Peter without 2 Peter. Indeed, the letter's rhetorical upgrade that envisages a decisive and expansive apocalypse of God's salvation—"the salvation revealed in the last time" (1 Pet 1:5)—makes clearer the historic *fulfillment* of God's promise without which there is no hope (cf. 1 Pet 1:6). Finally, by not bringing 2 Peter's eschatological theodicy to bear upon 1 Peter, the tension between present and hoped for but still future experiences of God's salvation is removed for a one-side preoccupation on the present.[29]

---

[28] Jerome Neyrey, *2 Peter, Jude: A New Translation and Commentary*, AB 37C (New Haven, CT: Yale University Press, 1993).

[29] Against this backdrop, we might allow that the principal contribution of 2 Peter to Petrine eschatology is its keen emphasis on the Creator's final judgment of the created order—an emphasis that underscores the decisive action of the Creator as purifier of a wicked creation (2:11-22) in readying it for a new creation in which holiness feels right at home. The apostolic community lives in a symbolic world mapped from beginning to end by biblical prophecy (cf. 1 Pet 1:10-12); thus, even as the community's scriptures herald Messiah's suffering as God's Servant (1 Pet 1:10; 2:22-24), so also they foretell his triumphant *parousia* as Lord (2 Pet 3:2-5) in the judgment stories of the Flood (2:4-5; 3:5-6) and Sodom and Gomorrah (2:6-8). According to this authorized witness, the Creator is perfectly capable of both the destruction of the ungodly (angels and cities) and the deliverance of the righteous (Noah and Lot).

But destruction comes first and is the condition of deliverance; this seems the eschatological calculus of the Petrine tradition. 1 Peter's belief in God's judgment emphasizes its *present* force within the community, experienced either as ethical incentive (1:17; 2:12) or as a cipher of its suffering (2:23; 4:17). This core belief is then expanded in 2 Peter with apocalyptic images, located at the coming triumph of God as Judge when both "living and dead" provide a moral accounting of their lives (cf. 1 Pet 4:5). What if the future of God's salvation is dismissed from the community's instruction? 2 Peter offers more than a reminder of scripture's prophecy-fulfillment hermeneutic; it suggests that without a future there is no anticipated judgment and believers are able to live according to its own moral code with impunity (2 Pet 2:19). This formative emphasis on an ethical Christianity, where God's soteriological verdict is based upon the performance of good works and not on the mere profession of faith, thematic of the CE collection, is made more precise by 2 Peter: "the Day of the Lord" (3:10) will bring a fiery destruction of all things, both human (2:1; 3:7) and material (3:7, 10-12), followed by "the day of eternity" (3:18) that dawns a more complete restoration of all things,

2) *Christology: 2 Peter appeals to the apostolic tradition when defeating the Christological error of false teachers.* Scripture's Petrine witness, if 1 Peter is received without 2 Peter, certainly would diminish its Christological affirmation. This seems counterintuitive given 1 Peter's significant contribution to NT Christology: what can 1 Peter's Christology possibly lack even without 2 Peter? Again, we are reminded of Käsemann's principal criticism that 2 Peter's eschatological theodicy "lacks any vestige of Christological orientation" (178) but harbors a "degenerate Christology" in which the primitive church's proclamation of Jesus's dying and rising has receded into the background.[30] This verdict, of course, has been overturned by Bauckham, Fornberg, and recent others.

But if we suppose that 2 Peter was added to 1 Peter's Christological affirmation, the impress of doing so is to shift 1 Peter's exclusive emphasis on the past of Jesus to include his present role as the exalted power-broker of God's salvation; the ascended Christ is *now* "the Savior" (1:1, 11; 2:20; 3:2, 18). A Petrine witness without 2 Peter, then, lacks this thickened sense of a *living* Christ's participation with God in the outworking of the church's salvation (1:11). In fact, significantly, 2 Peter's apostolic affirmation is confirmed by God's testimony that "the Lord Jesus Christ ... is my beloved Son with whom I am well-pleased" (1:17).

The effect of participating in this heavenly audition secures the epistemic criterion according to which the Lord Jesus Christ is known by his apostolic representatives in terms of his "power and *parousia*" (1:16) rather than only in the past of his obedient suffering and atoning death—points already covered by 1 Peter. Appropriately, unlike 1 Peter the theological crisis 2 Peter addresses is internal to the community and concerns the denial of Jesus's lordship (2:1) and "commandment" (3:2), both of which are linked to the denial of his *parousia* when he will mediate the apocalypse of God's judgment and repair of creation.

A canonical approach to 2 Peter affords, then, this observation: the effect of reading 1 Peter without 2 Peter impoverishes Petrine Christology especially as it relates to the dynamic of God's unfolding redemptive plans for the world. The tension that now exists between two discrete periods of Christ's messianic mission would be tamed. As things now stand, the rhetorical effect of 2 Peter's Christology constructs an *inclusio*, bracketing and concentrating 1 Peter's suffering Servant and his messianic death and resurrection by its prophecy on the holy mountain on one side, and by its cosmic and ultimate results at the coming triumph of the Creator on the other. In doing so, the Petrine witness as a whole not only refuses to isolate Christ's importance in the past and on the cross but then carries the results of the Christ event into the future in a way that continues to judge the present moment in salvation's history.

---

both human (3:11) and non-human (3:13). The community's baptism into a Christian hope because of Messiah's suffering (1 Peter) will be confirmed at his *parousia* (2 Peter).

[30] There is an interesting parallelism when comparing Pauline and Petrine witnesses. Early Paul placed keen emphasis on Christ's present and future work, whereas these accents receded as Paul became increasingly convinced that Jesus's return was delayed to a future after his death. In this sense, 1 Peter picks up where latter Paul leaves off; 2 Peter, on the other hand, links up with early Paul and his emphasis on an apocalyptic Christology.

Of importance in this regard is the shift of the pivot point back from the resurrection to the transfiguration of Jesus, which confirms the "power and *parousia* of our Lord Jesus Christ" (1:16-17) according to the Apostle's eyewitness authority (cf. 1 Pet 5:1). This appeal may well carry more rhetorical clout in the letter's argument against the scoffers of the *parousia* (3:3-4), who suppose that this article of Christian faith is a clever fiction (1:16) rather than a delayed reality (3:8-13), and so disbelieve that God is capable of either creation's destruction or its new beginning (3:3-4). The heretical teachers suppose on this basis that they can act with impunity as though the Lord issued no moral command (3:2; cf. 2:21).

3) *Ecclesiology: 2 Peter appeals to the righteousness witnessed in Jesus to correct the social identity of a community too accommodating of its secular moral economy.* The first half of 1 Peter concerns the formation of the church's social identity as a community of non-Jewish converts set within a pagan world, ironically by reclaiming key images from the synagogue's Bible. In continuity with Israel's calling and destiny, the church is chosen by a holy God for a salvation hoped for but yet to arrive; such a salvation obligates a people to form a counter culture of exiles and foreigners who suffer ridicule because of their beliefs and lifestyle.

1 Peter shapes a community's identity that assumes its marginal existence within a hostile environment, which forms patterns of interaction between its members and outsiders. The confidence required to endure a hostile setting, even to challenge it, is predicated on its theological claims: the church is a people chosen and reborn by a holy God to instantiate a "living hope" that heralds God's coming victory over evil (1 Pet 4:1-6) by its acts of doing right (1 Pet 3:13-17). In this sense, the church's moral practices transcend cultural norms and are rather inspired by prophetic witness of Israel's scripture and by the testimony of the historical Jesus whose suffering Peter is eyewitness.

The question might be raised, what effect on the reception of Petrine ecclesiology if there is "no 2 Peter."? Bauckham has carefully located the crisis to which 2 Peter responds a generation later for a new day in which the church no longer views itself as resident aliens of a hostile pagan world. In fact, the elect community is cleansed from past sins (1:9) to participate in God's power (1:3) and nature (1:4), not in Christ's sufferings, so that they are capable of living in the world apropos of pagan ideals (1:5-11). The conflict over social manners found in 1 Peter (cf. 1 Pet 4:1-6) has been replaced by a surprising agreement over the virtues of a well-lived life in 2 Peter.

Yes, the church of 2 Peter remains embroiled in conflict; but the struggle has moved indoors. The opponents are no longer pagans but other Christians who have diluted the gospel by relaxing its moral demands (thus compromising the very virtues of the pagan world it seeks to reach) and by voicing public skepticism about the apostolic proclamation of the community's "living hope."

Conclusion

The crisis 2 Peter continues to address faces any congregation whenever it seeks to translate the moral and theological goods of the gospel for a new cultural setting. The real opponents of change are not unbelieving outsiders—as 1 Peter would have it—but are those within the community who struggle over competing versions of the apostolic word. Reading 1 Peter without 2 Peter would compromise the church's reflection over those theological and moral agreements of the apostolic tradition that are most vulnerable to internal compromise—perhaps not apocalyptic eschatology as in 2 Peter but other elements of the church's Jewish legacy that have been Gentilized and muted.

Moreover, de-canonizing 2 Peter would vacate an important check on the church's potential drift from the moral rigors of a covenant-keeping life, set out in the second part of 1 Peter, to a morality compromised either by an over-determined desire to meet the pagan world halfway or by the spiritual laziness of an elect community whose living hope comes without conditions so that its participation in the new creation is a foregone conclusion. 2 Peter doesn't so much complete 1 Peter's ecclesiology but corrects a possible appropriation of it that foregoes Israel's calling as a light to the nations.

Perhaps nowhere is Käsemann's theological criterion more keenly expressed than by his criticism of 2 Peter's moral dualism. Not only its stunning eschatological claim that believers participate in God's nature (1:4), which is then clarified by a catalog of moral virtues, 2 Peter argues that moral rectitude is the norm by which the false teachers' departure from the apostolic heritage is recognized and condemned. The teachers deny the essentially ethical nature of apostolic religion: they refuse to live the "way of rectitude" (2 Pet 2:21; cf. 1:11; 2:2) which evinces the denial of the theological agreements of apostolic religion.

But is not 2 Peter's dramatic claim in 1:3 that πάντα ἡμῖν τῆς θείας δυνάμεως αὐτοῦ τὰ πρὸς ζωὴν καὶ εὐσέβειαν δεδωρημένης explanatory of 1 Peter's emphasis on moral rectitude (see 1 Pet 2:14-15, 20; 3:14; cf. 2:24)? 2 Peter elaborates this emphasis by elevating it as a feature of eschatological theodicy: those who imitate God's rectitude share in God's nature and will naturally oppose the moral abuses of false teachers (1:2, 3, 5, 6, 8; 2:20; 3:17). It is not orthodoxy, then, but "godliness" (1:3, 6, 7; 3:11) that delivers God's people from eschatological judgment.

Without 2 Peter's elaboration a principal check in resisting the modern tendency of reading 1 Peter (and scripture's Petrine witness) as though of a single piece with the Pauline witness is lacking.[31] Indeed, whereas the Pauline witness also speaks of "righteousness (or rectitude) by faith," the Petrine witness, especially inclusive of 2 Peter, emphasizes a "righteousness (or rectitude) of life": the moral character of a virtuous life marks a people out as belonging to God. Indeed, character matters in the reception of truth (cf. Acts). For this reason, the community must take responsibility to guard its theological borders but also its moral formation.

According to the deeper logic of the Pauline gospel, this same "righteousness" is a natural result of Christ's death in which the believer participates as beneficiary by faith; sharply put, Paul does not require the rigors of a spiritual discipline (1:5; 3:14) that habituates faithful acts of obedience to God's rule (1:9) called for by 2 Peter. Clearly, the deification of believers (1:4) does not result in an inevitable obedience to the commandment of the Lord (2:20-21). The church's appropriation

---

[31] Nicklas, "'Der geliebte Bruder'" (see fn 27 on p. 84).

of Paul at this point, even though perhaps uncritically (cf. 3:15-16), justifies a self-indulgent lifestyle (2:2, 10, 13, 18) that pursues personal pleasure (2:13) and private property (2:15-16) instead of a rigorous obedience to the "commandment of the Lord" (3:2; 2:21).

Part Three

The Pauline Letters Collection and Hebrews

5

Reading the Pauline Pastorals in Canonical Context (2012)

Introductory notes: The invitation to contribute a commentary on 1 and 2 Timothy and Titus to the Two Horizons New Testament Commentary *(Grand Rapids: Eerdmans, 2012) gave me an opportunity to explore various interests of a canonical approach to theological interpretation. I had already begun to register concerns regarding the effects of historical criticism's assessment of these so-called "Pastoral Epistles." My concerns were not so much over the now axiomatic verdict of their deutero-Pauline authorship or post-Pauline social location, even though I find criticism's conclusions in this regard overdetermined; my concerns are registered because of the de-canonizing (or disinteresting) effect criticism's negative judgment of these letters' "authenticity" has had on their current readers in both the academy and church. In the minds of many scholars and well-schooled clergy, if the Pastoral Epistles were authored by nameless pseudepigraphers who selectively remembered Paul's legacy and reinterpreted it for a post-Pauline setting in which a de-apocalypticized, politically domesticated "household of God" had become the ecclesial norm, then their apostolicity is suspect and their contribution to a canonical Pauline witness is set aside. This chapter has been extracted from the "Introduction" to my commentary to illustrate a canonical approach to a theological interpretation of this sub-collection of Pauline letters. Readers may note the tensions I continue to feel and explore between historical and literary criticisms that locate biblical texts in their ancient worlds and interpretations of these same texts as a word from God that targets today's church.*[1]

It strikes me as especially important that my introduction seeks to clarify the relationship between the particular problems that occasioned the composition of each individual letter in the first place and the hermeneutical role these letters came to perform within the canonical collection of Pauline letters by the end of the second century. The criticism that persists among some that a canonical approach to biblical exegesis removes any interest in a composition's historical origins is grossly misplaced.[2] Quite apart from the plain

---

[1] See Andrew Knapp's essay that constructively explores the contours of these tensions, "The Role of Historical Criticism in Wesleyan Biblical Hermeneutics," in *The Usefulness of Scripture: Essays in Honor of Robert W. Wall*, ed. Daniel Castelo, Sara Koenig, and David Nienhuis (University Park, PA: Eisenbrauns, 2018), pp. 24–46.

[2] See Darian Lockett, "Reading Scripture as Canon: Theological and Historical Commitments," unpublished paper presented to Westminster Theological Seminary, March, 2018, who refers to my

sense of the comments on the epistemology and methodology of a canonical approach that introduced this commentary (see below), a cursory reading of the commentary itself evinces an attempt to negotiate between two discrete "origins" of these Pauline letters—both each letter's origins as authored compositions and their postbiblical origin as members of a subcollection of Pauline letters that was added to the extant corpus of Pauline letters to complete it. I do not displace the earlier origins as a composition with the latter origins as canonical but seek to bring both into constructive dialogue.[3]

A Canonical Approach to Historical Prolegomena

A persistent objection to the canonical approach to the theological interpretation of scripture is that it refuses to read biblical texts as historically shaped. This is simply not the case: no one who approaches a text by the light of its textual setting within its canonical setting or in light of its canonical performances as the church's scripture doubts for a moment that a biblical text must also be approached as a human production with full awareness of the particular and various socio-historical forces at work during the long history of its composition and canonization. In fact, however, on the rare occasion that biblical writers actually reflect on what they are doing, they do

---

commentary on the Pastoral Epistles as an example of "reader-response criticism" that is "untethered from historical events" or to the communicative intention of the text's apostolic author (and so in his mind its canonicity). Perhaps the epistemic value of his criticism is self-evident to a conservative Protestant audience, but nowhere does he defend why a text's normative meaning should be linked to the intentions of a presumptive apostolic author. Moreover, such a comment reflects a failure to understand that a text's postbiblical readers are somehow "untethered" from historical events, which I sometimes find in more facile discussions of "reader-response criticism." In any case, had Lockett read beyond the commentary's introductory comments to the commentary itself, where I attempted to demonstrate a canonical approach to theological exegesis, he may have observed a sustained attempt to negotiate between the historic occasion and social world that shaped the compositions of 1-2 Timothy and Titus, and the historic occasion and social world of their postbiblical canonization and addition to an extant ten (or nine)-letter Pauline corpus. More crucial, in my mind, is the observation that Lockett's criticism of my canonical approach (in comparison to his own) logically follows from his evangelical Protestant theology of scripture that privileges a divinely inspired author's *production* of the biblical text and so the epistemic and methodological value of constructing the author's communicative intentions for that text. At this point, too, I depart somewhat from Childs's idea of "canonical intentionality," which may be distinguished from authorial or textual intentionality. Childs locates the "theology" of a divinely inspired scripture in the final form of its subject matter rather than in its presumptive author. I do not locate the divine intent of scripture either in its author or in the per se text but in the church's recognition of the Spirit's sanctification of those texts the church then canonized in the fullness of time. My conception of intentionality as it relates to scripture's nature and role in a way that secures my particular approach to scripture as an ecclesially performed (rather than author-produced) canon is worked out in Castelo and Wall, *The Marks of Scripture*.

[3] The very idea of a text's "apostolic" nature is also contested. Especially those scholars who continue in the stream of the Magisterial Reformation insist that the apostolic nature of a biblical text requires that the text is actually written by or in correspondence with one of the Lord's apostles. The greater distance the interpreter moves away from the historical beginnings of a composition, then, is to lose sight (and insight) from its apostolic nature and so subverts its religious authority for current readers. I rather understand a text's "apostolic" nature in theological terms: not as a text written by one of the apostles but as a trope for a text's alignment in both content and consequence with the apostolic witness of Jesus as God's Messiah and Son.

not characterize their writing as a magical performance or as divine dictation but as an occasional and conventional literary act in which they address real people when read aloud to particular congregations (e.g., Luke 1:1-4; Eph 3:3-4; 1 Tim 4:13; Rev 1:1-4; et al.).

In this sense, canonical exegesis is characterized by an abiding interest in this human, historical element of producing and editing a biblical composition. Like the apostolicity of Paul's gospel, the apostolicity of the text requires the interpreter to regard it as a "treasure in earthen vessels" (2 Cor 4:7). All the factors that shaped the earliest literary history of individual biblical compositions at their diverse points of ancient origins—language, date and location, religious experience, spiritual crisis, or social struggle—should also inform the exegete's understanding of what the text actually says, even if written and first read/heard for reasons that differ from why it is subsequently received by a later generation of readers/hearers as scripture. The aim of faithful exegesis is not to hunt down "the" normative meaning of a text based upon what the author or first readers intended; rather the aim is to address a text's lack of clarity as a major cause of its misuse or non-use among its present interpreters. The goal of critical exegesis is to build a consensus within a community of readers, agreeing what a text plainly says ideally in anticipation of its various performances as a sacred text.[4]

Exegesis that clarifies what a text plainly says should also aim at restoring to full volume the voice of every biblical witness. The endgame of this critical work is the recovery of the whole sense or "tenor" of scripture, which is vocalized as a chorus of its various witnesses to God's word. To presume the simultaneity between every part of the whole, without then adequately discerning the plain sense of each in turn not only shortchanges the diversity of the whole but undermines the integral nature of scripture thus distorting its full witness to God. If the penultimate aim of hard-nosed exegesis is to expose the theological pluriformity of scripture, its ultimate purpose is "to put the text back together in a way that makes it available in the present and in its (biblical) entirety—not merely in the past and in the form of historically contextualized fragments."[5] In this sense, then, exegesis of the literal or plain sense of scripture is foundational for scriptural interpretation, but has value only in relationship to a more holistic end.[6]

The linguistic priority of the exegetical task does expose the inherent elasticity of words and their grammatical relationships. Further changes in the perception of a text's meaning may result from new evidence and different exegetical strategies and from interpreters shaped by diverse social and theological locations. In fact, the sort of neutrality toward texts as human productions requires such changes in meaning to be made. Our experience with biblical texts in particular, layered into the history of their interpretation, cautions the exegete not to absolutize a particular textual meaning. Building a critical consensus regarding what a text plainly says is never a static process

---

[4] Although we disagree about the ends of exegesis, John Barton's *Biblical Criticism* is in my mind the best available discussion of this crucial point.
[5] Jon D. Levenson, *The Hebrew Bible, The Old Testament, and Historical Criticism* (Louisville: Westminster/John Knox, 1993), p. 79.
[6] Esp. Childs, *Biblical Theology*, 719–27.

and requires the more careful and current thinking of an entire community gathered to work toward this common end. Nonetheless, this text is canonical for a particular religious community. Exegesis intending to bring greater clarity to the Bible must then be aimed by the community's teachers at more practical ends: knowing more precisely what to believe and how to behave as God's people must.

Fortunately, several commentaries on the Pastorals have been recently published that do excellent work in locating these letters in their ancient social worlds. I stand on the shoulders of their authors to see my way clear on these historical critical matters.[7] What follows is a series of brief excurses on the standard topics of a modern historical prolegomenon but glossed by the interests of canonical exegesis. In my view, the modern quest of the historical Paul and a version of textual meaning predicated on authorial intent has largely been guided by a myth of originality that assumed a text's normative meaning is brought to clarity by a rigorous assessment of its author's social and literary worlds. However the interpreter reconstructs the text's "original" meaning by the tools of critical exegesis, this comes to serve as the regulatory norm that measures the validity of any subsequent meaning, especially to protect the text's author from his self-serving interpreters.[8]

While the historian is also interested in clarifying the plain sense of the text and in constraining self-serving uses of it, such interests hardly secure the text's theological value for today's reader. Therefore, these excurses make introductions of mostly indeterminate issues that nonetheless aim to make us more wakeful of what the Pastoral Epistles actually teach as textual treasures in earthen vessels.[9]

1. *The author.*[10] Attributing the author of the Pastoral Epistles to Paul is not secured in this case by historical analysis, since I find the hard evidence necessary to do so much too sparse and uncertain to secure such a claim. In any case, the Paul who addresses every reader of these letters is not the historical Paul, but the "canonical" Paul, whose continuing importance as Christ's apostle frames the church's use of his biblical letters in every age.

Even so, the historian's quest of the real author of the Pastoral Epistles remains important to their reception within the modern academy: did the historical Paul participate in writing the Pastoral Epistles as attributed or did someone else do so

---

[7] The reader is encouraged to consult especially the commentaries of Jouette M. Bassler, I. Howard Marshall, William D. Mounce, Philip H. Towner, Raymond F. Collins, Luke Timothy Johnson, Samuel Ngewa, and George W. Knight. A fluent primer by Mark Harding, *What Are They Saying about the Pastoral Epistles?* (New York: Paulist Press, 2001) is a good portal into these introductory matters.

[8] This is the essential conclusion of Robert Morgan, "Made in Germany: Towards an Anglican Appropriation of an Originally Lutheran Genre," in *Aufgabe Und Durchführung Einer Theologie Des Neuen Testaments*, ed. Cilliers Breytenbach and Jörg Frey, WUNT XII-1 205 (Tübingen: Mohr Siebeck, 2007), pp. 85–112.

[9] See Stephen E. Fowl, *Theological Interpretation of Scripture* (Eugene, OR: Wipf&Stock, 2009), esp. pp. 13–53.

[10] My construction of and response to this historical concern are set out in brief in an exchange with Stanley E. Porter; see his "Pauline Authorship and the Pastoral Epistles: Implications for Canon," *BBR* 5 (1995): 105–23, and my response, "Pauline Authorship and the Pastoral Epistles: A Response to S. E. Porter," *BBR* 5 (1995): 125–8. What follows offers a more pointed discussion of a canonical approach to this question.

under his name long after his passing and probably without his permission to do so? And if the evidence points us in this direction, did s/he do so to deceive or to assume a sacred duty to continue to write words in the spirit of the departed apostle? It has become axiomatic for modern criticism to deny Pauline authorship of 1 Timothy on historical grounds, and in most cases also of 2 Timothy and Titus.

Without repeating the arguments on every side of this ongoing debate, let me simply sketch the evidence typically used by those who contend the Pastoral Epistles are not written by Paul and are therefore "inauthentic," "deutero-Pauline," "fictive," or similarly named by other rubrics that effectively set them outside the Pauline corpus. (1) Pastoral Epistles' use of a different and distinctive vocabulary; (2) images of a more developed (= post-Pauline) church structure (e.g., 1 Tim 3:1-16; Titus 1:3-7); (3) routine appeal to traditions about Paul as an exemplary person worthy to be imitated (e.g., 1 Tim 1:12-17; 2 Tim 3:11-14) or to formulae of his teaching as the congregation's theological norm (e.g., 1 Tim 2:3-7; Titus 2:11-14; 3:3-7; cf. the "faithful sayings" of 1 Tim 1:15; 2 Tim 1:9; 2:11-13), which many contend are motivated to preserve the blessed memory of a now-deceased Paul; (4) the imprecise description of Paul's opponents suggest they are fictionalized and used for rhetorical ends; (5) inconsistent teaching or contrary practices; and (6) the Pastoral Epistles are shaped by a "sociology of domesticity" that points to a later time period when earliest Christianity's apocalyptic gospel and practices were replaced by a concern for long-term social stability and political respectability (e.g., 1 Tim 2:8-15; 6:1-2).

The body of hard evidence marshaled to support this historical construction generally fails to convince me. The diversity evident within the Pauline collection at every level makes it difficult to nail down any single letter as non-Pauline on the grounds that it is different than the rest.[11] Additionally, Paul may have followed ancient convention and wrote letters with the aid of secretaries or even co-authors; the collaborative nature of literary productions in antiquity may help explain the different vocabulary and distinctive literary character within Pauline letter corpus. Every Pauline letter is linguistically, theologically, sociologically inconsistent with every other Pauline letter due to variations of secretary/editors/co-authors, audience, occasion and Paul's own developing theological understanding.[12] This is true even within the Pastoral Epistles collection, where differences between them in language, purpose and theological emphasis can be easily detected and will be explained in a brief introduction to each.

---

[11] By and large, I accept Porter's rebuttal of this historical criticism and his counterargument in "Pauline Authorship;" the issue I have with his methodological interests does not lie here but rather with his epistemic assumption that authorship equates with apostolicity and apostolicity with canonicity. In this sense, authorial attribution is an epistemic necessity without which a text has no enduring authority.

[12] See Hermann Patsch's study of the reception of F. Schleiermacher's initial and highly controversial essay that first challenged Pauline authorship of 1 Timothy; "The Fear of Deutero-Paulinism: The Reception of Friedrich Schleiermacher's 'Critical Open Letter' Concerning 1 Timothy," *Journal of Higher Criticism* (Spring 1999): 3–31. Schleiermacher's argument was based almost entirely on his assessment of "non-Pauline phrases and a host of *hapaxlegomena* that provided the decisive evidence against Pauline authorship."

Suffice it to say that from the historian's perspective that if the historian's Paul did not participate in writing the Pastoral Epistles, if Timothy and Titus are fictional recipients of non-Pauline letters, if the date of composition is long after the apostle's death for a church that did not know him in person, if the opponents and problems mentioned in the letters are merely tropes that reimagine Paul's legacy for a later day, then the world behind the text that frames its exegesis would necessarily be cast in different ways than if it can be determined that Paul did actively participate in their production. In my mind, however, these speculations of who is responsible for the canonical letters (i.e., letters in their final form) are largely irrelevant considerations when deciding a text's canonicity. Moreover, the argument, often heard among conservatives, that a fictive letter would have been skunked out as a deception and rejected as canonical in antiquity strikes me as an anachronism, since what determines a literary fiction or a "real" author is itself subject to modern historical critical criteria.[13]

In this regard, the most striking feature of modernity's quest of the real author of biblical texts is the tacit connection made (at least since the Reformation) between the text's author and a letter's apostolicity. The modern marginalization of the Pastoral Epistles on the basis of their inauthenticity is rooted in what Andrew Lincoln calls an "authorial fallacy" (see above). According to this fallacy, the criterion of a text's apostolicity is based upon whether or not modern historical reconstructions "prove" a real apostle had a hand in the production of the text. A critical orthodoxy based upon the "assured results" of leading scholars on this point often predetermines a judgment about a text's usefulness or continuing authority. In fact, Luke T. Johnson implies that increasingly an *idola theatri* is in play as the principal reason Pastoral Epistles are marginalized within the academic guild, where scholars sometimes accept the verdict of critical orthodoxy without careful examination.[14]

The apostolicity of a biblical text is recognized by the church, not by modern historical constructions, and by its effects when using it. Most biblical compositions are anonymous or come with attributions that are difficult to nail down on historical grounds. Judgments about apostolicity are mostly intuitive, then, rather than critical, and are based upon a track record of practical use by Christians as a means of divine grace. The church's treasuring of these earthen vessels is not blindly given but predicated on hard evidence of a practical kind.

2. *The occasion.* Even though recent commentaries have offered elaborate reconstructions of the circumstances that occasioned the writing of each Pastoral Epistle in turn, most contend that the instructions and exhortation found in each respond in some way to early opponents of Pauline Christianity. While several opponents are sometimes named in these letters, their passing reference hardly explains the letters as a whole. Not only is their profile thinly drawn, the letters' instruction is practical and personal and not very concerned to correct the bad theology of Paul's opponents.

---

[13] The most able of these "deception" arguments is Terry L. Wilder, *Pseudonymity, the New Testament, and Deception: An Inquiry into Intention and Reception* (Lanham, MD: University Press of America, 2004).

[14] Luke T. Johnson, *The First and Second Letters to Timothy: A New Translation with Introduction and Commentary* (New York: Doubleday, 2001), pp. 52–4.

Put simply, the occasion of these letters is better understood as a response to the crisis of Paul's departure (cf. 1 Tim 1:3; Titus 1:5) and the effects his absence may have upon his unproven associates and their fledging households of believers in hard places. The variegated instructions, theological formulae and pastoral admonitions found in these letters are apropos of the succession of a Pauline apostolate to the ever-next generation of his tradents who must struggle afresh to get their religious bearings in the absence of their charismatic and experienced leader. Indeed, false teachers and teachings pose a real threat to apostolic succession because their correction must be executed by the church's leaders when Paul is no longer available in person to deal with their various needs.

The reading of the Pastoral Epistles, then, constructs what Charles Taylor has called a "social imaginary" of what an apostolic succession might look like on the ground.[15] That is, Paul's instructions to his successors, Timothy and Titus, define a set of normative practices and beliefs, both congregational and individual, which help every generation after Paul imagine how an apostolic succession should take place in a post-apostolic setting. Simply put, these letters help their intended readers—Paul's successors—imagine for themselves the root concern of any succession: what would Paul do were he here among us today? In helping to guide an apostolic succession, reading these letters forges an intuition of how a sacred household should be organized, why it should be organized in this way (practically and theologically), and also what ought it anticipate as the material effects of doing so.

In this way the interpreter's move from the particularity of an ancient (or authored) text to the more universal meaning of a canonical (or church's) text may be facilitated. For example, while the particular catalog of virtues found in 1 Timothy 3 profiles the sort of person best able to serve a congregation according to Paul's world, readers today can read the same catalog not as a checklist of leadership but as a guide to help cultivate a sense of who best to lead them in their own particular historical moment. In fact, the church's reception of the three letters to complete the Pauline canon for the not insignificant reason of providing "church orders" (according to the Muratorian canon) suggests an ongoing performance: the instruction of these letters form and guide local congregations of Paul's tradents in every age and place, who then safeguard the canonical goods of his apostolate to help people reimagine Paul from one generation to the next.[16]

3. *The genre.* Since the genre of sacred literature is a carrier of theological freight, it is an important element of theological interpretation: a composition is not only shaped by theology, its literary expression shapes the reception of that theology by its readers. In this regard, whatever occasions the writing of a letter also determines the form of

---

[15] Taylor's concept of a shared understanding of our political or social surroundings is fully articulated in his *A Secular Age* (Cambridge, MA: Harvard University Press, 2007).

[16] In explaining why the Pastoral Epistles were chosen as the first commentary of the *African Bible Commentary*, Samuel Ngewa says the focus of the letters is the same as the series: to focus on the church leaders and pastors of a new movement (Association of Evangelicals in Africa) who need to "examine themselves in light of Scripture to lead the people of God in a way that conforms to Scripture;" *1 and 2 Timothy and Titus*, African Biblical Commentary (Grand Rapids: Zondervan, 2009), p. xix.

written response. While the Pastoral Epistles are correspondence like other Pauline letters, they are written in response to a particular theological crisis when the leader departs and his work must be succeeded and continued by others. Letters of succession are paraenetic—they instruct and exhort, they present examples and models to imitate (cf. Acts 20:17-35). But in doing so they target a particular crisis occasioned by any succession of leadership, made even more critical in this case because the leader is an apostle who is providentially given a word from God for this moment of salvation's history (see comment on Titus 1:1-3). This is an apostolic succession; and its sacred deposit must be safeguarded for the next generation (see comment on 2 Tim 1:13-14; 2:1-2).[17] Significantly, this species of letter also facilitates the role the Pastoral Epistles perform within the Pauline canon.

Of course, letters took many forms in the ancient world. Most were written communication to bridge the distance between two parties. Oratory was an important social convention of Paul's world, and letters were the literary expression of speech. Among the various kinds of letters preserved from the ancient world, perhaps the most common is private correspondence, similar in function and form to the Pastoral Epistles. We now possess literally thousands of ancient papyrus letters, stored in museums across the world, which reflect a variety of transactions even though following a standard literary pattern: an opening greeting, the main body, and a concluding benediction.

Of the various functions performed by private letters, the Pastoral Epistles are letters of "instruction and order"—although the instructions contained in 1 Timothy and Titus are to order a congregation while those given in 2 Timothy are more personal and seek to order Timothy's life after the model exemplified by Paul. While there are few exact parallels to the Pastoral Epistles from the ancient literary world, they do bear a striking family resemblance to those letters of antiquity still in our possession. The paraenesis of 1 Timothy and Titus is roughly the same as a kind of administrative instruction found in letters we do possess and so allow the exegete to make general observations about the literary form of these letters (see below). One final note in this regard, in light of the prior discussion about the authorship of the Pastoral Epistles.

Letters of antiquity began with formal greetings so that the recipient would know the sender immediately upon unrolling the scroll. Paul's letters generally followed this well-known script: "Sender to recipient, greetings." In personal letters such as the Pastoral Epistles, this formula was amplified to highlight the nature of the relationship between sender and recipient; this in turn clarified the expected response of the letter's recipient to its instructions. In the case of the Pastoral Epistles, Paul's address does more than underwrite his personal relations with Timothy and Titus, but his spiritual authority as well. Especially when the NT reader has the Paul of Acts in mind, Paul's identification of himself as an "apostle of Christ Jesus" posits the religious importance of his mission and message for the future of the church, which Timothy and Titus are now delegated by him to organize in Ephesus and Crete.

---

[17] See Johnson's important discussion of literary form, especially in the connection between form and function, *1-2 Timothy*, 93–7.

The main body of a personal letter takes up the business at hand. (In this sense, it functions much like a sermon does in a worship service.) Differences of emphasis and vocabulary that the careful reader notes from Pauline letter to letter reflects the range of controversies and crises that Paul considers and seeks to resolve in the main body of his various letters. Advice is given, instruction rendered, commands made, doctrine corrected, false teachers rebuked according to Paul's understanding of scripture's roles within the faith community (cf. 2 Tim 3:16b). The purpose of the main body of a personal letter follows this strategy but ostensibly with a particular person rather than congregation in view. The subject matter of 1 Timothy and Titus is primarily concerned with conveying instructions that would order congregational life in pagan places—not unlike the early second century *Didache* as well as other Christian writings written across the next several centuries for a developing, expanding missionary church. The main body of 2 Timothy is quite different, with a heightened sense of Paul's passing and the importance of Timothy's role to carry on his legacy to the next generation—a kind of literary "last will and testament" of the revered apostle.

The concluding words of a Pauline letter, including these, hold together many elements. While always a benedictory blessing of some kind is found, miscellaneous greetings, exhortations, itinerary, summaries of concern, and other personal reminders are included as well. What this suggests about the Pastoral Epistles is that they were not intended by Paul as "private" letters but for a wider readership beyond Timothy and Titus.

The more personal tone and themes of 2 Timothy suggest a professional relationship between a mentor and apprentice that seems to require equal measure of encouragement with a firm reminder of the important mission at hand. This observation is important for understanding the particular literary genre of 1 Timothy as a private letter (see above) and underscores the astute observation of L. T. Johnson that 2 Timothy is written in the manner of a *personal paraenetic* letter, not as a farewell brief but as—I would call it—a succession letter. Likewise, 1 Timothy and Titus are in the manner of *mandata principis*—that is, an official letter from a superior to an administrative associate for use at a specific location, which mixes instruction (probably read publicly) with personal exhortation (probably kept private).[18] These literary observations not only explain their occasion but their continuing role for a church that does its work in absence of the apostle and is charged, as Timothy was, to safeguard the Pauline apostolate for the next generation.

4. *The social world.* The corpus of Paul's canonical letters, which is introduced and framed within canonical setting by his story in Acts, indicate that those converted to Christianity by his urban mission came from a variety of cultural backgrounds that reflect the makeup of the Roman cities in which Paul had his greatest successes as a missionary. In particular, recent scholarship has demonstrated that the Pastoral Epistles share an array of intellectual and ethical materials with Greco-Roman philosophy, both academic and popular and both in subject matter (e.g., virtuous life, truth claims/

---

[18] See Johnson, *1-2 Timothy*, 97.

falsehood, moral practices, household, and so on), and literary form (e.g., proverbs, paraenesis, biography, lists, biographic models, epigrams, and so on).[19]

No shift within the social world of earliest Christianity is more remarkable than the movement from the Palestinian and rural setting of the "Jesus movement" to the Roman and urban setting of Paul's missionary church. And no study of earliest Christianity is more critical to a critical reading of the Pastoral Epistles than an honest assessment of the "collision" between Paul's missionary practices and those cultural norms that shaped the Greco-Roman world.[20]

At a surface level, the Pastoral Epistles reflect considerable contact with the cultural horizons of the Roman cities of the day. (The student should note that Luke's narrative of the church's mission after Jesus in the Book of Acts takes place almost exclusively in cities, from Jerusalem to Rome. In part, this story world reflects the reality of Luke's own urban church at the end of the first century.) To a large degree, L. T. Johnson's reconstruction of the ways of being religious in the Greco-Roman world corresponds with the nature of social interactions and conflicts mapped by the Pastoral Epistles.[21] Each of the four modes of religious practice he notes, especially within Judaism and then earliest Christianity—participation in divine benefits, moral transformation, transcendence of the world through religious experience/confession, "household" practices that promote socio-political stability—is thematic of Paul's instructions to Timothy and Titus. Moreover, there is considerable ambivalence, if not real conflict, that recognizes the decisive and non-adaptive character of his apostolate and vocation: he suffers as a Roman criminal because of the gospel he proclaims and he fully expects his successors will experience a similar outsider status (see commentary on 2 Tim 2:8-13). Ironically, the Pastoral Epistles are deeply concerned about the redemption of the outsider—those who live outside the sacred household—while recognizing that Christian confession and practice are inherently marginal. In any case, the Pastoral Epistles are case studies of Christianity's apocalypse into a foreign world, complete with instructions that are formative of a confessing community—"God's household"—struggling to "lead a quiet and peaceful life in full godliness and holiness" (1 Tim 2:2b) as members of another, very different household.

The cities of Paul's mission, including Ephesus (mentioned in 1-2 Timothy) Nicopolis in Greece (mentioned in Titus), were typically important commercial centers of the Empire, cosmopolitan in social makeup, and conveniently located for travel by land and sea. Most cities were divided into ethnic neighborhoods, each with its own public places. Especially important was the large Jewish population in the Diaspora,

---

[19] Drawing this landscape, however inconclusively, remains the singular contribution of Martin Dibelius and Hans Conzelmann's influential Hermeneia commentary, *The Pastoral Epistles: A Commentary on the Pastoral Epistles*, Hermeneia (Philadelphia: Fortress, 1972) and more recently is elaborated by a series of important articles by Abraham J. Malherbe.

[20] Richard Horsley (see in particular his edited collection, *Paul and Empire: Religion and Power in Roman Imperial Society* [Harrisburg, PA: Trinity Press, 1997]) has led recent Pauline scholarship in mapping the difficult terrain between an emergent Pauline Christianity and the Empire's dominant Imperial cult and ideology.

[21] Luke T. Johnson, *Among the Gentiles: Greco-Roman Religion and Christianity*, AYBRL (New Haven, CT: Yale University Press, 2009), esp. pp. 111-41. See also C. Kavin Rowe, *World Upside Down: Reading Acts in a Greco-Roman Age* (Oxford: Oxford University Press, 2009).

which normally settled into enclaves within the city identified by its own synagogue (or "voluntary organization"). Otherwise, most Roman cities tolerated a diversity of religious cults devoted to the worship of local deities, deities of the Greek pantheon, "mystery" (or "new age") religions, and the Roman Caesar.

The family household is not only the principal metaphor of church in the Pastoral Epistles; it is so in part because it was the social context for much of Paul's missionary activities. Roman households were mostly larger "compounds" which combined shops, living accommodations, gathering places with play yards for children. As a Pharisee, Paul was bi-vocational, working to support his mission by day and teaching interested people by night. His missionary strategy and congregational gatherings, alluded to throughout the Pastoral Epistles and elaborated in conversation with the Book of Acts, were easily adapted to this household structure. Further, households were often large and always inclusive communities; each member held certain responsibilities and their relationships to others were predicated on these roles. The patterns of this political structure were also easily adapted to the congregational life. The "Christianization" of the Roman household curtailed any potential for internal conflict, even between household congregations within the same city, while also commending the gospel to outsiders who might measure its truth on the basis of Christian conduct. In part, this recognition explains Paul's abiding concern for virtuous character in his description of those who make up the Christian household/congregation.

At the same time, the household is a social institution shaped by a particular social hierarchy. The head of the house was typically the father or another older male; and indications of gender, social class and rank are everywhere noted in the Pastoral Epistles. For example, even though aspiring to the same virtuous persona, the poor widow occupies a different place within the Christian household (cf. 1 Tim 5:1-16) than does the married woman of means (cf. 1 Tim 2:9-15); and the instructions Paul gives to each reflect their very different social status. From the Book of Acts, one is able to discern that a broad range of social groups was represented within a Pauline congregation, reflecting the diversity within the city, including a substantial middle class. Paul's great "Magna Carta" of Gal 3:28 (cf. Col 3:11) is really a descriptive statement about the mixed membership of a congregation, perhaps asserted with the more revolutionary subtext that "in Christ" these different groups cut along social, gender, ethnic, geographical lines are able to achieve an uncommon solidarity because of the presence of divine grace.

The longstanding discussion of the household codes of Pauline *paraenesis* (and of the NT in general), besides drawing obvious parallels with the management scheme of Roman households (and the Greek philosophical tradition that shaped it), is mostly concerned with the role they perform within the Christian writings in which they appear, whether to improve relations with non-believers or to organize the internal relations of believers. Rather than a microcosm of the Empire, however, the Christian congregation is presented as a "household of God, the church of the living God" (1 Tim 3:15) and as such a microcosm of "God's way of stewarding the world" (1 Tim 1:4). Hardly a trope of social domestication as some insist, the ecclesial household shaped by this divine pattern challenges the world, changes the world. There is hardly a more powerful image of this than the distinctive epiphany passages of the Pastoral

Epistles according to which God's grace and friendship erupt into the world in order to rescue the world from sin and purify a people for good works (so Titus 2:11-14). The household trope, then, neither implies an inoffensive assimilation into the pagan world or a prophetic resistance to it; rather, the Pastoral Epistles presume a particular cultural setting in which the family household is the meeting place where people encounter God and are recreated or transformed into a family that belongs to God (cf. 1 Tim 3:15).

Additionally, the theological commitments of the Pauline gospel are sometimes juxtaposed with images of imperial Rome to create a deep sense of the church's counterculture. For example, the church is instructed to pray for its civil rulers (2:2) while at the same time to confess its allegiance to one God (2:3-4) who mediates humanity's salvation through the mediation of one Messiah (2:5-6) and instruction of a single Apostle (2:7). While the church is certainly not seditious, it is plainly intolerant of any claim of the Emperor's singular role or right to save and teach the world. Again in 1 Timothy, Paul reminds Timothy of Jesus's "good confession" before Pilate (6:13), who personified Rome's occupation of the holy land, as apropos of the kind of faithfulness demanded by "God, the blessed and only Ruler, the King of kings and Lord of lords" (6:15). Roman culture is engaged by a "good confession" of a divine who rules over Rome's Caesar. It should come as no surprise that Paul speaks of the costly effect of doing so in 2 Timothy—a letter in which his personal suffering is recalled more poignantly than in any other Pauline letter.

Diaspora Jews, such as Paul, typically settled in neighborhoods in which the synagogue was a central gathering point of religious and social life—probably in the common area of a Jewish household rather than a distinct building. Christianity began as a messianic movement within Second Temple Judaism—and was thoroughly Jewish in its core theological beliefs, ethical behavior, religious and exegetical practices, worship liturgy, and social patterns. While the church gradually separated itself from the synagogue, primarily over controversies related to the conditions for initiating repentant pagans into Christian fellowship, both remain intimately related in the world of the NT. The level of their discourse (and disputation!) is keenly reflected in the Pastoral Epistles, in which the false teachers appear to be Jews, perhaps Christians, who contest certain Pauline beliefs and perhaps even the manner by which converts are folded into the faith. These are intramural conflicts, probably arising within the same household of believers, which had as much to do with the social identity or structures of a congregation belonging to the God of Israel as with religious practices or theological beliefs.

Finally, it seems clear not only from Paul's autobiographical statements in his letters but from his story narrated in Acts that his missionary organization included several colleagues, to whom he delegated important responsibilities of his missionary enterprise (cf. Phil 4:2-3). Paul preferred to engage in the work of ministry in person (cf. Rom 1:10-11), no doubt believing that his apostolic gifts mediated God's grace in powerful and distinctive ways (cf. Rom 1:5). His missionary associates, such as Timothy and Titus, were faithful substitutes for his apostolic persona when he went missing for the hard work of preaching the gospel or establishing a congregation of converts to the Christian faith (cf. 1 Cor 4:16-17; 16:10-11; 1 Thess 3:2). In this sense, then, the instructions and charges a departed Paul gives to Timothy and Titus to establish Christian congregations or correct his opponents in Ephesus and Crete reflect a strategy and theological curriculum he would have used had he been there to engage in this ministry himself.

The Formation of a Canonical Collection of Pauline Letters[22]

The effect of the forming whole collections of individual writings for a single biblical canon creates a literary aesthetic that is substantively and functionally different than corpora scholars invent according to their historical reconstructions of authorship and social location. For example, the various corpora of "authentic" letters used to fashion a critical Pauline theology typically differ in shape and substance from the thirteen-letter Pauline corpus fashioned and fixed during the church's canonical process. The theological priority of reading scripture's Pauline witness at its ecclesial address compels the interpreter to shift an interest in an author's intentions for writing a text to the church's intentions for canonizing it. In this sense, the canonical approach drills down on a *second* point of origin that follows the postbiblical history of an authored text, written for a particular audience, to the church's recognition and reception of it as canonical for all subsequent Christians.

The deep logic of this shift of interest from a text's point of composition to its point of canonization, with its various ancillary claims of canonical rather than authorial intent and textual meaning, follows the epistemology of modernity's defense of a text's "original meaning." Any reasonable definition of historical critical orthodoxy can be re-appropriated for defining the interpretive contingency of a text's canonization, except now the readers of a *canonical* text (rather than an authored one) are located differently both in relationship to their social worlds and in relationship to the biblical text. In fact, we may know more about the circumstances of a text's canonization than we do of its composition, making it an even more practical critical measure than the reconstruction of an authorial original in protecting the sanctity of the text from interpretive abuse. But the primary warrant for making this move is, of course, meta-theological: indexing a biblical text's "original meaning" to the church's initial reception of a text as scripture illumines it within its canonical context, which is how any faithful reader should receive it as a means of grace. Even so, according to Gamble's assessment, the "early history of Paul's letters and the process by which they were collected are very obscure."[23]

---

[22] What follows revises my chapter "The Formation of a Canonical Collection of Pauline Letters," in *The Pauline Canon*, ed. Stanley Porter (Leiden: Brill, 2004), pp. 22–44. See also in this same volume James W. Aageson, "The Pastoral Epistles, Apostolic Authority, and the Development of the Pauline Scriptures," pp. 5–26, and Stanley E. Porter's essay on the various proposals of the formation of the Pauline canon, "When and How Was the Pauline Corpus Compiled? An Assessment of Theories," 95–127. I have been helped along in this case study, even if in a somewhat different direction, by Aageson's excellent monograph, *Paul, the Pastoral Epistles, and the Early Church* (Peabody, MA: Hendrickson, 2008).

[23] Harry Y. Gamble, *The New Testament Canon*, GBS (Philadelphia: Fortress Press, 1985), p. 36.

Most modern efforts at reconstructing the pre-canonical reception history of the Pauline corpus are concentrated by the following <u>four moments</u>: First, elements of a canonical Pauline biography found in the Pastoral Epistles, whenever composed and by whom, suggests that a collection of his writings is a logical "next step" following his death. The memories of his apostolic persona and mission along with the summaries (or "faithful sayings") of his message leave no doubt of Paul's God-given authority and his lasting importance to the church, especially when stipulated in contrast to his various rivals. In fact, one argument against the Pauline authorship of the Pastoral Epistles is the rather immodest picture of a canonical Paul that is drawn by this biography of him: Paul is a Christian saint and martyr whose unrivaled authority within the church insinuates the truth claims of his gospel and life as moral exemplar as the norm for all who believe. The memory of his piety and preaching has become the norm of a truly Christian life and witness.

In most letters, Paul routinely writes that he intends to make an apostolic "house-call" on the letter's recipients, presumably to check and see whether his instructions have been followed. As R. Funk argues in his now famous essay on Paul's "apostolic *parousia*," the rhetorical function of a tacit warning of an imminent official visit is to intensify the importance of the letter itself, which supplies an inferior although effective substitute for Paul's persona and the edifying charisms he conveys within the faith community.[24] Sharply put, the letter represents the "spirit" of the prophetic Paul, which communicates the word of the Lord in his personal absence. If so, then Paul himself offers support for the canonical perception that the NT collection of Pauline letters is an effective medium for continuing the true "spirit" of Paul's witness to God's gospel within the post-Pauline church.

Second, the emergence of the Pauline letter collection, perhaps already by the end of the first century and perhaps put into circulation by the Apostle himself, carries immediate value as the substitute for the personal presence of the now departed Paul. We should not be surprised, then, by the first actual reference to a collection of Pauline writings, with the implication of scripture, found in 2 Peter 3:16. Here a collection of Pauline writings serves the church as a Christian appendix to the Jewish scriptures.[25] Even without knowing the precise dating and *Sitz im Leben* of this letter, this text from a catholic epistle discloses two modest impressions of this early collection of Pauline letters: a collection of Pauline letters had been put into "catholic" circulation "according to the wisdom given him" (2 Pet 3:15b; cf. 2 Tim 3:15); its reception by Christians was not only difficult to understand but also susceptible to distortion by false teachers (2 Pet 3:16). The importance of this witness to the earliest reception of the Pauline canon should not be minimized by modern criticism's suspicions of this letter. In fact, I think it offers us the essential clue that explains the late arrival of the Pastoral Epistles to complete the extant ten-letter Pauline corpus (see below).

---

[24] Robert W. Funk, "The Apostolic Parousia: Form and Significance," in *Christian History and Interpretation: Essays in Honor of John Knox*, ed. William Reuben Farmer, C. F. D. Moule, and Richard R. Niebuhr (Cambridge: Cambridge University Press, 1967), pp. 249–68.

[25] F. F. Bruce, "Some Thoughts on the Beginning of the New Testament Canon," *BJRL* 65/2 (1983): 38–9.

David Trobisch speculates that an earlier edition of this proto-Pauline collection was actually fashioned and put into play by Paul himself.[26] Trobisch bases his hypothesis upon the contemporary convention of other teachers of important schools, such as Seneca and Cicero, who gathered their writings into a collection for future students. This prospect is even more likely if we place Paul, the missionary-teacher, in an urban (and thus well educated) church, and recognize that his letters are informed by the practices and rhetorical conventions of teachers. Trobisch suggests Paul's "authorized recension" included only Romans, 1 and 2 Corinthians, and Galatians.[27] Subsequent to his death, his most influential colleagues (Timothy or Onesimus?) added a 'posthumous collection' to Paul's volume, which they perhaps edited and expanded as encyclicals to meet the needs of a wider audience, and published them together as his "collected letters" with Ephesians serving as the collection's theological introduction (following the well-known thesis of Edgar Goodspeed followed notably by John Knox).[28] Trobisch includes all thirteen letters in this posthumous collection, because I gather its practical aim is to make available to subsequent generations Paul's best thinking in response to a wide range of theological and ecclesiastical issues. While I agree for theological reasons that all thirteen Pauline letters are required to cultivate a fully Pauline understanding of scripture's witness to the gospel (see below), Trobisch's historical basis for doing so is lacking. The evidence from the second century rather shows the widespread circulation within Pauline circles of a ten-letter collection but not yet of the canonical edition of thirteen letters.

Trobisch's essential hypothesis finds partial support in J. Barton's thesis that the frequency of quotation is tacit evidence of a letter's importance within the church and even its canonicity. When considering this citational evidence from the early second century, then, the letters Trobisch includes in Paul's own collection are the very ones cited much more frequently than his other letters combined.[29] Even if an early second century date is accepted for the formation of this proto-Pauline canon, Barton fails to account for the curious silence of Justin Martyr who never quotes from a known Pauline letter. Moreover, the more robust portrait of an authoritative Paul found in Acts (even though as prophet like Jesus and not as a letter writer) does not come on board until the end of the second century when two versions of Acts were put back into circulation. Yet, at the very least, the studies of Trobisch and Barton are highly suggestive of a Pauline collection mentioned in 2 Peter 3:15-16 and perhaps even alluded to in 2 Timothy 3:14-17 where Paul speaks of his own teaching (v. 14) as having the same influence of Israel's scripture in Timothy's spiritual formation.

Third, what recent studies have made clear is that the reception of Paul's letters was in the form of a collection of select letters rather than by individual letters received

---

[26] According to Trobisch, this collection includes edited (by Paul) versions of Romans, 1-2 Corinthians, and Galatians; see *Paul's Letter Collection*, 55–96.
[27] Trobisch, *Paul's Letter Collection*, 55–96. But see Porter's criticisms of Trobisch's thesis and evidence in *The Pauline Canon*.
[28] Ibid., 101 (fn 22).
[29] John Barton, *Holy Writings*, 14–24; cf. Trobisch, *Paul's Letter Collection*, 55–8.

one at a time.³⁰ The first known collector of a Pauline corpus was Marcion (160 CE). Given the prior history of the Pauline corpus to this point, Marcion's Pauline collection was likely an edited collocation of one popular version already in wide circulation.³¹ Marcion collected and used Paul, however, with clear theological intent, since his theology was predicated on Pauline theology.³² Often in sharp contrast to emergent catholic Christianity, which did not pay much attention to Paul, Marcion's innovation was to vest an extant Pauline collection with normative authority for Christian formation: that is, the Pauline corpus was no longer "scripture" (as in 2 Peter) but "*canon*."³³ This move was to push the catholic church in the direction of a Christian Bible of its own, perhaps sooner than would have been the case otherwise.

Most critics of Marcion, both ancient (e.g., Irenaeus, Tertullian) and modern (e.g., Harnack), infer from his canon list that he intentionally excluded the Pastoral Epistles as canonical for his faith community (see below). If so, his reasons for doing so remain obscure to most scholars, myself included, unless he recognized his own beliefs in the profile of the opponents whom Paul roundly attacks in these letters!³⁴ (I with a growing number of scholars doubt that Marcion or Valentinius and their followers knew the Pastoral Epistles.) In any case, the Beatty manuscript (P46) from the end of the second century follows Marcion's list, suggesting that indeed his ten-letter edition of Paul does not diverge from the corpus of Pauline letters generally in circulation at the time.

Almost certainly Marcion's use of this Pauline collection as scripture for the formation of a non-catholic version of Christianity triggered several counter-measures by the church's principal theologians. Ironically, one of these counter-measures was to promote the importance of Paul's gospel and piety for catholic consumption! That Marcion, perceived a heretic, would stipulate a Christian Bible for his faith community provoked Tertullian, his fiercest opponent and learned defender of catholic faith, to respond and offer his own version of a Pauline collection, which included the Pastoral Epistles, with Marcion's alleged omissions restored and the Book of Acts serving as its narrative and biographical introduction.

A second line of evidence is provided by the groundbreaking work of I. Dunderberg on the Valentinian school. Although the target of Irenaeus and frequently cited as an example of so-called "Gnosticism," Dunderberg locates Valentinius, and especially his moral teaching, *within* a fluid Pauline tradition of the second/third century. That is, Valentinianism is a Pauline insider rather than a sub-apostolic (i.e., Gnostic) school of thought. What is interesting about Dunderberg's study is the repeated note he sounds

---

³⁰ Cf. Andreas Lindemann, "Die Sammlung der Paulusbriefe im 1 und 2 Jahrhundert," in *The Biblical Canons*, ed. J. M. Auwers and H. J. Jonge, BETL 153 (Leuven: Leuven University Press, 2003), pp. 321–51.

³¹ Gamble, *New Testament Canon*, 41.

³² I find James A. Sanders' comment highly suggestive that the rich theological diversity found within the final form of the NT may well reflect the canonizing community's response to Marcion's exclusivist and hegemonic use of Paul; *Canon and Community*, GBS (Philadelphia: Fortress Press, 1984), p. 37. I suspect Marcionism is what Christianity looks like when using the Pauline letters as its "canon within the Canon."

³³ In distinguishing between a text's canonical and scriptural authority, see Charles Wood, *The Formation of Christian Understanding* (Philadelphia: Westminster, 1981), pp. 82–105.

³⁴ As John Knox famously speculates in his *Marcion and the New Testament: An Essay in the Early History of the Canon* (Chicago: University of Chicago Press, 1942).

that nowhere is found in the Valentinian literature a clear allusion to the Pastoral Epistles. On the one hand, the memory and apostolate of Paul are clearly contested from several fronts during the latter half of the second century; yet, on the other hand, all rivals for the true soul of the Pauline legacy look for and secure the real Paul in the ten-letter Pauline corpus.

Finally, this line of evidence brings us to a final moment at which time the Pastoral Epistles were added to an extant ten-letter corpus to complete its canonical edition. The precise moment of the church's earliest reception of the Pastoral Epistles as a collection remains indeterminate for lack of evidence; but here is the evidence with which we work. Quite apart from P^{46} (ca. 200), a papyri codex that contains the ten-letter Pauline corpus (2 Thess is missing but was probably in the original) but not the Pastoral Epistles,[35] the earliest papyri evidence of the Pastoral Epistles is P^{32}, a codex that includes a fragment of Titus dating roughly from the early third century. Still other early papyri that include a collection of Paul's letters do not mention the Pastoral Epistles. While the *Biblia Patristica* catalogs many apparent allusions to the Pastoral Epistles from the second century, most clearly from Polycarp (ca. 120), scholars are divided whether they allude to Pauline texts or oral tradition. Even if accepting this evidence indicates a likely date of composition from the first century, this datum alone does not indicate the more crucial date of canonization, which most scholars place at the end of the second century. While the apostolicity of the letters was attested quite early, then, their catholicity was not. Only by maintaining a distinction between dates of composition and canonization can one explain the broad circulation of the ten-letter Pauline corpus apart from the Pastoral Epistles throughout most of the second century.

What conclusion seems plausible from the evidence in hand is that the Pastoral Epistles were known as a collection and used throughout the second century, but only with limited circulation (principally among groups of the Pauline mainstream). Again, the church's reception of the Pastoral Epistles collection as canonical must be distinguished not by questions of authorship but by the scope of the church's use. Marcion, for example, evidently published and circulated the ten-letter Pauline corpus based upon commonplace practice among Christians of his era, but does not seem to know the Pastoral Epistles (see above).

In addition, Judith L. Kovacs's study of the contest between Valentinius and Clement over the Pauline legacy has substantially narrowed the gap between these two Pauline interpreters,[36] while Ismo Dunderberg has sought to retrieve the Valentinians from the Gnostic hinterland and place them among the Paulinists vying over the legacy of the canonical Paul.[37] Their work further illustrates my point because, like Marcion, Valentinius used the ten-letter Pauline corpus to support his

---

[35] However, see Philip H. Towner, *The Letters to Timothy and Titus*, NICNT (Grand Rapids: Eerdmans, 2006), pp. 6–7.

[36] Kovacs has published a series of important articles on this topic, which are now layered into her superb commentary on 1 Corinthians for *The Church's Bible*; *1 Corinthians: Interpreted by Early Christian Commentators* (Grand Rapids: Eerdmans, 2005). A précis for a forthcoming book on this debate was presented to the Nordic NT Conference in Joensuu, Finland, June, 2010, "Contending for the Legacy of Paul: Clement of Alexandria and the Valentinian Gnostics."

[37] Ismo Dunderberg, *Beyond Gnosticism* (New York: Columbia University Press, 2008), pp. 1–31.

teaching without a single reference to the Pastorals. And Dunderberg explains this silence by saying "there is no evidence that the author of the *Gospel of Truth* would have known (the Pastorals)."[38] Again, the real problem with the Pastorals has less to do with their Pauline authorship and more to do with their limited use among Paulinists of the second century.

This datum does suggest, in any case, that the Pastoral Epistles may have been added to complete the Pauline corpus in a way that settles this intramural debate between rival Christian groups over the identity of the canonical Paul.[39] The effect of forming a whole collection, then, is to form a coherent witness to Paul's persona and proclamation as exemplary of Christian faith for the whole church. And within this canonical setting, the Pastoral Epistles are appropriated as hermeneutical writings whose new role is to guide readers of the Pauline corpus to a right understanding of Paul's legacy as "teacher of the nations."

Two more ideas from earliest Christianity's polemic against Marcion may illumine this point. In concluding his discourse against Marcion (*Against Marcion*, V.21), Tertullian seems to suggest that Marcion's Pauline corpus knew the three Pastoral Epistles but had rejected them (*quod ad Timotheum duas et unam ad Titum de ecclesiastico statu composites recusauerit*) because they are brief and written to individuals. Not only this, but to Marcion's religious detriment the Pastoral Epistles treat "ecclesiastical discipline," among the very elements in which Marcion was lacking. In effect, Tertullian's concluding pericope is a crucial summary of Marcion because it implies that he is heretical *because* his Pauline canon is incomplete. While anyone can easily point out the flaw in Tertullian's argument by noting that Marcion included Philemon in his canon, which is also a brief Pauline letter written to an individual, his intuition about an incomplete Pauline canon appears right.

Jerome Quinn further appeals to this text in Tertullian to supply patristic evidence for a collection of three Pastoral Epistles at the time of Marcion and Valentinius.[40] Accordingly, the subsequent Muratorian fragment[41] envisages distinctions already widely understood within the ancient church between the nine congregational letters (plus Philemon) and these three briefer letters written to individuals about church orders. Thus, the *Muratorianum* commends two discrete Pauline collections, adding

---

[38] Cf. Ismo Dunderberg, "The Reception of Paul in Valentinianism" (paper presented at the annual meeting of SNTS, Berlin, July, 2010), p. 3. In private conversations, Dunderberg suggested to me that had Valentinius known the Pastoral Epistles, he would surely have made use of them, especially the sayings about sin and the moral catalogs.

[39] There is no patristic evidence that any one of the three Pastoral Epistles circulated independently of the other two. The problem of the similarity of 1 Timothy and Titus—why include Titus with 1-2 Timothy when 1-2 Timothy has an integrity all its own—is perhaps best understood by the aesthetic principle, since "three is a satisfactory and symbolic number, implying a true collection;" Richard I. Pervo, *The Making of Paul: Constructions of the Apostle in Early Christianity* (Minneapolis, MN: Fortress, 2010), p. 84.

[40] Jerome D. Quinn, "P46—The Pauline Canon," *CBQ* 36 (1974): 381–4.

[41] The list's date and provenance are notoriously contested, especially since Albert C. Sundberg's case for a fourth-century date and a provenance in the Eastern (not Roman) church; "Canon Muratori: A Fourth-Century List," *HTR* 66 (1973): 1–41 and more recently defended by Geoffrey M. Hahneman, *The Muratorian Fragment and the Development of the Canon* (Oxford: Oxford University Press, 1992).

that the authority of the second three-letter collection is based on their effective performance "for the ordering of ecclesiastical discipline."[42]

This phrase, which also suggests a theological function of the Pastoral Epistles, and the final shape of this list, which combines the ten-letter corpus with the Pastorals, are remarkable innovations—especially when compared to other contemporary lists of extant Pauline letters that do not include the Pastoral Epistles. The *Muratorianum* assessment of the Pauline corpus almost surely reflects anti-mainstream politics, not in a petty way but to correct the broader consensus within the emergent catholic church. In fact, it seems highly unlikely, as Tertullian avers, that Marcion/Valentinius rejected this second collection for the same facile reasons that would have prompted him logically to exclude Philemon as well. Nor is there any evident reason for excluding them on theological grounds. In fact, as Charles Nielson rightly argues, the Pastoral Epistles display many of the characteristics of the church from which Marcion emerged and theological beliefs with which he would have agreed.[43] Given the fluid nature of the canonical process, it therefore seems more likely to me that Marcion did not exclude this second collection for due cause and more probably simply did not know about these writings—and we can only wonder why.

What we can observe, then, is a phenomenon of collection-building as a type of evolutionary mechanism. New external threats present by the mid-second century and on the horizon, a change of audiences, new responsibilities that come on line to meet the internal pressures of an expanding religious movement all forge a different ecclesial environment than Paul's original mission so a collection of his letters must be adapted in order for his apostolate to survive. Put positively, subsequent readers of Paul about the time the Pauline canon reached its final canonical form, such as Irenaeus and especially Tertullian, found the sweep of its concerns readily adaptable to this new environment. When the dust finally settled on the Marcion controversy at the dawning of the third century, so pivotal in the formation of the New Testament canon, the theologians of the early church had not only given us the very idea of a Christian biblical canon but also formed its Pauline corpus that now included the Pastoral Epistles. It is important to read them today in this ancient light.

The Final Form of the Pauline Letters Collection

In his neglected 1955 monograph, *The Formation of the Pauline Corpus of Letters*, Leslie Mitton signals a shift of interest in Pauline letters as separate literary entities

---

[42] Even though modern biblical criticism has taught us to read each letter independently from the other two, so that the different themes and occasion of each are more easily recognized, the similarities between the three (e.g., individual addressees, churchly themes, literary form and conventions, common occasion) compel the reading of the three together as "Pastoral Epistles," which may explain why the church received them together into the Pauline canon.

[43] Charles M. Nielson, "Scripture in the Pastoral Epistles," *PRSt* 7 (1980): 4–23. In my mind, had he known the Pastoral Epistles, almost certainly Marcion would have used them to secure his teaching, especially about Christ. For example, it seems inconceivable, based upon the little we actually know of his teaching, that Marcion would not have used 1 Timothy 3:16 or Titus 2:11-14 or any of the five "canonical sayings" of the Pastoral Epistles had he known them.

to a consideration of them as a whole collection.[44] While overly optimistic that a scholarly consensus had emerged in settling the various historical critical problems of individual Pauline writings, he rightly points out that consideration of the literary whole necessarily concentrates on a range of different problems, mostly indeterminate and unsettled: Why were these individual letters preserved together into a corpus? When and where did this formative process take place, by whom, by what process, and according to what criteria did the Pauline canon reach its final thirteen-letter form? The nature of these questions presumes the historian's hard work is sifting through available evidence, most of it indirect, to reconstruct the canonical process within the ancient church.

While the formation of the Pauline canon is profitably studied as an historical phenomenon—what might be termed a "canonization from below"—it should also be mined for what this process implies for Bible practices in an ecclesial setting. Most scholars of canonization are not interested in explaining the choices made in forming the biblical canon theologically as a process of spiritual discernment led by the holy Spirit—a "canonization from above." A canonical approach is interested in a careful reconstruction of the canonical process as a deep reservoir of important interpretive clues for using scripture to inform the witness and form the faith of today's church. The church's discernment of the Spirit's leading role in the production of the biblical canon is not predicated on the identity of a text's author but on its effect in forming a congregation that is wise for salvation and mature for good works.

Most modern constructions of the canonical process follow individual books through their earliest history, whether in the West or East and whether evinced in mss., in allusions and citations of the earliest Christian writings, or in the various canon lists. While useful in helping track the sociology and theology that attends the canonical process within antiquity, this kind of work largely ignores the phenomenology of the process itself: almost every individual book entered the biblical canon as an integral member of a whole collection (e.g., Torah, Psalter, Book of the Twelve, Fourfold Gospel, Pauline collection, Catholic Epistle collection, et al.). The final redaction of a collection, therefore, evinces an aesthetic that is maximally effective for performing the authorized roles of a biblical canon. In Pauline idiom, these roles include to make believers wise for salvation and to bring them to maturity to perform the good works of God (so 2 Tim 3:15-17). If a reader recognizes this theological dimension of the Bible's formation, instantiated in its final literary form, then the phenomena of canonization, and in particular the "canonical shaping" of discrete collections of biblical books and their placement within the final form of the biblical canon, will be mined for interpretive prompts that continue to guide how these texts are faithfully used as the church's scripture.

In this sense, I contend that the final literary form of the biblical canon is a work of aesthetic excellence. That is, the formation of a canonical collection or even of the biblical canon as a whole concluded with its final shape fixed at the moment the church recognized that a *particular* literary shape of a collection or the canon had sufficient aesthetic excellence to function effectively as scripture. While certainly

---

[44] C. Leslie Mitton, *The Formation of the Pauline Corpus of Letters* (London: Epworth Press, 1955).

related to what the church affirms about the Bible's authority and holiness, its formation into a textual analog of the apostolic Rule of Faith is the end-result of a vast repertoire of choices spiritual leaders observed being made when gathering individual texts into discrete collections and then putting these collections together to form a single biblical canon.

But this observation begs a more practical question that is more to the present point: *what prompted the church to make those editorial decisions that put collections of individual sacred writings together into a particular shape and size?* Even if we are to believe these decisions merely recognize the Spirit's will, Harnack observed that a century before the church discerned which way the wind was blowing its various canon lists and mss. traditions evinced multiple different possible shapes and sizes of this canon of sacred texts. This debate continues into our own day, whether to set aside the very idea of a biblical canon or to open it up to additional texts. The tenor of this debate begs the question, why did the church settle on the biblical canon it did and in particular on a thirteen-letter Pauline collection that includes these three Pastoral Epistles? Why this canonical shape and not some other?

From our routine experience as humans we might allow that how objects are formed is an important factor of their utility. How individual bits work together as a whole and for what purpose are decisive measurements of an object's performance, whether it will be well received and well used by its future practitioners. In objecting to what he calls "high art" that is momentarily valued for art's sake but is unused in any practical way and so soon forgotten as a passing fad, Nicholas Wolterstorff advances a more functional conception of the aesthetic excellence of an enduring work of art.[45] In his view, any work of public art should be shaped and sized in a way that makes it accessible for ever changing audiences, constantly performing in ways that inspire them to do good work or to live more virtuously as a result. While defining aesthetic excellence in this more activist direction, Wolterstorff allows for inherent properties of color and texture, shape and proportion that distinguish a good work of art from one of lesser quality. People are naturally drawn to a particular work of art or line of poetry or landscape because it inspires them but also because they are able to recognize the sheer excellence of its nature.

In applying Wolterstorff's definition of aesthetic excellence to the final literary form of the biblical canon, I would argue that in addition to a deep sense of the Bible's completeness and coherence as a trusted witness to the word and ways of God,[46] the Bible's shape may be appraised as an artifact of aesthetic excellence with the following implications. First, the church discerned when the Bible got shaped into that particular literary form that would more effectively enable the Spirit to use it in performing those

---

[45] See Wolterstorff, *Art in Action*, esp. in his proposal of a distinctively "Christian aesthetic," 65–174. Wolterstorff is therefore not primarily interested in whether art can be used as a source of Christian theology or as an auxiliary of divine revelation, although I take it he would allow that great art which deals with themes central to the Christian faith might better function in drawing people to God.

[46] So, e.g., Christopher Seitz allows that the final literary form of the canonical text "bears the fullest witness to all that God has said and handed on within the community of faith"; "Canonical Approach," in *Dictionary for Theological Interpretation of the Bible*, ed. Kevin J. Vanhoozer (Grand Rapids, MI: Baker Academic, 2005), p. 102.

religious roles that form a holy people who know and serve God. Every collection of texts was received and folded into the biblical canon on the basis of a résumé of ecclesial performances that would commend its future productivity according to the purposes of God. The church's decisions, in this sense, were rational and based upon solid evidence of a text's spiritual utility. It was first well-used and widely so for congregational teaching, reproving, correcting, and training before it was received into the biblical canon. My point is that the enduring excellence of a particular form is recognized from among other possibilities by its capacity to perform the workload intended for a biblical canon. Scripture is a beautiful thing because it performs its public roles well.

Second, there are literary properties inherent to the biblical canon that might naturally draw readers to its wisdom or into its narrative world as advice or a story of higher quality. Are there norms of excellence that may be applied to the biblical canon that might help clarify the church's choice as one based upon its aesthetic as well as religious excellence? Indeed so. For example, the Bible's diverse parts are noteworthy because of their rich texture. As a literary genre, the biblical canon is a collection of collections made up of artfully told stories, memorable lyrics, vivid poetry, exacting law codes, all of which aim us at ultimate meaning. Yet these diverse and discrete parts are nicely fitted together into whole collections and then into a single biblical canon whose internal unity of theological and moral content renders a more coherent—and perhaps for this reason compelling—word about God. Moreover, the effects of reading scripture in the company of the Spirit and worshiping community enable the reader to experience God's holy presence, and the joy and peace, the conviction and judgment elicited by the divine word.

Finally, similar to the artist who changes the wording of a poem or a line of a painting because it makes the poem better or the painting's image more arresting, we might allow that the indwelling Spirit forms a community's capacity to recognize which particular bits and in what form are necessary in constructing a single biblical canon that is most effective in accomplishing its holy purposes. The church's decisions in forming the collections of the biblical canon, if they are directed by the holy Spirit, will effectively help to accomplish God's redemptive desires for the world. In other words, if a loving God has created us for loving communion with God and each other, then the church's production of scripture in its present canonical form and so the church's practices of scripture—its careful exegesis, its theological interpretation, its vibrant proclamation—must target this same holy end.

The Contribution of the Pastoral Epistles to Paul's Apostolic Witness

The question may be reasonably asked, in what way does the addition of the Pastoral Epistles to complete the Pauline collection also complete its apostolic witness? Let me in broad brush strokes consider three important themes, which are emphasized in the Pastoral Epistles, that reconceive the Pauline apostolate as important for the future of the church.

1. *The church as the "household of God."* Even a cursory reading of the Pastoral Epistles within the Pauline canon witnesses to a different conception of the church. For example, "church" (ἐκκλησία), used often in the other Pauline letters, is used only three times in the Pastoral Epistles, all in 1 Timothy (3:5, 15; 5:16) and perhaps a later Pauline gloss on its earlier use. The distinction is not between a voluntary organization—"church"—and a more structured "household," since both address a congregation of believers. Nonetheless, noting the Muratorian canon claim that these letters are "for the ordering of ecclesiastical discipline," von Campenhausen famously concluded that the Pastoral Epistles envisage a church structure and male authority of earliest Christianity, a more domesticated social organism that replaced the more free-wheeling charisms of the church's apostolic leadership.[47] This analysis seems to draw support in part from the evident shift in the Pastoral Epistles from the charismatic community of 1 Corinthians, where the church is a community of "kindred spirits" who live and worship together as the "body of Christ" under the aegis of the Spirit, who gives various "spiritual gifts" to believers to empower their congregational ministries and who gives them various "spiritual fruit" to empower their corporate solidarity (this "body" idea is elaborated especially in Ephesians and Colossians).

But Hans von Campenhausen's highly influential analysis of the Pastoral Epistles idea of the church is overdetermined. As Johnson rightly notes, we do not find in the Pastoral Epistles what we should expect if von Campenhausen (and many others who follow his lead) are right: an elaborate hierarchy more similar to later ecclesiastical models of "official" Christianity, details of a leader's roles and responsibilities, and a theological defense for such church orders. We find nothing in these letters that suggests the creation of a new organizational structure. Rather what we find is a congregation fashioned after a household (cf. Gal 6:1-10), much more like the synagogal structure of diaspora Judaism[48] or the Greco-Roman *collegia*—both social models, of course, familiar to Paul.[49] 1 Timothy and Titus, the two Pastoral Epistles most interested in church orders, are more interested in the moral character and spiritual maturity of the congregation leaders than in rigid requirements or job descriptions. In fact, the titles designated for these leadership posts in the Pastoral Epistles are probably common tropes of common household positions—a supervisor or household servant—rather than formal ecclesial offices. In any case, they are used elsewhere in the Pauline corpus (Rom 16:1; Phil 1:1) and are hardly unique to this material.

My intent in questioning the current critical conclusion about the Pastoral notion of an institutionalized "church" is to shift the connotation of "church discipline" from a concern for social structure to the practices of and relations within a "household of God" (1 Tim 3:15). The Pastoral Epistles are primarily concerned with the protocol

---

[47] Hans von Campenhausen, *Ecclesiastical Authority and Spiritual Power in the Church of the First Three Centuries* (Peabody, MA: Hendrickson, 1997), pp. 106–23.

[48] Philip Towner's conjecture that the catchphrases "people of God" or "church of God" used in the Pastoral Epistles echo OT teaching that asserts Israel belongs to God, central to the social identity of the diaspora synagogue, seems relevant here; see his *The Goal of Our Instruction*, JSNTSup 34 (Sheffield: Sheffield Academic, 1989). That is, the distinctive idiom for the church in the Pastoral Epistles reflects a synagogal social identity, and by implication also its social structure.

[49] Luke T. Johnson, *Letters to Paul's Delegates*, NTC (Valley Forge, PA: Trinity Press, 1996), 14–16.

and importance of Christian formation: the congregation functions as a household of believers who receive the apostolic word and practice its truth in an orderly, caring manner.[50] This is a missionary church, steadfastly on-guard against all manner of opposition to maintain the word's theological purity, since their salvation from sin depends upon it.

As is well known, "teaching" words, διδασκαλία/διδάσκαλος/διδάσκω, are featured in the letters' special vocabulary, used far more here than anywhere else in the NT: that is, a Pauline congregation is formed by "healthy" (i.e., Pauline) teaching (cf. 1 Tim 1:10-11, et al.).[51] Theological formulae are scattered throughout, sometimes introduced as "faithful sayings," which supply the curriculum for authorized instructors of the Pauline school (e.g., Timothy, Titus). What must be said here is that the theological substance of this curriculum coheres to the theological substance of a Pauline rule of faith,[52] even seeking to extend its formative significance for a setting where Paul has departed by vesting the core claims of his gospel and the memory of his missionary practices with a different language and additional layers of meaning.[53]

Paul's successors are enabled to teach, remind, and transmit to others the goods of his apostolate by the Spirit's "special" gift (so 1 Tim 4:14; 2 Tim 1:6). Even von Campenhausen must admit that the authority of the "teaching office" in the Pastoral Epistles is established more in terms of Paul's own prophetic authority than in those terms associated with an "office" established by a religious institution.[54] That is, the gifted teacher—including Paul's immediate successors—is not granted authority by ecclesial review of their character and academic credentials; the gifted teacher is set apart by apostolic appointment (2 Tim 1:6) and prophetic utterance (1 Tim 4:14). In this regard, it is a category mistake to understand the teacher as the holder of an ecclesiastical office; rather, the teacher is more like the prophet of God, who carries God's word to instruct God's people under the Spirit's anointing—the Spirit of "power and love and self-control" rather than of "timidity" (2 Tim 1:7; cf. 1 Cor 2:13).

These various thematic probes allow a discussion of the nature of Titus and Timothy's delegated authority within the congregation. The only title given the pastoral team of Titus and Timothy is "man of God," which trades on its use of OT prophets, carriers of God's word to God's people (see comment on 2 Tim 3:14-4:4). Otherwise the duties and practices given them by Paul are apropos of delegated leadership: they teach and preach Paul's gospel as a word of truth and they instruct congregations founded by Paul's missionary endeavor; they safeguard the memories and practices of the Pauline apostolate and pass it on to other tradents; Timothy is called "the pillar and foundation

---

[50] See Francis Young, *The Theology of the Pastoral Epistles*, NTT (Cambridge: Cambridge University Press, 1994), pp. 79-85.

[51] Consideration of the entire semantic subdomain for teaching (L&N 33:224-50) would extend and deepen this impression enormously: there is a keener emphasis in the Pastoral Epistles on the activities and substance of Christian teaching, along with the moral character of the "apt teacher," than anywhere else in scripture.

[52] I take it this is what Jouette M. Bassler means when she calls the Pastoral Epistles' theological argot "mundane;" *1 Timothy, 2 Timothy, Titus*, ANTC (Nashville: Abingdon Press, 1996), pp. 31-4.

[53] Cf. Childs, *NT as Canon*, 387-95; *Reading Paul*, 69-74.

[54] Hans von Campenhausen, *Ecclesiastical Authority*, 116; although von Campenhausen remains true to his larger polemic and thinks this move back towards a genuinely Pauline idea is fictional.

of the truth" (1 Tim 3:15) and so must practice and parade this truth (1 Tim 4:13) according to his ordination (1 Tim 4:14); he is held responsible for the congregation's salvation (1 Tim 4:16). In fact, the political structure of the "household of God" vests considerable authority to the successor of the apostolate, not in the form of a church office but of Paul's hands-on ordination (2 Tim 1:6-7), precisely because the word of God that the "man of God" carries into the *missio Dei* is none other than the word disclosed to Paul "in due time" (cf. Titus 1:3).

The Pastoral Epistles teaching about the church completes but does not move Pauline ecclesiology in a different direction: "the ecclesiology of the Pastoral Epistles (is) akin to that of Paul."[55] This teaching is hermeneutical of what else the Pauline witness may teach us about the covenant community. In this sense, to imagine the church as a "household" belonging to God, shaped by teachers of the Pauline word, is to clarify the church's vocation, introduced and elaborated in other Pauline letters, for a setting in which the powers of Paul's apostolic persona are absent. They are the successors of the Pauline apostolate who must absorb the instructions given them in these letters to establish a protocol and working principles/rules, much like those found in a "household," that will effectively transmit Paul's theological and personal legacy into the ever-changing "next generation" of his spiritual progeny (2 Tim 2:2). Only then will the church be able to extend his witness to God's gospel to the ends of the earth.

2. *The test of the real Christian is the performance of "good works."* Abraham Malherbe has located the keen emphasis on moral formation found in the Pastoral Epistles in the intellectual culture of the wider Greco-Roman world.[56] The various catalogues of virtues found here identify Christian faith with the competent person who is moderate, modest, and self-controlled, a good citizen whose conscience protects him against imprudent conduct. In essence, the interplay between the moral character of theological confession found in the Pastoral Epistles, already mentioned to make a different point, underscores this fundamental structure of Pauline thought: that "there is an indissoluble connection between beliefs and behavior," between Pauline orthodoxy and social orthopraxis.[57] Conversely, where this connection appears broken apart, where moral chaos is found, there is evidence found of opposition to the core claims of Paul's gospel. Thus, for every virtue list there is a contrasting vice list, together delineating the real difference between embodied truth and falsehood—this is also consistent with both Jewish theology and Greco-Roman moral philosophy. There is also clear continuity between the evangelical purpose of Paul's mission and this "indissoluble connection" between "healthy (i.e., Pauline) doctrine" and virtuous character (so 1 Tim 1:8-11).

Given this fundamental continuity, then, are there distinctive emphases found in the Pastoral Epistles that round off the Pauline profile of the believer's lifestyle? I have already suggested that the differences one finds between the Pauline paraenesis generally and the Pastoral Epistles paraenesis particularly is best explained by the keen

---

[55] I. Howard Marshall, *Pastoral Epistles*, ICC (London: T&T Clark, 1999), p. 521.
[56] Among several important studies on this topic, see especially his *Paul and the Popular Philosophers* (Philadelphia: Fortress Press, 1989).
[57] Bassler, *1 Timothy, 2 Timothy, Titus*, p. 34.

interest in teaching discussed above. Sharply restated, Pastoral Epistles paraenesis defines moral character in terms of that species of faithful disciple who can teach "healthy doctrine" to others who make up a "household of God" dedicated to Christian instruction. Yet two features of this profile of the "apt teacher" stand out and supply a moral standard for all faithful disciples: namely, their "godliness" (εὐσέβεια; 1 Tim 2:2; 3:16; 4:7, 8; 6:3, 5, 6, 11; 2 Tim 3:5; Titus 1:1) and "good (ἀγαθός/καλός) work(s) (ἔργον; 1 Tim 2:10; 3:1; 5:10, 25; 6:18; 2 Tim 2:21; 3:17; Titus 2:7, 14; 3:1, 8, 14), catchwords critical to the Pastoral Epistles "special" language. Rather than providing full-bodied word studies, which many others have already done, I want to make a couple of related points relevant to my thesis. First, the implicit consistency between the believer's internal (spiritual) character (εὐσέβεια) and the character of the believer's external (public) life (ἔργα ἀγαθός) subverts any attempt to internalize and privatize Christian formation—again, no doubt, in service of the community's missionary vocation. Godly believers produce good works as the concrete demonstration of the gospel's truth, and this "indissoluble connection" within Pauline Christianity between beliefs and behavior.

The idea of "good works" in the Pastoral Epistles, so pivotal to how they portray the Christian life, defines those moral habits that result from the work of God's grace. "Good works" characterize the life, brought to maturity by Bible practices (2 Tim 3:16b), that accords with God's will and is therefore pleasing to God (2 Tim 3:17). In fact, the paraenetic contrast between evil and good works, which typically frames the Pauline polemic against false teachers (who perform evil works), also illustrates the public effect of God's salvation-creating grace in the true believer's life (cf. Rom 12:1). This idea, then, is not only theologically considered but also the *necessary* evidence of the gospel truth that Paul and his successors preach. No matter the apparent agreements between the idea and character of these "good works" with contemporary secular philosophy, it is deeply grounded and reflective of what stands at the epicenter of Paul's thought world: the sinner who believes the gospel is initiated into a new life with God, whose grace transforms the believer from doing evil to doing good.

This stress on "good works" in the Pastoral Epistles as the effective, moral yield of receiving God's grace brings out in bold relief a point that is made elsewhere in the Pauline canon, most effectively in Rom 12:1, 2 Cor 9:8, and Eph 2:8-10. The net result is to correct what I think is a dangerous tendency of the (especially) Protestant misreading of Paul, which demonizes good works as somehow subversive of the sinner's dependency on Christ's death for salvation. Further, the Pastoral Epistles stress on the formation of a "godly" character as the distinguishing mark of the faithful believer, who is then morally competent to perform "good works," corrects another tendency of a (especially Protestant) misreading of scripture's Pauline witness: namely, the emphasis on teaching a saving orthodoxy to the exclusion of any instruction in a practical divinity that embodies confessed truth in the hard work of Christian charity and virtue. In this regard, too, the emphasis of the Pastoral Epistles, intensified by the addition of the Catholic Epistles collection, brings a necessary balance to the church's appropriation of the Pauline canon.

3. *The Pastoral Epistles portrait of the canonical Paul.* A final illustration is the expanded résumé of the apostle Paul found in these letters. Even though it is commonplace these days to suggest the reception of Pauline traditions in that the Pastoral Epistles present a post-Pauline apologia in support of his legitimacy as an exemplar and apostle, this purposeful presentation of Paul may be viewed as especially crucial at the moment when the Pastoral Epistles were added to complete the Pauline canon toward the end of the second century. At this historical moment, the formation of a canonical witness of Paul was made necessary by an intramural debate over Paul's legacy and importance for the church's future (see below). Within the social world of the canonical process, the portrait of a canonical Paul that emerged in the Pastoral Epistles and in Acts intended to secure a particular account of his enduring importance as an apostle for subsequent generations of believers.

This characterization can be gathered under different rubrics. For example, from these materials one might sketch a biography of Paul that includes his experience of conversion (cf. 1 Tim 1:12-16), his apostolic calling (cf. 1 Tim 1:12-16; 2 Tim 1:8-12; Titus 1:1-3), his reception of God's word at a *kairos* moment in salvation's history (Titus 1:3; cf. 1 Tim 1:10-11), and on this basis his distinctive appointment by the risen Christ as teacher of the nations (1 Tim 2:7; cf. Acts 13:47). This biography is extended to include exemplary missionary experiences (e.g., 2 Tim 3:10-13) and the names of personal opponents and supporters (1 Tim 1:20; 2 Tim 1:15-18; 2:17; 4:9-21; Titus 3:12-14). This is an extraordinary example of the canonical Paul since the eternal destiny of real (i.e., named) individuals is related to their personal relations with Paul—not unlike the frightened sailors on the ship in stormy seas narrated in Acts 27: safe haven finally is located wherever Paul is! The memory of this Paul regards the security and continuity of his apostolate.

There is nowhere a more expansive definition of the Pauline apostolate and its religious purchase for the church than Titus 1:1-3. Even a cursory comparison between this greeting and the equally lengthy one that begins Romans and so the Pauline corpus shows that while in addressing the Romans Paul is concerned to set out the core beliefs of his gospel, which is preached to empower the salvation of the nations, in Titus the core concerns regard the importance of Paul himself for the salvation of God's elect. In the address of Titus, it is not the risen Christ that sets out the terms of the gospel as in Romans but God's word delivered directly to Paul at a καιρός ἴδιος! On this basis a "knowledge of the truth" is delivered to fashion the faith of God's elect so that God's promise to them, made in ages past, might now be fulfilled. Paul is now front and center in the outworking of God's promised salvation!

This evocative greeting agrees with the claim, nowhere else made in the Pauline canon, that Paul was appointed "a teacher of the true faith to the nations" (1 Tim 2:7). What he taught is compressed into canonical sayings spread across the Pastoral Epistles (1 Tim 1:15; 2:15-3:1a; 4:9; 2 Tim 2:11-13; Titus 3:4-8) as well as in dense theological formulae (e.g., 1 Tim 3:16). These texts are less useful for catechesis as they are the kind of soundbites that summon the community's teachers to a curriculum for instruction organized around these big ideas.

Even more crucially, this portrait and its various bits underwrite the importance of the Pauline apostolate that is now passed on to others to safeguard, with the Spirit's help, and transmit to still other teachers (1 Tim 6:20; 2 Tim 1:13-14; 2:1-2). There is a peculiar eschatology that emerges in these letters that is linked to the apostle Paul, which not only concerns the eternal destiny of certain individuals but also of the (esp. Gentile) church. Even as Jesus is concerned what choices his disciples will make in his absence, since these choices concern eternal life, Paul is similarly concerned in these letters with respect to following his example and instruction.

The Hermeneutical Role of the Pastoral Epistles within the Pauline Canon

At the moment when a canonical collection of Pauline letters was finalized, the Pastoral Epistles were added to an extant ten-letter collection to complete the Pauline canon. In the messy and contested world of the second century church, the legacy and content of Paul's apostolic tradition was still up for grabs. There was no agreed upon "canonical Paul" yet in play within the church catholic. Marcion v. Tertullian, Valentinius v. Irenaeus were intramural battles over Paul that took place along a broad trajectory throughout the second century (and perhaps into the twenty-first!). Richard Pervo's study of the second century ferment and foment along this trajectory, while contested at several points, nonetheless raises important questions for a theological reading of the Pastoral Epistles. For example, even though most interpreters routinely discuss the relationship between the apocryphal *Acts of Paul and Thecla* (APT) and the Pastoral Epistles especially in connection with particular people mentioned or common themes, Pervo aims their relationship at the reception of an authoritative Paul, which by 175 CE had become "a rather murky and frothy pool" of competing ideas and images.[58] The author of APT is the broker of a particular reading of an apocalyptic, ascetic Paul and as such is highly critical of rival readings including the one envisaged by the canonical Paul of the Pastoral Epistles. In fact, according to Pervo's close comparison, the most obvious thematic disagreements between APT and the Pastoral Epistles—over household life (i.e., marriage, women, celibacy, child-raising), spiritual gifts, political authority, for example—suggest that the Paul of the Pastoral Epistles has been rejected by the narrator of APT for the purpose of discrediting its version of the Pauline apostolate and so of its succession to the next generation and beyond. The reception of the Pastoral Epistles as scripture envisages the triumph of a particular understanding of Paul and his apostolic legacy; but more critically the canonization of the Pastoral Epistles reflects the triumph of a particular way of remembering Paul and teaching the goods of his apostolate to others, which confirms the trustworthiness of his portrait in the canonical Acts (see below). Put in practical terms, the church not only found the apocryphal Paul unreliable; its verdict in favor of the Pastorals

---

[58] Richard Pervo, "To Have and to Have Not: Receptions of Paul in the *Acts of Paul*" (unpublished paper presented at the annual meeting of SNTS, Berlin, July, 2010), p. 13. A comparison between the Paul of the Pastoral Epistles and the Paul of the apocryphal "Acts of Paul and Thecla" (APT) is instructive for our general thesis. Without commenting on the various theories of its composition or its connection with the canonical Acts, the date of APT's composition and the Pastoral Epistles' canonization is roughly the same.

Paul suggests the apostolate of this apocryphal Paul cannot be trusted for Christian formation. *Simply put, at the point of their canonization, the Pastoral Epistles formed an intellectual rejoinder to competing interpretations of the Pauline apostolate in a way that fixed a normative understanding of his memory and message according to which the Pauline corpus is read.*

2 Peter 3:15-16 remains, especially when glossed by 2 Timothy 3:14-17, a pivotal text for understanding the continuing role of the Pastoral Epistles within the Pauline corpus. Depending on the date of this text, it seems likely from this passage that the valorization of the Pauline corpus, which 2 Peter claims is a fount of spiritual "wisdom" (3:15), shares the same effect as Israel's scripture, which conveys "wisdom" necessary for salvation (2 Tim 3:15). But 2 Peter also indicates that Paul's letters' lack of clarity opens them up to potential abuse by the very teachers it castigates. This passing reference of a Pauline collection hints at a hermeneutical crisis that might threaten the future of the community.[59]

The addition of the Pastoral Epistles collection to the extant Pauline corpus subsequent to the cautionary note sounded in 2 Peter may therefore be understood as a response to such a crisis. Not only does its portrait of a canonical Paul (see above) respond decisively to the battle over Paul's legacy within Pauline Christianity, the canonical sayings and the theological formulae that fashion a Pauline rule of faith, along with the instructions about personal and congregational practices that illustrate how the rule is applied, are spread across its pages to commend a particular version of Pauline Christianity that chooses sides—I would argue at the holy Spirit's bidding—in a challenging and contested succession.

The hermeneutical props alluded to in the Pastoral Epistles are what one should expect in a collection that helps a community respond to the intellectual crisis provoked by disagreements over the canonical Paul. For example, opponents are sometimes named with clear allusion made to other Pauline letters in which a contested belief (e.g., resurrection) is set out in a way that agrees with the Pastoral Epistles (see comments on 1 Tim 1:18-20; 2 Tim 2:8-20). Other allusions to antecedent Pauline letters seek to clarify practices unique to Paul's apostolic office from those that are normative of Christians (see 1 Tim 5:18-19). In part, one of the hermeneutical props of the Pastoral Epistles is to help Pauline tradents distinguish the unique apostolic practices of Paul (e.g., 1 Tim 1:20) from the "pattern of healthy teachings" (2 Tim 1:13) that are received from Paul but then passed on to others (so 2 Tim 2:1-2). Such a distinction may well include restrictions about marriage and celibacy, which an ascetic, apocalyptic Paul may well have advanced in his lifetime (1 Cor 7) but which have been lifted for a

---

[59] In a similar way, Margaret M. Mitchell proposes that Paul's Corinthian correspondence marks the origins of Christian hermeneutics made necessary by the "confusion and even alienation" generated by his earlier letters when their instructions were not adequately explained; *Paul, the Corinthians and the Birth of Christian Hermeneutics* (New York: Cambridge University Press, 2010), pp. 5–6. Significantly, she examines the "rootedness of early Christian exegesis in rhetorical training," observing that the "leaders of tomorrow" (i.e., successors) were trained how to use texts according to what Mitchell calls "the agonistics of interpretation" (21)—that is, interpretive tools that enabled leaders to settle debates over the meaning of texts within the law court or town square. Although she is working with different Pauline texts (1-2 Cor) and from a different angle, her important study supplies insight that secures my point more firmly.

post Pauline community. Vivid memories of Paul's conversion (see 1 Tim 1:12-17) and body of work are scattered across these letters that exemplify what is expected of his successors (see 2 Tim 2:1-7; 3:10-14). Well known are the canonical sayings (cf. 1 Tim 1:15; 2:15–3:1a; 4:8-9; 2 Tim 2:11-13; Titus 3:4-8a) and important theological formulae or syntheses (e.g., 1 Tim 2:3-7; 3:16; Titus 2:11-14; 3:4-8) that fashion a Pauline rule of faith, which continues to regulate how the community should adapt Paul's gospel to everyday life. These same theological agreements, which focus on the pattern of God's redemption of everyone, also guide the community's use of Israel's scripture for wisdom of salvation (so 2 Tim 3:15). A controversial example of this prop is found in 1 Tim 2:13-15a where Paul's biblical Eve instantiates the redemptive plan of Israel's God set out in 1 Tim 2:3-6 and proclaimed to the nations by Paul (2:7). Still other memorable aphorisms are found throughout the Pastoral Epistles, which aid the church to this day in the catechesis of new believers.

Rather than approaching the Pastoral Epistles as a marginal collection of biblical letters, whether because they are addressed to individuals rather than to congregations, because of authorship doubts or a late date of composition, or because certain instructions seem offensive to contemporary sensibilities, they should be read within their present canonical setting as of indispensable importance in guiding faithful readers of the Pauline corpus as a distinctive apostolic witness to God's gospel.[60]

Pastoral and Catholic Epistles: In Prospect of an Intracanonical Conversation

If we agree on evidence that the formation of the CE collection occurred sometime during the third century and was canonized sometime during the fourth, we should also agree on evidence that this process occurred after the fourfold Gospel and thirteen- or fourteen (+ Hebrews) letter Pauline canon was completed and already in wide circulation. The primary purpose anticipated for this new letter corpus, then, would likely have been to forge a more viable use of the biblical canon, which was still under construction. In this sense, any new reading of the life of the canonical Jesus narrated in the fourfold Gospel or the Pauline witness safeguarded in the thirteen/fourteen-letter corpus would have been thickened by the addition of the CE collection.

At the very least, this added collection promises to prevent a distorted reading of the Pauline gospel by the church. Given the history of heretical currents emanating from Pauline traditions in the early church, one should not be surprised that a substantial Pauline criticism, an important hallmark of the James tradition within the early church (e.g., the Pseudo-Clementines, Gospel of the Hebrews), is largely retained in the letter of James, especially (but not exclusively) in 1:22–2:26. Moreover, the Jewish roots of these traditions are hardly obscured in the letter.[61] The viability of such an

---

[60] See again James Aageson's *Paul, the Pastoral Epistles, and the Early Church* for a comparison between the Pastoral Epistles and the undisputed Pauline letters, which reflects the multiple layers of multiple Pauline authors who contributed to an emerging, coherent Pauline Christianity.

[61] The Jewish background of James has been constructed by modern criticism; however, this background has more to do with maintaining a distinctively Jewish "ethos" than with the ongoing

intracanonical conversation between Pauline and Catholic, then, would not rest on the prospect of conceptual harmony but on a mutual criticism that does not subvert the value of the Pauline canon but rather insures that its use by the church coheres to its own *regula fidei*.[62]

By the same token, the internal calculus of a catholic collection consisting only of 1 Peter and 1-2 John, when viewed through the lens of Acts, merely supplemented (rather than added anything distinctive to) the extant Pauline canon. The addition of James as its frontispiece and Jude as its conclusion, also of 2 Peter to 1 Peter and 3 John to 2 John, the initial Peter-John grouping was recalibrated into a more robust (some might say "louder"!) conversation partner for the canonical Paul. The relations between the "Pillars" and Paul recalled from Galatians 2:1-15, and hinted at elsewhere in his letters and Acts, are transferred differently to gauge the relations between the two epistolary corpora that are regulated by the canonical motives of the catholicizing church and by the theological grammar of the *regula fidei*—as textual representatives of partners engaged in a self-correcting and mutually informing conversation. The first element of a unifying theology of the CE is thus conceived in more functional terms. The reception of James cues the church's critical concern about a reductionistic use of Pauline tradition that edits out the church's Jewish legacy, especially an ethos that resists any attempt to divorce a profession of orthodox beliefs from an active obedience to God's law in a pattern of salvation (see below).[63]

An intriguing aspect of this emerging intracanonical dialog is the relationship between the Pastoral Epistles and the CE collection, mostly because they came on line roughly at the same time of the canonical process. That is, toward the end of the second century, the same pressures at work that prompted the church to add the three Pastoral Epistles to complete the canonization of the Pauline corpus also prompted the church to add a second letter corpus to its emerging NT canon (see above). I mentioned earlier three themes in particular are distinctive to the Pastoral Epistles; they are apropos for the study of the CE collection as well. Each theme may be considered as a response to a crisis within and upon the church that threatened its apostolic message and evangelical

---

performance of particular elements of a Judaic religion, whether from the Second Temple or the Diaspora. In this sense, James's rejection of supersessionism is neither formalistic nor legalistic but adheres in a principled way to a Jewish way of life—a way of life that James contends is threatened in part by certain tendencies of the Pauline tradition. I would add that the addition of the catholic collection to the NT canon serves this "canonical" function of delineating the boundary between Christianity and Judaism, not by doing so sharply but rather by underwriting the continuity between them.

[62] Ironically, Luther's negative appraisal of James—that it fails a Pauline test of orthodoxy—illustrates this same methodological interest in reading James and Paul together; yet Luther fails to engage the two according to the hermeneutics of the canonical process. To do so would have led him to recognize that the CE collection as a whole might actually render a Pauline "justification by faith" gospel more faithful to the church's *regula fidei* and for the very reasons he rejected James!

[63] My formulation of the relationship between the Pauline and Catholic witnesses draws on an insight of James A. Sanders who long ago commented that the Pauline witness concentrates upon the "mythos"—or unifying narrative—of God's salvation as articulated/promised in the Torah and fully articulated/fulfilled in Christ; cf. Sanders, "Torah and Paul." In our opinion, it is the *ethos* of the Torah—obedience as loving response to God's saving mercies—that the CE collection concentrates upon. The result of reading *both* corpora together, then, is a fuller presentation of God's gospel. See Wall and Lemcio, *NT as Canon*, 232–43.

mission and prompted the church to delineate its witness for future generations. My hunch is that the common ground occupied by the Pastoral Epistles and the CE, the canonization of each occasioned by similar social forces and theological questions, may help readers better understand the roles and interplay between the two canonical corpora of letters.

1. *Church as the "household of God"* (1 Tim 3:15). The Muratorian canon list adds that the Pastoral Epistles are "for the ordering of ecclesiastical discipline." The use of the "household" metaphor in the Pastoral Epistles is primarily concerned with the protocol and importance of Christian formation: the congregation functions as a household comprised of believers where Christian tradition is passed on to the postapostolic generation wherever Christian instruction is practiced in a disciplined, orderly manner.[64]

This same theme of "ecclesiastical discipline" is supported by the CE collection. As introduced by James, the community's internal discipline extends to what is said and what is done, elaborations of which are found everywhere in the CE. Instructions to maintain church order are similarly attached in both the Petrine and Johannine letters to the prospectus of apostolic succession (see introductions to both). In fact, the metaphor "household" is explicitly used in 1 Peter (2:5; 4:17) and "church" in 3 John (4, 9, 10) in response to different threats to congregational life that may subvert the congregation's reception of and perseverance in the truth. Clearly for James, the reception of "the implanted word" depends upon a humility instantiated by the community's spiritual leaders who are quick to defend the poor (cf. 2:1-7, 15-16) and who use their teaching office wisely to build up rather than to tear down (3:1-17).

2. *"Good works" as the hallmark of real Christians.* The repetition of an exhortation to engage in "good works" in the Pastoral Epistles underscores that "there is an indissoluble connection between beliefs and behavior."[65] The stress on "good works" as the effective, moral yield of receiving God's grace brings out in bold relief a point that is made elsewhere in the Pauline canon, most effectively in Romans 12:1, 2 Corinthians 9:8, and Ephesians 2:8-10. The net result is to correct a dangerous misreading of Paul, which demonizes good works as somehow subversive of the sinner's dependency on Christ's death for salvation. Further, the Pastoral Epistles stress on the formation of a "godly" character as the distinguishing mark of the faithful believer, who is then morally competent to perform "good works," corrects another misreading of Paul: namely, the emphasis on teaching a saving orthodoxy to the exclusion of any instruction in a practical divinity that embodies confessed truth in the hard work of Christian charity and virtue. In this regard, too, the emphasis of the Pastoral Epistles brings a necessary balance to the whole of scripture's Pauline teaching.

The keen emphasis of the CE on a community's covenant-keeping practices, introduced by James 2:14-26, complements this same emphasis and so helps to correct the church's use of Paul to promote a false sola fideism. The community's confession of faith is embodied and so confirmed by its moral practices. Faith alone does not work with God and so the Christian who claims faith but does not live it cannot be

---

[64] See Francis Young, *The Theology of the Pastoral Epistles*, 79–85.
[65] Bassler, *1 Timothy, 2 Timothy, Titus*, 34.

befriended by God. This is the deep logic of the second collection: faith is confirmed by faithfulness. I would argue that the theme of "good works"—the performance of God's will (1 Pet 2:20; 3:17)—is a necessary condition of the believer's final salvation. While faith and not works alone is covenant-initiating, works and not faith alone are covenant-keeping.

A keen emphasis of the Christology of the CE collection highlights the role of Jesus as messianic exemplar of good works. He demonstrates that faithfulness to God saves human lives. In James those saved lives are poor and powerless (so James 2:1); in the Petrine witness, those lives are non-believers (2:18–3:7); in the Johannine witness, those lives are confessing believers (2:3-6). The messianic mission of Jesus is extended beyond his atoning death, appropriated by faith, to include an obedient life, followed in faithfulness.

3. *Portrait of the canonical Paul.* The reception of Pauline traditions in the Pastoral Epistles funds a final theme: the expansive résumé of a canonical Paul. This portrait and its various bits underwrite the importance of the Pauline apostolate that is now passed on to others to safeguard, with the Spirit's help, and transmit to still other teachers (1 Tim 6:20; 2 Tim 1:13-14; 2:1-2) after the departure of the Lord's apostle. There is a peculiar eschatology that emerges in these letters that is linked to the apostle Paul, which not only concern the eternal destiny of certain individuals but also of the (esp. Gentile) church. Even as Jesus is concerned what choices his disciples will make in his absence, since these choices concern eternal life, Paul is similarly concerned in these letters with respect to following his example and instruction.

The importance of the apostolic witness as recipient of God's word and then the importance of receiving it from trusted others is a critical feature of the CE collection. The addition of 2 Peter to 1 Peter and the Johannine letters to the CE collection have the overall effect of securing this apostolic impress for the entire corpus. In an epistemology necessarily different than the Pauline witness but for the same ends, both 2 Peter 1:12-21 and 1 John 1:1-4 ground what is preached and written in the memory of those who were ear- and eyewitnesses of Jesus. This apostolic memory establishes an epistemic criterion of truth and every departure from it is condemned. False prophets are exposed by the church's faithful proclamation of the truth (2 Pet 2:1-3; 1 John 4:1-6), Christian faith is secured and formed according to its instruction (2 Pet 1:12; Jude 3-4), and God's future judgment is measured by it (2 Pet 2:2-3; cf. 3 John 12). Simply put, salvation results from coming to knowledge of this apostolic-shaped truth (cf. 1 Tim 2:4).

6

A Canonical Approach to the *Paratext* of Hebrews (2019)

Introductory notes: Despite the spate of recent studies on the canonical process, highlighted by the magisterial two-volume work of Lee M. McDonald on the formation of the biblical canon in antiquity (2017) and by David Trobisch's insistence (with a chorus of other voices) that manuscript knowledge is of decisive importance in shaping the very idea of a biblical canon, most scholars continue to assume the canonical process was a serendipitous moment in the history of the Bible's reception without much relevance for biblical interpretation. Of a piece with this presumption is that canonization happened on an individual case-by-case basis and as such the reception of particular biblical books was preserved and protected by local communities. But Trobisch, supported by the work on early canon lists produced first by D. C. Parker (2008) and more recently updated by Edmon Gallagher and John D. Meade (2017), has put forward historical evidence that suggests otherwise. Not only were NT books gathered during their postbiblical transmission into four discrete volumes, these collections were deliberate productions with a role to perform—namely, to preserve the canonical witnesses of the Lord's apostles for the benefit of the whole church in a social world where the character and content of these witnesses were contested. Trobisch points out that such purposeful productions were not an innovation but followed the literary convention of antiquity: other thought leaders (e.g., Cicero) or their tradents collected their most important or useful writings and eventually published final, canonical editions to teach future followers of their now departed leaders.

While I agree with Trobisch that the formation of each canonical collection that constitutes the canonical edition of the NT (and that the Synagogue followed a similar path in forming the canonical edition of Tanakh) was purposeful and deliberate, the NT letter, Hebrews, is something of an outlier in this regard and requires special treatment. On the one hand, even though difficult to nail down with precision, the manuscript evidence seems to suggest that the early church's canonization of Hebrews was secured by including it as a member of the Pauline collection (even if placed in various locations within the collection depending on the canon list or codex). And yet, on the other hand, its anonymity, its idiom, and some of its most pressing Christological commitments are different than what is found elsewhere in the Pauline canon and was so noted early on by Patristic interpreters. This early ambivalence toward Hebrews is reflected in the manuscript tradition by the letter's fluid movement within (and eventually outside) the Pauline collection.

This ambivalence is picked up by modern biblical criticism, which hardly can consider an anonymous Hebrews to be a Pauline pseudepigraphon (however, see Claire K. Rothschild's speculation about Pauline authorship). More typically, scholars tend to read Hebrews as a "non-Pauline book" without a canonical home—neither Pauline nor a member of the CE collection. Hebrews more typically is placed in a collection of textual miscellanea, "labeled 'General Epistles' as little more than a matter of organizational convenience."[1] The purpose of this essay is to demonstrate another possibility.

A principal subtext of this chapter offers a response to the uneasy relationship modern criticism makes, especially in Protestant scholarship, between a text's apostolicity (and so its presumptive authority) and the identity of the text's "real" author, whether an apostle or not. Quite apart from the practical problem of reconstructing the author's identity when his anonymity seems purposeful, the ambivalence of locating Hebrews within the NT canon testifies to the problem of linking the identity of a text's author with the church's final recognition of its apostolic authority. It simply is not the case that a writing's eventual canonicity is made inevitable or self-evident by the presumption of an apostolic author. Quite apart from those letters probably written by the historical Paul that were not then included in the Pauline canon (e.g., the lost letter he mentions in 1 Corinthians), Hebrews is an anonymous letter probably neither written by the historical Paul, nor was his name ever added to it, but nonetheless initially circulated with the Pauline canon. I would add that whenever commenting on the act of composing a biblical text, its author never presumes that he is writing scripture but rather is engaged in an ordinary literary act (e.g., Luke 1:1-4). That is, a composition's canonicity is not predicated on the mere identity of an apostolic author but by the postbiblical recognition of its apostolic content and effects that were detected over considerable time and distance.

Especially Pauline criticism tends to settle the question of a text's canonicity by settling the question of its authorship; the earliest reception history of Hebrews would suggest this is a fallacious move. The invincible anonymity of Hebrews, which is maintained throughout its earliest reception history even when included in a 14-letter Pauline corpus in which attribution of authorship would seem necessary for admission (hence, the inclusion of letters most historians think are pseudonymous), suggests a different way of formulating the connection between a composition's authorship and its reception as apostolic. I contend that a study of the paratextual elements of this letter may help us understand this "different way."

Introduction

The NT Letter, "To the Hebrews," is surely one of scripture's most enigmatic books. Not only is its esoteric language strange-sounding to most readers, its anonymity and final placement within the biblical canon envisages a kind of textual homelessness (or

---

[1] Neil Elliott, "Introduction to Hebrews, the General Epistles, and Revelation," in *Fortress Commentary on the Bible* (Minneapolis: Fortress Press, 2014), 2:623.

restlessness) prescient of the history of its interpretation. The church finally placed Hebrews between the two canonical collections of apostolic letters, which is perhaps indicative of its ongoing role within the biblical canon as a bridge-builder or moderator (see below).

Readers have also found that the various comparisons made in Hebrews between the exalted Christ of Christian faith and Israel's OT story place a hard wedge between the church and synagogue as though the one has replaced the other in the economy of God's salvation. The effect of reading Hebrews as scripture within the church has shaped the belief that to trust Christ for our salvation requires believers to detach themselves from the church's Jewish legacy and from the spiritual equipment passed on to Christians from our Jewish ancestors. The worse example of this wrongheaded belief is to deny the authority of the OT and even to engage in the racial politics of anti-Semitism.

These sometimes dangerous effects of reading Hebrews sound a cautionary note: handle with care! Even faithful readers who pick up Hebrews as Spirit-appointed scripture are bound to ask, how does this strange and dangerous book address Christians as God's word for today's faith? Quite apart from the inability of modern scholars to locate this composition in its original historical setting or to identify who wrote it, for whom, when and for what reason, the more important question is this: why should Christians read this odd letter addressed "to the Hebrews" as the church's scripture? This chapter proposes a modest response to this question.

It is axiomatic among Bible scholars that the titles of New Testament books are not authorial properties but rather postbiblical additions by later editors, cued by the literary conventions of antiquity,[2] by secondary traditions, and by a common sense reading of the composition itself. As such, book titles rarely attract critical attention and are routinely dismissed as the misunderstandings of the second/third century church whose quest for a book's original address was well-intended but simplistic.[3] Surely if book titles are assessed by whether they contribute reliable historical markers of a composition's original address, they are deemed of little help.

We would argue, however, that an historian's approach to book titles is misplaced in two ways. In the first place, titles are not authorial properties at all and should not

---

[2] For example, Harry Y. Gamble argues that titling the four canonical Gospels became necessary in response to the practical need of distinguishing between four different versions of a single Gospel so then to catalogue the four in congregational libraries and to order their use for liturgical readings; *Books and Readers in the Early Church* (New Haven, CT: Yale University Press, 1995), pp. 153–4.

[3] See F. F. Bruce's discussion of the title, "To the Hebrews," as a viable if not vague entry point to his reconstruction of the letter's original address; *Commentary on the Epistles to the Hebrews*, NICNT (Grand Rapids: Eerdmans, 1964), pp. 3–9. Most scholars think the title given Hebrews in the first printed editions, "An Epistle of Paul to the Hebrews," is mistaken at every level: it isn't an epistle, nor is it written by Paul, and the author's audience is not Hebrews—at least in the sense of Acts 6:1, since the audience is Greek-speaking. Such an assessment, however, misses the paratextual point entirely. Most commentators do not bother to discuss the title at all because it preempts a critical assessment of internal evidence that may lead to a plausible identity of the letter's addresses. The indeterminate nature of this quest of the letter's point of origin, which characterizes virtually every modern introduction to commentaries on Hebrews, may in fact commend a different approach that shifts readers away from speculations of a book's composition to refocus on its subsequent reception as scripture.

be approached as though they tell us something of a book's original address. They were attached by editors to texts during an early stage of their reception history when the text's enduring authority for subsequent generations was initially recognized by the church's episcopacy. Titling a book, then, is a phenomenon of the canonical process and may reveal something of the church's initial reception and intended role for a composition included in its biblical canon.

Additionally, recent literary theory proposed by Gérard Genette has called attention to the importance of those ancillary or "fringe" productions that surround a text even though not belonging to its main body. Genette calls these later additions, whether by the author or subsequent editors, the "paratext of the work."[4] These additions include the book's title and its precise placement within a larger textual field, as well as other literary conventions such as the author's name (whether real, a pseudonym, or an anonym) and a preface or epilogue, all of which present the principal text in a manner that assures its reception and performance—its "transaction" with the reader as Genette calls it.[5] He adds that the paratext of a work is typically modified to adapt the work to readers of a particular time and place to assure their transaction with the work will respond effectively to "differences of pressure."[6]

Following Genette's insight, then, I would argue the paratext that frames the church's "transaction" with Hebrews as scripture includes at a minimum its title, its anonymity, and its placement within the final redaction of the NT canon, and if these productions were added during a postbiblical canonical process as I would argue, then the elements that constitute the paratext of Hebrews has a certain illocutionary force in clarifying the letter's role within the church's biblical canon for its current readers.[7]

---

[4] Gérard Genette, "Introduction to the Paratext," *New Literary History* 22 (1991): 261, and his expanded introduction in *Paratexts: Thresholds of Interpretation*, ET (Cambridge University Press, 1997), pp. 1–14 in which he considers ways in which the paratextual elements of a primary text are added during the course of its history to control how it is received and read. See a suggestive application of Genette's theory to the final placement of Hebrews within the NT canon by Gregory Goswell, "Finding a Home for the Letter to the Hebrews," *JETS* 59 (2016): 747–60. I acknowledge my debt to Professor Goswell whose study pointed me to Genette's body of published work.

[5] I find David Trobisch's connection between manuscript production and their oral performances in the earliest stages of the canonical process illuminating. Trobisch reminds us that mss were written and copied with punctuation markers, paragraph divisions, chapter headings and the like. When canonical stories or letters were read aloud in a small community of mostly illiterate auditors, the reader needed to make interpretive moves to tell the story or read the letter in ways that communicated God's word to God's people. That is, something so elemental as the divisions and headings of the critical text is another paratextual element to consider; see his "Oral Performance of Biblical Texts in the Early Church," *ConJ* (2011): 277–84.

[6] Genette, 262. This feature of a paratext shares with rabbinical midrash a vital concern to contemporize biblical texts for current readers. An approach to the book title, "To the Hebrews," as midrashic (see below), then, is apropos of its paratextual role. I would simply add that the paratext itself is a critical element of the canonical shaping of texts for inclusion in and continual use as the community's scripture.

[7] Some interpreters contend the final chapter of Hebrews, which differs from the rest of the letter in genre and idiom, was a secondary addition to the text perhaps by the author himself. The motive for doing so remains unclear and contested. Childs, for example, argues that this addition indicates a canonical shaping of a non-letter, adding a Pauline-like benediction so that Hebrews would fit more easily within the Pauline canon with which it circulated early in its reception history; *NT as Canon*, 417. Recent scholarship has dismissed this hypothesis, however, and virtually all recent interpreters accept the thirteen-chapter work as an integral whole. Not only is this conclusion secured by ms. evidence but also by its rhetorical design. See Craig B. Koester who considers Hebrews 12:28–13:21

In addition, as properties of the canonical process, the importance of a book's paratext is not retrospective of its particular origins or of the communicative intentions of a particular author for a particular audience located in a particular social world at a particular moment in time. The effect of canonization (and so of each element of a book's paratext) was to universalize and globalize the intended audience. The interpretive act, then, is also transformed, evident in the history of a book's reception, to contemporize its meaning for its current readers. In this special sense, then, the title, "To the Hebrews," is affixed to this ancient word of exhortation to continually encourage different communities of faithful readers who use Hebrews again and again to inspire their worship and catechesis to interpret and forge their lives and witness as disciples of Jesus within their respective time-zones.

The Title, "To the Hebrews"

We may suppose that when the book was titled, "To the Hebrews," probably sometime late in the second century, Paul was viewed as its best candidate for apostolic authorship. Even though Paul's name was not added to the letter's address,[8] the letter's title was formulated to correspond to the linguistic form of the titles of Paul's canonical letters (see below). Especially since a Pauline canon would undoubtedly have already been in wide circulation by this time, the title's implication of Pauline origins is puzzling, even apart from its anonymity, since nowhere in his canonical letters does Paul speak of a mission "to the Hebrews." In fact, the Pastoral Epistles identify him categorically as God's appointed teacher of non-Hebrews (1 Tim 2:7; Titus 1:2-3).[9]

---

as the conclusion or "peroration" of a public speech or homily, *Hebrews*, AB (New York: Doubleday, 2001), pp. 554–84.

[8] Among the most persistent exegetical problems facing the interpreter of Hebrews is its anonymity. Considered as a paratextual property, the letter's lack of authorial attribution—and one might even say the deliberate decision to retain its anonymity—may actually help clarify its function within the NT if the intent of doing so was to place the letter *outside* of the Pauline canonical collection (contra Childs). Especially if apostolic attribution (i.e., pseudonymity) was an accepted convention of the so-called "Pauline circle"—since most Pauline scholars suppose Pauline attribution was added to several "disputed" Pauline letters for inclusion within the canonical corpus—the interpreter must ask why not then also add Paul's name to Hebrews during the canonical process. In my view, leaving the author unknown is a deliberate decision of its canonization and perhaps may help explain its final location within the NT canon; cf. Gabrielle Gelardini, "'As if by Paul?': Some Remarks on the Textual Strategy of Anonymity in Hebrews," in *The Early Reception of Paul the Second Temple Jew*, ed. Isaac W. Oliver and Gabriele Boccaccini, LSTS 92 (London: T&T Clark, 2018), pp. 267–86. I will return to this prospect later in this chapter. In any case, I would allow that the doubt or even neglect this letter has suffered during its reception history, especially in the West, is often due to a lack of clear apostolic attribution. In passing I would note that I am deeply suspicious of a line of reasoning that links authority with authorship and think the claim for a text's apostolicity based upon its real author is fallacious. The claim of apostolicity to secure a book's authority was registered because of its content and usefulness in forming the community's faith and public witness. Hebrews in particular perhaps presents a good case study in this fallacy of securing a text's apostolic authority by historical reconstructions of authorship.

[9] In *1 & 2 Timothy and Titus*, I argue that the late addition of the Pastoral Epistles to the Pauline corpus intended to perform a hermeneutical role by defining the settled terms of Paul's apostolic tradition. Central to this role is the depiction of a "canonical Paul" as the apostle *par excellence* whose missional vocation, now followed by his tradents, is to present the gospel to the nations/Gentiles. See the chapter included in the present volume.

Perhaps the reader may suppose, however, that among the canonical performances of the Book of Acts, especially if read as the NT's introduction to the apostolic letters, is to delineate the borders of Paul's mission as including Jews according to his commission by the risen Jesus (see Acts 9:15-16). One might speculate on this basis that perhaps the final placement of Hebrews in the NT at the tail-end of the Pauline collection intends to register this point: Paul's personification of Israel's vocation as a "light to the nations" is concentrated by a gospel message that the saving grace of Israel's God is international. This conviction is surely thematic of the story of Paul in Acts. The canonical process merely reifies this theme by appending the Pauline corpus to include Hebrews to correct the supersessionist impression shaped by reading the Pauline collection without Acts, which seems to present Paul's gospel as exclusively for non-Hebrews. In any case, I will turn our attention to the interpretive importance of the final placement of Hebrews within the NT canon in concluding this study of the interpretive importance of its title.

While many titles given to biblical writings seem perfunctory, some provide their readers with initial interpretive clues of a book's particular role or its relationship with other books within the biblical canon.[10] If we allow that a book's usefulness as scripture was first recognized by its congregational practice within catechetical, liturgical, or missional settings, the same may be inferred of its titles. Much like the superscriptions that were added to various Psalms to recall episodes from David's biblical narrative to contextualize their use in worship settings—an example of what Boyarin calls, "the intertextuality of midrash"—titles may also have been added to compositions or whole collections (e.g., "The Gospel") by later editors to guide their subsequent performances as scripture in worship and catechesis. Titles, then, are hermeneutical of a new setting where canonical compositions or collections are now used by the church catholic as sacred scripture to guide its mission, worship, and catechesis for generation after generation of faithful readers.[11]

C. Koester follows the clear majority of interpreters when he concludes that the title of Hebrews reflects a common sense reading of the letter's contents—its use of the synagogue's Bible (even if in Greek translation) and sustained commentary on the temple and its priestly practices.[12] This naturally leads exegetes to assume historical referents stand behind the Pastor's exhortations and Christological exposition; most proposals present, then, some version of the "back to Judaism" scenario with a "my gospel is better than yours" polemic in response. What should be said in this regard is that the historical record is silent about such an intention. Koester does allow, however, that "the Hebrews" may provide a more symbolic address of the letter's intended audience. He goes on to note the choice of "the Hebrews" may symbolize a community of pilgrims to a Greek-speaking audience, which he finally dismisses on the grounds that such an audience would be hard-pressed to recognize the wordplay.[13] But his

---

[10] Brevard Childs introduced this essential insight of this phenomenon in his important study, "Psalm Titles and Midrashic Exegesis," *JSS* 16 (1971): 137-50.

[11] In this regard, see Wall, *The Canon Debate*, 535-8.

[12] See in particular Eyal Regev's unpublished SBL paper (2017), "Hebrews' Priestly Christology and the Understanding of the Death of Jesus: Taking the Temple Cult Seriously" who takes these references to temple and priesthood as literal, not figural descriptions of Judaism's principal institutions.

[13] Koester, *Hebrews*, 171-3.

criticism is based on linguistic grounds rather than the potential of "the Hebrews" as a midrashic device that recalls a particular biblical narrative in which the Hebrews played a central role as the antecedent text (or "co-text") for reading the letter within canonical context. I will return to this prospect below.

Apart from any other claim implied by a book's title, its literary form often placed it within a particular canonical collection, which when recognized as completed was added to the biblical canon with a particular role to perform within the whole. This observation is especially decisive for a canonical approach to Luke and Acts, whose respective roles within scripture are cued in part by their different titles. On the one hand, Luke's title, κατὰ Λουκᾶν, locates its story of Jesus within the fourfold Gospel collection rather than as a continuous narrative of Christian beginnings with Acts as though a canonical Luke-Acts. On the other hand, the title added to Acts, Πράξεις Ἀποστόλων, refocuses the reader's attention from the signs and wonders of Jesus from Nazareth (Acts 2:22) to those of his apostles, which authenticates their spiritual authority as successors of the risen Lord.

In any case, what finally emerged during the canonical process is an ordered anthology of canonized collections—an ordered collection of ordered collections—whose sequence intends to target the spiritual benefaction of one, holy, catholic, and apostolic church. We contend, then, that some book titles may actually cue more than a precise location within a canonical collection and also may evoke a canonical book's theological potential when performed by faithful congregations in worship and catechesis. Further, even though a title often reclaims the address given by the book itself, which is typical of Pauline letters, it often implicates an apostolic tradition thereby securing its authority for subsequent use. This canonical move seems especially important for the NT's other anonymous compositions (Gospels, Acts 1-2-3 John). I would add this is also true of the composition's superscription, Ἀποκάλυψις Ἰωάννου, which actually relocates its opening attribution, Ἀποκάλυψις Ἰησοῦ Χριστοῦ ἣν ἔδωκεν αὐτῷ ὁ θεὸς (Rev 1:1), to the apostolic tradition founded by his beloved disciple.

Unlike the Pauline letters, however, the title, "To the Hebrews," is not cued by the letter's internal address. Nowhere within the book are its intended readers identified as "the Hebrews." In fact, the closest marker we have of this audience is registered in 2:3-4, where they are addressed as second generation recipients of a gospel first proclaimed by the Lord and subsequently confirmed as God's word by the "signs and wonders" of the Spirit of Pentecost. Whether these recipients of this saving message are Jews or non-Jews, the text simply doesn't say. A second clue is provided by 10:32-34, which speaks of these new converts to Jesus as mistreated by others, which they accepted in confidence of a future with God. The Pastor's concluding focus on the community's leaders (13:7-17) may indicate that this intersection between conversion and subsequent suffering is exacerbated by their unwillingness to follow the spiritual direction of their leaders.

In light of the book's own markers, however faint, criticism's lingering presumption that the title addresses disaffected "Hebrews" whose conversion from Judaism to Christ is threatened by unexpected suffering is hardly secured on evidence. The theological crisis addressed by the Pastor is more likely the sort of existential weariness that sometimes faces the second generations of socially marginal religious movements even today. This crisis does appear to be deepened by a realized soteriology that has mistaken their dramatic conversion to Jesus and its Pentecostal confirmation as an exodus from sin "once for all," which would bypass any subsequent experience of temptation and suffering before entering into the blessed "world to come" (2:5). As Lindars puts it, "nothing was said to them about post-baptismal sin; they simply assumed they would remain in a state of grace until the *parousia*."[14] If this is the situation of the book's intended readers, the title given it does not direct the Pastor's "word of exhortation" (13:22) toward disaffected Jewish believers but all believers who struggle to remain faithful to their confession of Christ and approach this scripture to hear a word from God on target.

The question remains as Childs has sharply put it: how does the title, "To the Hebrews," function to guide those Christians who practice this canonical letter as scripture in their worship and catechesis? Childs is surely correct that the theological problem occasioned by Hebrews regards the intertextual relationship between Israel's prophetic/biblical word and its definitive interpretation in the apostolic witness to the incarnate One.[15] But he does nothing to explain how the title functions hermeneutically to cue this intertextuality. In my mind, Childs provides a way forward in his earlier study of the Psalter's superscriptions as midrashic prompts that recall biblical stories of David to contextualize various Psalms for their subsequent performances as scripture in the community's worship and catechesis. Childs's insight may help us understand better the function of this letter's title, especially to provide a canonical context to guide those believers who struggle to keep on the pathway to full salvation.

(1) If prospective of its use as scripture, then, I commend an approach to the title that understands, "To the Hebrews," as midrashic of antecedent traditions, intended to recall the biblical narrative of "the Hebrews" as hermeneutical of the existential situation that continues to face every generation of the letter's Christian readers. Put differently, "To the Hebrews" is the figural address of *any* community of readers who confess Jesus as their "apostle and high priest" (Heb 3:1).[16] The title is an evocation for Christian readers to identify with Israel, not only with its biblical narrative but also with the theological grammar of God's covenant people who in "these last days" have been chastened by the apocalypse of God's incarnation in the historical Jesus and called to a life of faithfulness for their wilderness journey to the coming world (so Heb 1-2). In this broad sense, I agree with Childs that the OT's story of Israel continues to vocalize God's eternal word in a way that links old with new, Christianity with Judaism,

---

[14] Barnabas Lindars, *The Theology of the Letter to the Hebrews*, NTT (Cambridge: Cambridge University Press, 1991), p. 13.

[15] For a somewhat different (but not incompatible) response to this same question, see Chistopher R. Seitz's treatment of Hebrews' use of the OT as Christian scripture in, *The Character of Christian Scripture*, STI (Grand Rapids, MI: Baker Academic, 2011), pp. 115-35. Seitz follows the lead of Brevard Childs's programmatic treatment of Hebrews in its canonical (i.e., Pauline) setting in his *NT as Canon*, 400-18.

[16] For an excellent study of biblical Israel as a figuration of the church (and synagogue), see now Frank A. Spina, "Israel as a Figure for the Church," in *The Usefulness of Scripture*, 3-23. Especially important is Spina's trenchant rejection of the heresy of supersession, which is an implication of the close intersection of Judaism and Christianity as figurations of biblical Israel. His study could be extended to include Hebrews as a case study of this very point, thereby subverting the persistent use of Hebrews to secure various theologies that claim Christians have replaced "the Hebrews" in the economy of God's salvation.

in a way that derails any effort to move Christian theological freight along separate tracks of the divine economy, for "there is neither Jew nor Greek for all are one in Christ Jesus" (Gal 3:28; cf. Eph 2:13-16).[17]

(2) I would argue the more particular episode of Israel's biblical narrative recalled by this title is the Exodus story—what Walter Brueggemann calls the elemental, non-negotiable story that lies at the heart of Israel's faith.[18] While "the Hebrews" may have reflected a mostly Gentile (non-Jewish) church's preferred name for Jews when the letter's canonicity was first recognized, its evocative power when approached within its present biblical setting may recall the moment when the naming of God as "the God of the Hebrews" (Ex 3:18) prepares a people for their Exodus into the wilderness to worship the God who promised land and progeny to Abraham and Sarah.[19]

While the word, "Hebrews," surely refers to God's elect people, it is used sparingly and strategically of Israel in the biblical narrative. Its general use in the OT (including 1 Sam and Jonah's opening declaration, "I am a Hebrew" [Jon 1:9]) would seem to underscore Israel's outsider status as justification for its abusive, derogatory treatment by more powerful others.[20] More significantly, several uses of "Hebrew" in Genesis mark out a particular group and prepare readers for God's naming in Exodus as "the God of the Hebrews." The first use is of Abraham (Gen 14:13) in a context that seems to indicate his alien and nomadic status.[21] The subsequent uses of "Hebrew" in Genesis are more telling. The two people who call Joseph a "Hebrew"—Potiphar's wife (Gen 39:14, 17) and a member of Pharaoh's staff (Gen 40:12; cf. 43:32)—do so in a clearly derogatory manner: Joseph the Hebrew is an outsider who is glibly devalued and accused of wrong. While this negative connotation does not continue in the story of Moses, the use of "Hebrew" to classify the midwives who saved him for his future as elect Israel's messiah locates them as members of an enslaved, oppressed people.

Repeatedly in the narrative that stages scripture's pivotal story of Israel's journey to its promised land, God encounters Moses with the name, "The God of the Hebrews" (Exod 3:18; 5:3; 7:16; 9:1, 13; 10:3). While God's initial revelation (3:18) is addressed to Moses and marks out a primary way in which Moses should confess God publicly, its repetition frames how Moses introduces God to an obdurate Pharaoh, who nonetheless responds by asking the right question: "Who is this whose voice I should listen to so that I send away the children of Israel?" (LXX Exod 5:2).

---

[17] Childs, *The NT as Canon*, 414–15.
[18] While Johnson is certainly correct that the Pastor's appropriation of the wilderness tradition is hardly "innovative," since the post-exodus story had become "an essential moment in Israel's history … as the prologue to covenant" (120), he expresses no surprise regarding how infrequently it is used in the NT. Perhaps this is because the NT receives the prophetic tradition that uses the wilderness story to interpret the exile, which many thought had ended with the risen Messiah.
[19] The function of the genitive "of the Hebrews" is debated but probably expresses a special relationship between God and "the Hebrews" that should be privileged by outsiders (e.g., the Pharaoh).
[20] So James LaGrand, *The Earliest Christian Mission to "All Nations" in the Light of Matthew's Gospel* (Grand Rapids: Eerdmans, 1999), pp. 49–55; cf. Matthew Akers, "What's in a Name? An Examination of the Usage of the Term 'Hebrew' in the Old Testament," *JETS* 55 (2012): 685–96.
[21] The plausible linguistic connection between the word "Hebrew" and its Akkadian cognate, *'apiru*, which means "alien" or "migrant," is well-known. At its root, the word "Hebrew" refers to a people's status as aliens and strangers whose nomadic life put them on the margins of civil society.

The naming of God is not incidental but central to the Exodus tradition received in Exodus. To know the name of God is to know something of who God is (cf. Ex 33:19; 34:6-7). In this case, the Creator God of the universe has a privileged relationship with a particular, elect people. Moreover, the naming of "the God of the Hebrews" shapes the identity and worship of a people who belong to God while at the same time enduring conflict with the Pharaoh, who personifies unrelenting, fierce opposition to God and God's people. There is a sense in which this naming of God is a wake-up call for Pharaoh's benefit: it intends to put him on notice that God not only plans to liberate the Hebrews from his death-dealing oppression but then to separate them for worship of a holy Creator God. The endgame of the Exodus is announced with dramatic irony as "as journey into the wilderness to sacrifice to our Lord God" (Exod 3:18). Because of the concentration of this witness to God's naming as "God of the Hebrews" to frame the Exodus event, I would contend that we can't read the title, "To the Hebrews," without having the biblical narrative of the Exodus in mind. That's the intertextuality of this title's midrash.

This makes sense of the letter's description of its audience's social status in Hebrews 10:32-34 as well as mention of their "shame" in Hebrews 12:2-3 (cf. 13:13). Lincoln concludes, "From the perspective of the writer, the real question in regard to social humiliation, as in regard to physical persecution and possible martyrdom, is whose approval, judgement and reward ultimately count—those of God or those of humans."[22] This could be said of the occasion facing the enslaved Hebrews as they prepared for their journey to the land God had promised their ancestors.

(3) I would argue that more important than recognition of the title's address "To the Hebrews" as allusive of the church's identification with Israel's marginal social status is its use in the Exodus narrative as harbinger of God's plan to deliver the chosen Hebrews from their oppressive slavery for a future land of promised blessings. That is, the title, "To the Hebrews," alludes to God's initial self-presentation to Moses as "God of the Hebrews," which provides a decisive theological claim that interprets the entire Exodus narrative as the liberation of an oppressed people from their slavery to an evil, death-dealing power for a blessed future with a faithful God. It is this theological marker that introduces and frames the Sinai revelation. I would contend that this same "transaction" (as Genette might call it) stipulates the canonical context for reading the Pastor's word of exhortation as scripture. Sharply put, the letter of Hebrews is read as a Christian commentary on the biblical story of Exodus.

An additional comment in this regard. God's self-presentation to Moses specifically indicates this Exodus event as a deliverance from Egyptian oppression for a three-day journey into the wilderness for a season of worship. This study will concentrate on the wilderness as the in-between place of Israel's journey from slavery in a land not their own to salvation in a promised land God gifts them. Despite what else we may think of the "wilderness," it is the liminal place that Israel necessarily must pass through in order to receive the blessings promised to them. What happens there, whether to worship the Lord, the God of Hebrews, or another god made of gold in the image of a

---

[22] Andrew Lincoln, *Hebrews: A Guide* (London: T&T Clark, 2006), p. 56.

calf, is the necessary means to a hoped for end. What also seems true is that the Exodus is God's *elected* means of fulfilling the promise of land to Sarah and Abraham.

(4) Modern criticism has succeeded in reconstructing in general terms the changing historical contingencies, independent sources, diverse literary genre, and different theological traditions that helped shape the final redaction of the Pentateuch. Various interpretive methods especially borrowed from the social sciences have helped us understand the reception history of this material not only in the OT (also non-canonical Jewish writings such as *Jubilees*) and the synagogue but then in the NT and the church where it is picked up and read as Christian scripture.[23] Nonetheless, the theological function of this Pentateuchal narrative is to make clear the constitutive elements of Israel's faith and life. It is in the mess and muck of the desert, where a Hebrew people's allegiance to their God is tested and their identity as God's people is forged, in this place where they lack everything material promised to them in their future homeland.

Three brief observations may prove useful in framing how the Pentateuch's wilderness story was appropriated by the Pastor in his word of exhortation "to the Hebrews." First, the NT's reception of this wilderness tradition is relatively infrequent. While the Exodus story remains central to Christian identity, its wilderness element does not. The desert stories of Jesus in the fourfold Gospel certainly allude to Israel's wilderness struggles and evidently link his messianic mission to God's promise to restore Israel, but these allusions are infrequent. Paul's appropriation of the story in 1 Corinthians 10 to warn his readers of moral indiscretion (see below) is the only clear wilderness intertext in his canonical letters. While spiritual testing is thematic of Christian discipleship in the NT, other biblical tropes are used to score this point.

Second, two different interpretations of Israel's wilderness tradition are evident in this material. Both interpretations conceive of the wilderness as a place of danger and spiritual testing. Walter Brueggemann calls wilderness a place of lifeless chaos. It is, in his phrase, "a land without promise, without hope, where no newness can come."[24] Simply put, it is a place where God's promise of newness will go unrealized and choices of loyalty to the "God of the Hebrews" who delivered them from past evil are called for but where present evils make such a choice uncertain.

On the one hand, the wilderness stages a "murmuring" community's protest movement against God and the leaders God has sanctified (cf. Acts 7:23-43[25]). This is the exodus (i.e., first) generation of the Hebrews whose persistent grumbling responds to hardship and suffering of a newly found freedom for which they are unprepared. The images of God, especially in the Numbers 13-14 version of the story, characterize

---

[23] See *Israel in the Wilderness*, ed. Kenneth E. Pomykala (Leiden: Brill, 2008), especially the essay by Susan L. Graham, "The Next Generation: Irenaeus on the Rebellion in the Desert of Paran" (183-99) as an example of early Christianity's reception of the wilderness tradition read through Christological lens and applied to Christian existence in a way similar to the Pastor's use in Hebrews.

[24] Walter Brueggemann, *The Land*, 2nd ed. (Minneapolis: Fortress Press, 2002), p. 28.

[25] Stephen uses the story of Moses in the wilderness to introduce his "two-visit" formula of prophetic ministry in Acts, which the story-teller then applies in particular to his narrative of Paul's mission: people whom Paul evangelizes have two chances to turn to Jesus; typically they reject or are ambivalent to Paul's message in response to his first visit but upon his second visit their choice is made firm.

an angry God's response to unfaithful, ungrateful Israel. This response strikes me as odd. There are several lament psalms in which a people's complaint occasions a gracious God's deliverance. God's response is not anger but mercy. Moreover, the Exodus 16 version of the tradition seems to have edited out divine anger to the people's murmuring, perhaps awaiting the later episode of the Golden Calf, Israel's "original sin." The subtext of Israel's failure is bookended by the songs of Moses and Miriam in Exodus 15 who celebrate in song and dance the community's exodus from Egypt and expectation of life in a promised land of plenty, and the covenant renewal service of Exodus 34. What isn't part of this narrative of Israel's post-Exodus life is a wilderness that lacked everything they had come to expect of a future with God and it took them by surprise.[26]

On the other hand, the wilderness is also a place that discloses God's responsive grace in the gifts of provision and presence for a people in constant need of goods for their journey to the promised land. The central character of this tradition is Israel's covenant-keeping God who promises Sarah and Abraham a homeland for their future family and who providentially keeps the promise and whose acts are characterized by the Pastor's apt phrase, "with well-timed mercy" (Heb 4:16b). Though they lacked resources, God's provision resulted in a covenanted people who "lacked nothing."

Perhaps for comic relief, the inclination of Israel is to save and store what meat and bread of God's daily provision goes uneaten, only to find it unfit to consume the next morning. That is, God's provision is precisely regulated to a community's existential need. In any case, I take it that the people who are primary beneficiaries of God's well-timed mercy are the wilderness (i.e., second) generation; the current wilderness generation is who the Pastor has in mind when writing Hebrews.

A final observation I would make of this Torah tradition is concentrated by the rabbi's well-known phrase that the synagogue's Torah consists of "five-fifths" of its whole.[27] While this shibboleth recognizes the discrete literary nature of its five books, God's people receive them for worship and catechesis as a fivefold, interdependent whole (much like the fourfold Gospel, Torah's NT parallel). Almost surely, the reception of the Pentateuch in Hebrews—the Pastor doubtless received the LXX Torah written on a single scroll as was typical of its production in the Diaspora—is as a whole consisting of five interdependent parts.[28]

The importance of this observation when applied to an analysis of the complex literary architecture of Hebrews is a reconsideration of the relationship between its discrete units. Almost all the book's commentators, ancient and modern, arrange these units in a way that separates the exposition of the community's wilderness sojourn (cf. Heb 3:1–4:16) from the expositions of Christ's high priestly ministry, its location in the heavenly temple, and its relationship with the new covenant (cf. Heb 5:1–11:40).

---

[26] See Graham, "The Next Generation," who traces Irenaeus's figural use Moses's warnings to the second generation in *Demonstration*, especially those found in Numbers 13–14 and Deuteronomy 1, already in the second century as typological of his warnings against Marcion and other post-apostolic Christians who dispute the apostolic gospel.

[27] See Robert Alter's marvelous reflection on this way of thinking of the Pentateuch's composition in the introduction to his *The Five Books of Moses* (New York: Norton, 2004), pp. iv–xvi.

[28] James A. Sanders, *Torah as Canon* (Philadelphia: Fortress, 1972).

However, if these themes—covenant, law, tabernacle, priesthood, sacrifice—are all received and read as elements of a single desert tradition, the Pastor's exhortation has a coherence that it otherwise doesn't. Christ's priestly ministry—past, present, and future—is an integral part of sustaining a wilderness people on their journey into the covenant blessings promised them by God (cf. Heb 12:1-29).

(5) The special role Deuteronomy performs in transmitting the wilderness tradition needs comment, especially because of Deuteronomy's allusive role in Hebrews. The Pastor's appeal to LXX Ps 94:7b-11 to provide God's commentary on Torah's wilderness narrative (Heb 3-4) rereads the prior narrative through the lens of the Deuteronomist: what is crucial is the community's covenant-keeping response to God's revelatory word (= Torah), which brings God's promised blessing rather than curse.[29] This point is scored as an exhortation to a people not yet in the promised land. The genre differences between Deuteronomy and Exodus/Numbers is important to note. Like Hebrews, Deuteronomy is a word of exhortation, not a story. What is made clear in the use of Moses's exhortation in Josiah's renewal movement 700 years later is that the desert is the place where Israel's identity, its covenant with God and the Torah that guides it are disclosed. The wilderness sojourn is not forgotten in any revival meeting precisely because this is where the motives and plotline of covenant renewal are made clear. First, the character of a people in need of renewal is made clear by the rebellion of a people who have quickly forgotten their experience of liberation. Second, the character of their God who renews is made clear by God's persistent presence and by the well-timed mercy of God's provisions—so that God's elect people who once lacked everything now lack nothing. The wilderness narrative (Deut 29:16-29) is God's word brought near (Deut 30:1-14; cf. Rom 10:5-13).

The Pastor's use of Psalms 94 cues yet another exegetical puzzlement (why is this particular Ps selected for use?); besides the centrality of obedience to God's word (see Heb 4:11-13), the Psalmist's reception of the wilderness narrative (esp. the tradition found in Num 14) adds two elements to the wilderness tradition that the Pastor exploits. First, is the idea that the destiny of the wilderness journey is entering into God's "rest"—a creational idea (cf. Gen 2:1-3; Heb 4:2-6) that may allude to the prospect of a new creation as the community's future inheritance (cf. Heb 12:27-28). The Pastor reinterprets the Psalm's "rest" as a future "sabbath rest" not realized by Jesus since the first "Jesus" (= Joshua) entered a "rest" that did not endure.

Second, and perhaps more critically, the Psalm dates the choice Israel must make in obeying God's word as "today." Both spatial and temporal aspects of the wilderness are tropes of Christian existence. The wilderness is a sacred space in which believers make their way into God's "coming world" (Heb 2:5; cf. Deut 32:8) and their "resurrection to a better life" (Heb 11:35), a new creation (cf. Heb 12:27-8). Wilderness is a place where

---

[29] The intertextual relationship between Hebrews and Deuteronomy is critical to the letter's exegesis. The Deuteronomist's commentary on the Exodus—Israel's journey to Canaan—is viewed as exemplary of the community's future life with God in the land; see David M. Allen, *Deuteronomy and Exhortation in Hebrews*, WUNT 238 (Tübingen: Mohr-Siebeck, 2008) for an expansive treatment of this intertext.

the community's faith is tested and challenged daily—as long as it is still "today" (i.e., any day of "these last days" prior to the coming Day of the Lord).

(6) In my view, then, the title cues the Pastor's Pentateuchal-shaped conception of Christian discipleship in a "word of exhortation" that not only concentrates readers on the biblical story of Israel's wandering in the wilderness but does so in a way that integrates both traditions into this letter's dialectical design. Simply put, the Christological exposition throughout Hebrews emphasizes the provisions of the exalted Son who "pioneers" and pastors his church through the temptations and hardships of the wilderness of this present age into the world to come. Especially in the opening, programmatic portion of the letter (1:4–4:16), disciples are addressed as the current wilderness generation; they are the people who belong to "the God of the Hebrews" who is incarnate in the Son.[30] The Pastor's exhortations in dialogue with this exposition trade on the Pentateuch's narrative of spiritual failure in which the exodus generation failed God because they could not endure their suffering and gave in to their temptation to refuse God's covenant and return to Egypt.

The integration of these two wilderness traditions, both canonical, places a keen emphasis on the existential conflict that characterizes Christian discipleship. Surely it is impossible to describe the post-baptism state of Christian existence in ways that promise a life without suffering and temptation as though one's exodus from death and sin prompts an immediate leap into the blessings promised by God. Discipleship is marked by a constant struggle to remain faithful to God, provoked in part by an aggressively hostile world. It is a wandering "on to perfection" (Heb 6:1) when a people's existence is, in James's apt phrase, "perfect and complete, not lacking in anything" (Jas 1:4b). Allusions to the Golden Calf story are never far from the hortatory sections of Hebrews and its implicit warning to the wilderness generation not to follow the example of the exodus generation.

Trading on the wilderness narrative, the Pastor locates his highly creative commentaries on the priesthood, the tabernacle/temple, and the covenant as theological constructions of God's provision. Virtually every proposal of Hebrews' rhetorical design separates out these different expositions from the opening exposition of the wilderness generation and exhortation to remain faithful to the Christian confession in the midst of temptation and suffering. This misses the integral nature of the Pentateuch's wilderness narrative, which introduces these resources as part of God's Sinai theophany.

In passing I would contrast Paul's (in 1 Cor 10:1-13) and the Pastor's reuse of the wilderness traditions as an example both of their common ground but then how differently the Pastor appropriates biblical traditions shared with Paul.[31] In both texts, the analogy to Torah's wilderness tradition lies in the possible failure of Christian readers to understand and apply a biblical theology of grace freighted by the canonical story of Israel's Exodus according to scripture. That is, both Paul and

---

[30] The images of a "second generation" abound in Hebrews beginning with 2:3-4.
[31] Cf. Carla S. Works, *The Church in the Wilderness: Paul's Use of Exodus Traditions in 1 Corinthians*, WUNT 2/379 (Tübingen: Mohr Siebeck, 2014).

the Pastor use wilderness as a trope of Christian discipleship that warns believers how not to respond to their experience of God's saving grace enacted through Christ (cf. 1 Cor 10:9-10). In the case of 1 Corinthians the intended audience is conflicted and spiritually/theologically immature and struggle with the very same problems (1 Cor 10:8). The warning issued is very real. In the case of Hebrews, however, there is no indication the intended audience is struggling with moral failure in a bid to retain their faith. The problem confronting the Pastor's readers is the effect of their theological immaturity and existential weariness in their struggle against sin. Additionally, while Paul argues the effect of Christ's death liberates believers from their slavery to sin to be instruments of righteousness (= moral rectitude), the application of God's grace in Christ does not provide cover for a free-wheeling discipleship, which in particular allows for conflict between believers from different social classes. Paul's concern is with an Easter=Exodus people's newly enabled capacity to practice grace toward others. The Pastor's warning, however, seems more confessional than ethical. The worry is rather a puny Christology that may in turn shape a distorted or disaffected discipleship whenever a rigorous catechesis of the congregation, led by its spiritual leaders, is not enjoined (so Heb 5:11–6:12; 13:7-19).

(7) The text used by the Pastor to shape his conception of discipleship is one particular version of the LXX. Susan Docherty's study of the biblical quotations of Hebrews concludes not only that he has reproduced his scriptural citations accurately without theological tampering but has used a variant of the LXX without recourse to other versions (Greek or Hebrew) at his disposal.[32] Docherty supposes his variant is simply the one and only scripture in use within the authorial community. This surely comes into play, for example, in the Pastor's use of LXX Ps 39 in Hebrews 10, where the Greek variant translates Psalms 39:7, θυσίαν καὶ προσφορὰν οὐκ ἠθέλησας, σῶμα δὲ κατηρτίσω μοι, changing the Hebrew word for "ears," אָזְנַיִם, for σῶμα in a midrash that concludes saints are made holy through the bodily sacrifice of Jesus Christ "once for all" (Heb 10:12).

We all recognize the massively complicated textual and social histories of the LXX: the axiom holds that no translation envisages a purely pragmatic or philological sensibility and so a translator's choices typically communicate her theological or ideological preferences. For many readers, Hebrews 10 evinces a "hermeneutical problem" precisely because the author uses the OG Psalm 39 rather than the MT Psalm 40 to score his Christological point and so to secure a related interest in a manner of Christian existence that embodies holiness. The problem is more than a practical one, of course, having to do with the decision to make the MT our canonical first testament rather than the OG, a decision which then is put at odds in Hebrews 10. It has also to do with our theology of scripture whose nature as a divinely inspired text is related to its production. That is, the inspired author of the MT Ps 40 conflicts with the inspired author of Hebrews 10 over whether to use an ear or a body when speaking of Messiah.

---

[32] Susan Docherty, *The Use of the Old Testament in Hebrews: A Case Study in Early Jewish Bible Interpretation*, WUNT 260 (Tübingen: Mohr-Siebeck, 2009).

The Placement of Hebrews within the NT Canon

Even a cursory review of the relevant manuscripts and canon lists of early Christianity recognizes that the placement of Hebrews within (or outside) the Pauline collection of an inchoate NT canon was itself a moving target. Most early canon lists say "the fourteen epistles of Paul" simply to avoid listing them all (e.g., Eusebius, Cyril, Epiphanius, Apostolic Canons, Rufinus, Innocent); other lists name and place Hebrews between the Pauline letters to churches and letters to individuals (Laodicea, Athanasius, Jerome, probably also Claromontanus); still others list them according to length with Hebrews falling between Romans and 1 Corinthians.[33] While I am mostly interested in the placement of Hebrews within the final redaction of the NT as a critical element of its paratext, it pays to mine the earliest history of Hebrews for clues about the editorial intention of its placement within the final form of the NT canon.

Settling the critical prolegomena that may otherwise locate Hebrews in earliest Christianity—its date and location, its occasion and intended audience, its genre and literary idiom—remains contested and most admit indeterminate and of no help in explaining its reception as a canonical letter. At the same time, most of its principal interpreters would allow that this history is problematized by the letter's anonymity.[34] Several data suggest it was initially received as a Pauline text even if its authorship was disputed. Its location in P[46] where Hebrews is sandwiched between Romans and the Corinthian correspondence, along with the form of its title and mention of Paul's protégée, Timothy, in the letter's benedictory, suggests an origin within the Pauline circle. Moreover, even though the portrait of the canonical Paul in 1-2 Timothy identifies him as apostle of the gentiles, the reception of similar Pauline traditions in Acts clearly includes his mission to the Hebrews.

David Trobisch's pioneering work with extant manuscript evidence, complemented by D. C. Parker and more recently by Edmon Gallagher and John Meade,[35] has successfully dismantled the old consensus that the NT canon was arbitrarily formed one book at a time until the process spontaneously ceased and achieved its final form sometime during the fifth century. The textual evidence simply does not support this historical construction, represented in the English-speaking academy by Bruce Metzger's work on the NT canon.[36] More likely, the NT is the deliberate compilation of four discrete collections, each produced in three stages and ordered not only according

---

[33] Clare K. Rothschild, *Hebrews as Pseudepigraphon*, WUNT 235 (Tübingen: Mohr Siebeck, 2009). Her argument that the placement of Hebrews in P46 between Romans and the Corinthian correspondence is hermeneutical challenges Trobisch's explanation that this manuscript's editor departed from literary convention (ordering books within a collection by their size) for unknown reasons and is in any case an isolated exception; *Paul's Letter Collection*, 98.

[34] See Craig Koester's summary of the letter's pre-Reformation history, *Hebrews*, 19–33.

[35] David Trobisch, *The First Edition*; D. C. Parker, *An Introduction to the NT Manuscripts and their Texts* (Cambridge: Cambridge University Press, 2008); Edmon L. Gallagher and John D. Meade, *The Biblical Canon Lists from Early Christianity* (Oxford: Oxford University Press, 2017). Framing this entire discussion is the magisterial body of work on the biblical canon produced by Lee M. McDonald, most recently his two volume treatment of *The Formation of the Biblical Canon* (London: T&T Clark, 2017).

[36] Metzger, *The Canon of the New Testament*.

to prevailing literary convention but in response to sociological and theological pressures, whether in response to Marcion's theological claims or to the internal chaos of earliest Christianity's struggle to find and secure an apostolic consensus amidst competing proposals. The NT is an authoritative collection of canonical *collections*. The fluid movement of Hebrews among the church's early canon lists and manuscripts does nothing to unhinge Hebrews from this essential typology of the canonical process. Its movement and final placement instantiates the struggle of an anonymous letter, which looks and in many ways performs differently than any other Pauline letter, to find a home in the Pauline canon.

Trobisch clearly elevates the interpretive importance of the editorial shaping of four discrete collections (Gospel, Acts and Catholic Epistles, Pauline Epistles and Hebrews, and Revelation).[37] The order of these four collections was relatively stable as was the sequence of books within each volume. Because this phenomenon was part of the canonical process, Trobisch considers this sequence normative, even if without continuing theological or hermeneutical importance. He therefore devalues the subsequent reordering of these four canonical volumes during the Middle Ages and especially in preparation for the Bible's printed editions, when Acts was separated from the Catholic Epistles and the Pauline collection was placed between them. Among the various effects of this move was to fix the location of Hebrews within the NT after (and perhaps outside of) the Pauline canon, which in Trobisch's mind misrepresents the editorial intent of the original arrangement.

While I accept in general Trobisch's reconstruction of the canonical process and his assessment of its religious content, I think the fluid placement of Hebrews mostly within but sometimes outside the Pauline canon during the canonical process may envisage a more ambivalent posture toward its role within the NT.[38] In part, my own ambivalence is due to the invincible (and I think deliberate) anonymity of Hebrews, which I believe frustrates any prospect of its inclusion within a Pauline canon as a canon-conscious pseudepigraphon, since clear attribution of Paul's authorship is a *sine qua non* feature of a Pauline letter, whether it is written in collaboration with Paul, by his amanuensis or a scribe copying a letter's draft for public reading (Col 4:16), or by a pseudepigrapher after Paul's death. In fact, Pauline pseudepigraphy of various canonical letters is not only a consensus of modern criticism since the nineteenth century but it now is widely viewed as an accepted literary convention of his apostolic tradition. *Anonymity just does not seem an option of compositions produced for a canonical (and postbiblical) edition of Pauline letters; it is not only a deliberate literary strategy of its author but also*

---

[37] *First Edition*, 78–106.

[38] For the ins and occasional outs of Hebrews in its relationship with the Pauline collection, see Reinhard F. Schlossnikel, *Der Brief an die Hebräer und das Corpus Paulinum*, GLB 20 (Freiburg: Herder, 1991). In his reconstruction of the Pauline collection, Trobisch has Hebrews added during the final or "comprehensive" stage of its formation; *Paul's Letter Collection*, 20–2. The thirteen Pauline epistles were consistently arranged in two groups: letters to congregations and letters to individuals, and within each group according to size. In this formulation, Hebrews is a notorious outlier, often disrupting this sequence. While I do not think this disqualifies Hebrews from membership within the original Pauline collection nor certainly from its canonical claim, I do think it suggests the early church's ambivalence toward its role as scripture.

of the church's reception of Hebrews as scripture and so its inclusion (and placement) within the NT canon must be viewed as a purposeful part of its paratext.

While the form of the letter's superscription, "To the Hebrews," follows Pauline convention and therefore would seem to incline it toward a special relationship with Paul's canonical witness,[39] the studied ambivalence registered toward this relationship during the history of its reception within the church and now by the modern academy would seem to harden this sense of the letter's homelessness. In fact, the consensus among scholars, reflected in every critical introduction of the NT, is that Hebrews is a non-Pauline letter (i.e., neither written by the historical Paul nor in line with the theological grammar of his undisputed letters). Years ago I chaired the SBL section that included the study of Hebrews with other "non-Pauline" and "deutero-Pauline" letters under the familiar rubric, "The General Epistles." In this case, "general" is the academy's rubric for "miscellanea." Naturally, each of these canonical epistles, including Hebrews, was studied in isolation from the others, an independent broker of religious meaning from God-only-knows authors for God-only-knows audiences in God-only-knows places in antiquity.

This brief rehearsal of the early history of Hebrews leads me to make the following programmatic suggestions about what the final placement of Hebrews may suggest as an element of its paratext. The prospects of each suggestion will require more careful testing than this study allows; but I set them out in advance of and perhaps to guide such an investigation.

Hebrews and the Pauline canon. The evidence from the earliest history of its reception suggests that canonical Hebrews (i.e., Hebrews within its canonical context) should be approached and studied as part of scripture's Pauline witness. It was received and preserved as such, and the title confirms it. Whatever conclusions a consensus of modern criticism forwards about the letter, the church must use it as a member of the Pauline canon, if only on its margins. Indeed, the long and steady struggle to find a place for it within the sequence of Pauline letters is at the least suggestive of its importance: everyone (in the East, and eventually in the West) agreed that the Pauline canon was in some way incomplete—less than "excellent" to use aesthetical language—without the arresting presence of Hebrews.

At the very least, such a prospect should be tested by the gains made by *relating themes in common between Hebrews and the Pauline letters, mostly to find whether Hebrews adds anything to their full exposition.* In this regard, the studies of Rothschild and Gelardini, which attempt to locate Hebrews within the Pauline circle are useful

---

[39] Here is what I tell my students: the ancient placement of Hebrews with Paul raises the question, if not Paul, who? In response, scholars are sharply divided. On the one hand, scholars search for candidates within the so-called "Pauline circle," perhaps with a Jewish bent. Barnabas (Tertullian), Apollos (Luther), Priscilla (Ruth Hoppin, Harnack), Luke (Clement of Alex), Clement of Rome, who cares. Don't get distracted by who wrote it at the expense of what is written. This is an important move since it recognizes the possibility of reading Hebrews with scripture's Pauline witness. On the other hand, others are quite content to disentangle the book from Pauline letters, not only on literary grounds—since Hebrews they say is not written as a letter—but also on theological grounds. Andrew Lincoln recently has placed Hebrews with the "Catholic Epistles," not only because of its Jewish theological sensibility, with its emphasis on purity and on an exemplary Christ, but because its expansive use of LXX seems more in common with books like James and 1 Peter than with Paul.

not in defense of its Pauline origins but of the themes and texts that might center an intracanonical conversation between them, especially with Romans as a gateway into the Pauline canon. Especially useful in this regard is Rothschild's idea of an "imitated Paul," which explains certain portions of Hebrews that sound like Paul and may even be read as Pauline fictions (e.g., Heb 13:20-25), as well as a comparative study of key catchwords such as ἐφάπαξ ("once for all") as a critical expression of the singular effects of Jesus's messianic work in both Romans and Hebrews.[40]

In consideration of the canonization of Hebrews, however, we suggest another possible role: as an *appendix to the Pauline canon*. If the rhetorical function of any appendix placed at the end of a book is to add information that is non-essential to a proper understanding of the collection but nonetheless useful in clarifying or illustrating the book's argument, then one might imagine the final shape of scripture's Pauline witness as excluding Hebrews because it was deemed aesthetically complete within its thirteen letter corpus but including Hebrews as the collection's appendix because it further clarifies an unwritten but indispensable element of the Pauline witness: namely, what Acts makes clear by its story of Paul that a mission to the gentiles must reject any scent of supersessionism and retain the Jewish legacy of the faith in order to be fully Christian.

To illustrate the problem of a Pauline witness without the addition of Hebrews, only consider the portrait of a canonical Paul found in the Timothy correspondence, which defines the singular importance of Pauline apostleship (no other apostles are named!) in relationship to his mission to the gentiles. In fact the apocalypse of the divine word targets only him (Titus 1:2-3) and the disclosure of the divine "mystery" of God's election of gentiles for inclusion in the covenant community (cf. Eph 2-3). Such a sentiment may naturally lead tradents into the heresy of supersessionism. The traditions of Paul received in Acts shape a portrait of his mission and message as of singular importance for the future of the church but never at the expense of his Jewishness. While the inclusion of repentant gentiles in the elect community is thematic of this narrative as well, the portrait of Paul in Acts presents him as actively preaching the gospel to the diaspora synagogue. In fact, the risen Jesus commissions him to do so (Acts 9:15-16). Throughout Acts Paul adapts his gospel for various audiences of devout Jews, even if with mixed results.

If these two pictures of a canonical Paul, Acts and Pauline, are considered together, a conflict in need of resolution emerges. In this regard, then, Hebrews may function as an appendix that purposes to resolve this textual tension by articulating Paul's gospel to the Jews but in a way that is in continuity with the essential theological grammar of the Pauline corpus. Moreover, the interplay of Jewish and Hellenistic materials as well as the peculiar nature of the theological crisis that occasions the reading of Hebrews fills in a narrative gap that teases out more the theological implications and its fallout when Jesus is preaching among the Jews. In any case, this is material apropos of an appendix.

Hebrews as canonical bridge between the two letter collections. Another possible role suggested by the final placement of Hebrews between the letter corpora, however, is

---

[40] Rothschild, *Hebrews as Pseudepigraphon*, 63–118.

that of a canonical bridge whose role is to facilitate mutually informing conversations between the different apostolic witnesses. If the traditions received in Acts help to contextualize a Pauline mission to the Hebrews and so in some sense legitimize its location within the Pauline canon (see above), but if Acts is placed not with Paul but with the CE during the early stages of the canonical process to form the *Apostolos* volume, then perhaps we have an historical basis for defending the hypothesis that Hebrews supplies a working glossary of themes that engages scripture's reader with a living "word of God" that envisions a manner of discipleship that resists either a Pauline or Pillars reductionism.[41] Its distinctive and complex portrait of a priestly Christ, for example, has this capacity. Although bits of this portrait recall and interpret a Pauline Christology, especially the centrality of Jesus's atoning death for putting the faith community into covenant with God, other bits prepare the reader for the Christology of the CE, which depicts his exemplary life—and his suffering in particular—as the pattern of the community's covenant-keeping.

I would argue that this study of the paratext of Hebrews commends its role as a facilitator of two important intracanonical conversations. The *title* cues the mutually-glossing conversation between scripture's two testaments, old and new, in a way that concentrates readers on the OT story of Israel's wilderness journey from its exodus from death to a promised land of plenty. The letter's conception of Christian existence is shaped by this narrative of temptation and potential failure of God's people and the ever-present provisions of a faithful God.

The *placement* of the letter within the final form of the NT canon, possibly to evoke an ambivalent response to the letter's purposeful anonymity, envisages its role as a facilitator of a conversation between the two canonical collections of apostolic letters, Pauline and Pillars. This prospect needs further elaboration but I would suggest it focus on Christology, especially in light of the importance of the congregation's catechesis to secure its confession of Christ for the difficult journey ahead.

---

[41] The scriptural allusions shared by Hebrews and Romans 9-11 where Paul responds to the theodicy occasioned by his gentile mission—is God faithful to promises made to Israel according to its scripture—and also found in the CE collection may provide a text-centered way forward in securing this prospect.

Part Four

The Revelation of John

7

The Church in John's Revelation (2015)

Introductory notes: This chapter comes from a book that seeks to demonstrate a canonical approach to a thematic study of scripture rather than to a biblical book or to a canonical collection—in this case, the theme is the church in the NT; cf. Robert W. Wall, Why the Church?, NTT (Nashville: Abingdon, 2015). It also seeks to reflect on the interaction between the church's creed and canon, which follow a parallel track of formation through the fourth century. These two textual products, creed and canon, create an enduring and interpenetrating conversation that targets the global church's theological formation. I've given structure to this idea by considering the church's creedal identity in the Niceno-Constantinopolitan Creed (381 CE), roughly at the same time the biblical canon had reached its final form. In my view, the formation of creed and canon during the same moment of early Christianity was guided by the same rubric—namely, the apostolic Rule of Faith. According to the Creed, the church confesses itself as one, holy, catholic, and apostolic. There is a keen sense in which scripture's instruction helps the church's membership understand what it means to live into each of these four marks. This chapter is a slightly revised version of the book's chapter on The Book of Revelation. Its vision of one holy catholic apostolic church is especially strategic because it brings scripture's metanarrative of God's salvation to conclusion. In this chapter I attempt to draw out the implications of Revelation's placement at the end of scripture as a canonical conclusion for NT ecclesiology.

Introduction

For most of the second century, the Apocalypse circulated with a "Johannine" corpus, which included the fourth Gospel and 1-2 John.[1] The church had collected and circulated this corpus based upon its theological agreements, common vocabulary, and a shared legacy that linked these anonymous writings to St. John's apostolate. For reasons now unknown to us, this small corpus of writings had been dismantled by the end of the third century (if not earlier): John's Gospel was placed in the fourfold canonical collection, the Epistles had found their way into a second collection of

---

[1] Charles E. Hill, *The Johannine Corpus in the Early Church* (Oxford: Oxford University Press, 2004).

"Catholic" letters, and the Apocalypse, left to fend for itself against various opponents, was finally placed at the end of the NT (although not until the eleventh century in the East after much handwringing).

This brief summary of a long and complex history introduces this chapter to make a key point: although we can now only speculate about the bumpy route the Apocalypse took in getting there, the church's reception of it into the biblical canon appears to be independent of other Johannine writings. That is, the role intended for it to perform within the NT, cued by its canonization, appears distinct from other Johannine writings and may be envisaged by its placement as scripture's last book.

The reader's intuition may very well agree with the church's decision to place the Apocalypse at scripture's end since it envisions the end-times of God's redemptive plan. The rhetorical role of a book's concluding chapter, however, is not precisely the same as "the end." A conclusion need not end things once and for all, but simply sets out the conditions for the plotline's imagined continuation into a future still to unfold of a story not yet complete. The role the Apocalypse performs in scripture is a conclusion, not an ending: readers are guided to envision God's victory over death and renewal of creation as the conditions of life eternal whose narrative is not yet told.

The book's odd title, "Apocalypse of John," is another property of the canonical process and not of the author's composition. The church gives the book its title to help readers recognize its authority—despite its strangeness and the controversy that swirled around it from the beginning. The first word, "apocalypse," recognizes this is the only biblical book so-named, thereby securing the community's sense of its distinctive role and theological character within the biblical canon. This is a standalone book.

The title's reference to John cues the contradiction we observe in the book's opening sentence: this apocalypse does not belong to John but is rather the "apocalypse of Jesus Christ" that God gave John via angelic intercession. One must assume such an obvious contradiction in such an important place is purposeful, targeting by doing so a special authority that underwrites its reception into the biblical canon as God's authoritative word. But the predicate of John's authority is not apostolic, since nowhere does the prophet refer to himself as an apostle. Rather his authority is due to his status as Christ's "servant" who is commissioned with the task of authoring a book of revelation "in the Spirit" (Rev 1:9; 4:2; 17:3; 21:10) based on visions sent him by a heavenly "son of man" (Rev 1:13-19).[2]

The deep impress of this move to wrap biblical compositions around the point of canonization helps secure the timelessness of their ecclesial address: scripture is always read in the present tense by its faithful readers. Against the emphasis of modern historical criticism, which seeks to explain the Apocalypse's visionary world against the background of antiquity (sometimes freezing its meaning there) or the emphasis of conservative theological interpretation, which seeks to signify this same word as a cipher for the end of time, a canonical approach to this book follows the lead of the church's first interpreters (e.g., Tyconius, Augustine, Bede): this is a book, like every

---

[2] This apocalyptic figure alludes to Dan 7:13-14 where the prophet envisions the appearance of a heavenly king who arrives on earth looking like a human being with the God-given task of ruling the nations forever.

other biblical book, that seeks to disclose God's gospel to the church of every age and time-zone. "The one who has an ear, hear what the Spirit says to the churches!" (2:29; 3:6, 13, 22; cf. 22:16-17).

This way of approaching the book finds support in its literary architecture. Although the genre of its composition is apocalyptic—that is, it is a book filled with other-worldly visions that reveal behind-the-scene mysteries about how the world really operates—these visions are formatted by the prophet into a pastoral letter. The symbolic, vivid images, characteristic of apocalyptic, does not disguise the practical bent of its canonical shape, which is to provide pastoral comfort for the afflicted and prophetic affliction against the comfortable so that the whole church is prepared for the coming victory of God—on earth as it is in heaven.

This is a book for, of, and about the church as the opening vision makes clear. The exalted Lord appears to the prophet "in the middle of seven lampstands" (1:13), which he subsequently interprets as the sevenfold (i.e., catholic) church (1:20). He commissions John to write down the visions he is about to receive for this same church, which the Lord is about to address (Rev 2-3). From start to finish, then, the Apocalypse is a vision about the eschatological church, past, present, and future (see the scope of John's commission, 1:19).

But the book's apocalyptic idiom is cosmic and dualistic. Its visions of the church constantly run between heaven and earth, between an old order that is passing away and ruled by an unholy trinity (= the evil one and two beasts; cf. Rev 12-13) already defeated, and the promised new creation ruled over by the eternal holy Trinity that is soon to come to earth as it now is in heaven. The apocalypse of God's salvation with Christ triggers a loud collision between these two worlds, the reverberations of which are everywhere observed and experienced. John sees, feels, and hears it, mostly from a distance, but on occasion even he participates in its arresting results. What seems clear from the beginning of this pastoral letter, when the exalted Christ addresses John's seven-point parish (Rev 2-3), is that the church presently has one foot in each world. In different ways and to different degrees, today's church experiences firsthand the collision between the passing old and the coming new. This is what I mean by reading the Apocalypse in the present tense: when one holy, catholic, and apostolic church gathers on earth to worship God, its heavenly ecclesial counterpart, which is wholly one holy catholic and apostolic, gathers in worship of the holy Trinity knowing that evil and death are already defeated foes. Today's church is constantly becoming by God's grace what it already is. The exegetical question that controls the following exposition is this: *how does the Apocalypse's adumbration of the church's four marks conclude and so complete scripture's witness to what it means to be God's people and to do as they ought?*

The Church Is One

Any coherent discussion of the church in the Apocalypse is concentrated by the Lord's address of the sevenfold church in chapters 2-3. The sender's greetings found in the personal letters of antiquity is typically shaped by his perspective of the readers/auditors. This frames whatever else he writes them in the rest of the letter. In the case of this apocalyptic letter, the prophet's pastoral theology of church is shaped by the vision that elaborates his opening address of the "seven congregations of Asia" (1:6).

The history of the church's use of these two chapters indicates the vision's "sevenfold" address is routinely taken to symbolize the church's catholicity.[3] Readers often find their own congregations here; the forces and factors that threaten the oneness of John's church in Roman Asia is taken as roughly analogous to those that threaten the eschatological standing of their own congregation, even if located in a very different time-zone.

One suspects this interpretive track is rightly directed by the prophet's repetition of the same "thus says" formula used by OT prophets when speaking God's word to Israel: "these are the words" of the exalted Lord to seven local congregations that define what will attract or discourage his presence and participation with his people. Like OT prophets, John casts his vision of the sevenfold church as the oracle of a prophet who both diagnoses the community's current spiritual health but then prognosticates what it must do to "overcome" evil to live with God forever. These are therefore crucial chapters in finding our theological legs in tracking down God's word for the church catholic of every age.

Moreover, John uses ἐκκλησία fifteen times in these two chapters but then only once more in the rest of the book. The book's theology of church from the risen Lord's angle of vision is clearly concentrated here. The primary idea of church evidently targets a particular community of believers gathered together in real places for worship and witness. The canonical mailing address is the sevenfold congregation of the church catholic; but the messy mixture of local culture and Christian faith that the living Jesus found in the local congregations over which the apostle John had oversight is the same he might find in the whole church at any given time.[4]

The prophet writes down what he sees and hears in a carefully crafted literary pattern, so that those hearing the Apocalypse read aloud (1:3) will not miss the Lord's message for them. First, his messages for each congregation follow the same outline for effective communication. Each opens with a description of the community's experience of its exalted and living Lord (2:1, 8, 12, 18; 3:1a, 7, 13) who is present in their midst and closely observant of how they conduct their spiritual and moral lives (see 1:13, 20; 2:1).

For this reason, the second part of each oracle begins with an ominous, "I know your works" (2:2, 9, 13, 19; 3:1b, 8, 15), which introduces a catalog of accusations and/or commendations that evaluate the congregation's readiness to receive the Lord upon his any-moment return (2:5, 16, 25; 3:3, 11, 20) so to participate in his final conquest over death (2:5, 10, 25-28; 3:5, 11-12, 21). The steady mention of a congregation's "works" (2:2, 5, 6, 19, 22, 23, 26; 3:1, 2, 8, 15) makes it clear that he is a Lord who measures discipleship by works in keeping with his example, characterized by loving

---

[3] The symbolic value of the number seven for Christians derives from the sum of three (= holy Trinity) and four (= four corners of creation), which come together in the realization of the new creation because of Christ's life and work. This new creation, of course, has a past, present and future that are plotted by the visions John receives and writes down in this book.

[4] The canonizing of Revelation universalizes its address, signifying that the sevenfold (= whole) church of chapters 2-3 targets the church catholic in every age and time-zone.

relationship and a firm rejection of the various evils (religious, cultural) that surround and threaten their communion with God.

A final part of each oracle regards the congregation's responsiveness to the Lord's exhortation, "If you can hear, listen to the Spirit" (2:7, 11, 17, 29; 3:6, 13, 22); whether or not to repent and restore a right relationship with the Lord mostly depends on its spiritual need and capacity to do so. Those who need to "repent" (i.e., to reorient themselves to a life like Christ) and those who do so will "emerge victorious" at day's end and participate in God's new creation—the markers of which are everywhere mentioned in concluding each oracle (e.g., "the tree of life in God's paradise," 2:7 par 22:2; "the hidden manna and the white stone," 2:17 par 21:5; "sit with me on my throne," 3:21 par 22:3).

How one listens to these "words of the prophecy" (1:3), whether in terror at the warnings to repent from present sin or face God's end-time judgment or in shalom at the exhortations to hope for the Lord's coming victory, depends on the congregation's responsiveness to the divine word. In fact, John's sevenfold oracle is precisely arranged so that the two congregations in gravest danger are those first and last mentioned (Ephesus and Laodicea), while the congregations in best shape (Smyrna and Philadelphia) are placed after and before these two in stark contrast. The other three congregations, noteworthy because of the description of their middling spiritual life, are appropriately found smack in the middle (Pergamum, Thyatira, Sardis)!

The contrasting pairs that begin and conclude the prophet's address have gained the most attention during the history of Revelation's interpretation for good reason. The haunting images of the abandoned "first love" of the Ephesian believers (2:4) or of the Lord spitting out the "lukewarm works" of the Laodiceans remind every reader that giving up a demanding discipleship by giving into a feel-good or secular religion undermines a community's union with Christ.

Indeed, the threats come from all directions, both within the churches, especially from teachers who have departed from the apostolic witness (e.g., 2:13-15, 20-23), and from the pressures of cultural expectation. The pressure of being a patriotic citizen in Caesar's empire is no different from what Christians experience today, when being a loyal citizen invites compromise of our allegiance to God's reign (cf. 2:9-10); or when routine business practices emphasize financial profit at the expense of Christian virtue (cf. 3:17-18). God's people are responsible for God's reputation in the world and therefore must resist any practice that subverts our "love and faithfulness, service and endurance" (2:19). This is a fundamental feature of the church's oneness with Christ.

Nonetheless, the centerpiece of John's address of the sevenfold church is what the Lord has to say for the congregation at Thyatira (2:18-29), and we should read this passage accordingly. There are three literary clues we should pick up in recognizing the importance of this often-neglected oracle. First, it stands at the center of an inverted parallelism or chiasm (ABCDC'B'A'), which pairs the first and seventh, second and sixth, and third and fifth members by their common form and linking words. What the careful reader finds where these two parallel lines intersect—where "X marks the spot"—is most important. Everything else funnels down to there and so intends to attract the interpreter's close attention. The Thyatira oracle is this vision's pivot-point, where "X marks the spot."

Second, this oracle is the longest and most complex address to the seven congregations. The sheer length of a biblical passage is often a cue of its importance; at least it should heighten the reader's interest to slow down and study it more carefully.

Finally, the use of Ps 2 in vv. 26-27 introduces one of the Apocalypse's essential co-texts (cf. 11:15, 18; 12:5; 14:1; 19:15): the entire book envisions the victory of the triune God over the rebellious nations currently under the control of an unholy trinity (= the evil one and two beasts; cf. Rev 12-13).

But the real importance of Thyatira is that its congregational profile expresses vividly the theological crisis that occasions any faithful reading of John's Apocalypse. This is a membership of rank-and-file believers whose everyday struggles and the practical concerns are those that face congregations in every age. In this sense, this is a good concluding text for scoring the mark of oneness in the NT.

Thyatira was a city known for its trade guilds (think: labor unions), membership in which would have involved idolatry. There was precious little idol-free space for urban Christians of antiquity. Their activities of daily life required decisions in business and social life that implicated one deeply in local traditions of idol worship (not unlike our own world of social media and personal technologies that preoccupy us and integrate us into a culture of self-absorption). The OT prophets speak of idolatry as a failure of attentiveness, the inability or unwillingness to focus our attention and desire upon God in the face of myriad distractions. John draws upon this prophetic criticism to frame the congregation's divided attention (v. 20) but then also of a false prophet (= Jezebel; cf. 2 Kgs 9) who apparently tolerated the routines of this idolatry with impunity as a way of getting ahead in business and social standing (2:20).[5] Compromise, whether theological or moral, is the essential threat of the church's oneness, which is measured by its solidarity with the risen One.

The Lord's concluding note promises himself to those who "overcome" (i.e., repent; v. 22) and continue to do "my works" (vv. 26a, 28). Jesus is "the morning star" (22:16), which is yet another striking metaphor of his messianic reign (cf. Num 24:17; Isa 60:3), specifically of the "light" that dawns at the daybreak of the new creation to illumine the nations of God's victory. The remnant of those believers in Thyatira and Seattle who repent and do the Lord's works—by rejecting the false prophet and avoiding idols—bears witness to this bright future.

The Church Is Holy

No other passage gives readers a better expression of the holy church in the Apocalypse than the vision of the 144,000 disciples on Mt. Zion, who have followed the Lamb wherever he goes and now stand in solidarity with him (see Rev 14:1-5). But first the context. John's flashback of God's victory over the evil one (12:10-12), already cued by the exalted Son's homecoming (12:5) and ensuing war in heaven (12:7-9),

---

[5] The specific reference of the curious phrase, "the deep secrets of Satan" (v. 24), is uncertain. Evidently, it is a label used of Jezebel's teaching, probably mentioned here sarcastically: there is nothing "deep" about it! Its content is thin because it is satanic; and will be proven false when Jesus returns (v. 25).

prepares readers for the terrifying vision of "What now?" We are told without much fuss or fanfare that the devil's defeat and demotion from heaven to earth has made him furious, not only because he has lost his heavenly status (and decisively so), but because he now knows "he only has a short time" left to unsettle God's plan of salvation before God's victory is made final. The devil's current target is the woman's "children who keep God's commandments and hold firmly to the witness of Jesus" (12:17)—the decisive image of a holy church in this biblical book. Holiness is not covenant-being but covenant-keeping.

The prophet sees the devil from a distance standing on earth's seashore (12:18), a fierce but defeated foe without anything more to lose and so ready to make a stand against God's people one last time. It is fitting the evil one recruits his partners from the sea, since in John's apocalyptic world the sea is home to evil and so an appropriate resource to draw allies skilled at violence and injustice. Two beasts are noted in particular, one from the sea and another from the land to form an unholy trinity. Together they rule over earth's anti-God kingdom in which the woman's children live.

If the devil is evil's representation of the first person of the holy Trinity, the beast he recruits from the sea similarly represents the second person (13:1-10). As we would expect the first two persons of this unholy trinity are one; they bear a striking family resemblance (cf. 12:3 and 13:1). John also recognizes this beast under the light of Daniel's vision of four beasts, which represent the four anti-God kingdoms of his world (cf. Dan 7:1-8). Bits and pieces of those four beasts fill out the picture of the anti-Christ that John draws for us. But the seven heads, the total of Daniel's beasts, now wear crowns, symbolic of kings rather than kingdoms. The prophet recognizes kingdoms are personified by their rulers, whether Roman Caesars or American Presidents; even though the structures and institutions of their nation-states shape the opposition to the practices of God's reign, these crowned (or elected) individuals are vested with "power, throne, and great authority" (13:2) to give direction that shapes the people and places under their rule. Evil rulers beget kingdoms that practice evil.

Likewise, the faithfulness of a single king, Christ Jesus, results in the triumph of God's reign (cf. Rom 5:18-21). Holiness is formed within those communities ruled by the holy Trinity who practice holiness. Perhaps for this reason, John at last recognizes the powerful beast as an "anti-Christ" who resembles God's Paschal Lamb who also was "slain and killed" and whose "deadly wound was healed" (13:3; 5:6).[6] The result is the global deification of both dragon and beast (13:3b-4), adorned with "blasphemous names" given them by their worshipers (13:1). This image, of course, is full of irony since their act of worship, rooted in unbelief and ignorance of God (see 9:20-21; cf. 13:8), mistakes who really controls earth's destiny: the Almighty One who sits on heaven's Throne and the messianic Lamb—a very different kind of slain beast—who stands beside it. But it also suggests that the failure to repent and turn to God has the

---

[6] We could also take this analogy between beast and Christ more literally: the beast was slain but then resuscitated while Jesus was slain on the Cross but then resurrected. The difference, of course, is that the beast's healing is temporary—a resuscitation to do more mischief "for a short time," not a resurrection to bring life eternal.

consequence of supporting, even worshiping, those in charge of the political/social institutions opposed to the redemptive purposes of God.

The catalog of brutal practices the evil beast is authorized to perform (13:5-7) offers a razor-sharp contrast to the redemptive practices of the faithful Lamb. Yet John hints at a divine purpose behind the beast's madness: the beast's lies and use of violence to bring submission to his rule of evil occasion a time of spiritual testing, when those faithful to the gospel should expect to suffer and even die (3:8-10). The present age on earth remains evil and the forces of evil, now in closer proximity with the devil thrown down to earth, seem to be in charge. The response of God's people called for by the Apocalypse is not to take up arms in retaliation but to face up to the reality of the present moment: to resist is futile (13:10) but also unnecessary since "salvation and power and kingdom of our God (not the dragon) and the authority of his Christ (not the beast) have now come" (12:10).[7]

A second monster emerges from the polluted land to complete this unholy trinity. Called elsewhere "the false prophet" (16:13; 19:20; 20:10), its "priestly" role is to direct the global worship of the other beast (13:12). The idiom of its various malevolent activities (all stated in present tense)—to exercise the authority of the first beast (13:12), to make fire to come down from heaven (13:13), to give breath that animates the beast's image (13:15) and mirrors and so seeks to subvert the Spirit's sanctifying work on Christ's behalf. The purpose of the Apocalypse's subversive representation of the triune God is to underscore the earlier claim that the evil one's work is to deceive the whole world (12:9). Evil works its magic by convincing people that falsehood is truth, what is bad is really good for you, God is not good, and there is salvation in something other than the Lamb. Deception, especially when the beast and its henchman open their mouth to speak blasphemies against God (13:6), is the principal instrument in the devil's toolbox.

But the impression shaped by John's vision is of the effectiveness and pervasiveness of evil's reign. The unholy trinity seems in charge. Evil is winning; its deceptions are easily believed; God's ways are marginalized and even removed from the public square. And this deadly pair of beasts leaves no wiggle room, so that everyone is forced to submit and be "marked" as belonging to the beast's people (13:16); their very survival depends upon it (13:17). If God's people are not for them, they are against them; and if God's people are against them, they are either led into exile (where their witness is no longer heard) or killed by the sword (13:10).

This terrifying vision depicts the essential struggle of the church's holy life in the present tense: living in a manner that pleasing a holy God is a slugfest. It is a life that is not cultivated in a "me-and-thee" vacuum but in a world organized by institutions that

---

[7] Revelation 13:8 speaks of names written in the "scroll of life" from "the time the earth was made." Some have embraced this text literally as a biblical justification for the doctrine of predestination. In context, however, this idea that salvation is something God grants some people (but not others) before salvation was even needed makes nonsense of the importance John places upon the decision to repent and turn to God. The better reading is to understand the phrases "from the time the earth was made" and the Lamb's "scroll of life" as tropes of God's faithfulness to realize the full plan of salvation written down on another scroll (see 5:1). Those who repent and follow the Lamb wherever he goes are willing participants in this salvation and on this basis they are named among the Lamb's people for life.

are fiercely opposed to God. In such a world, covenant-keeping is constantly subjected to brutal assault. An embattled holiness does not win out without suffering and even martyrdom.

The stirring vision of the 144,000 saints, now standing with the Lamb on Mt. Zion (14:1), must be understood in connection to the previous vision of the oppressive regime of the two beasts. Much has been written about the numerology of 144,000 (cf. 7:1-4). Simply put, it is a large compound of twelve, the number that symbolizes God's people. John now sees the heavenly community, which he had earlier only heard (cf. 7:4). What John actually "sees," then, is the Messiah's tribe: "a great crowd that no one could number" (7:9)—the same crowd of folks "from every nation, tribe, people, and language" that the messianic Lamb purchased for God with his shed blood (see 5:9).

If the Apocalypse 12:1-12 is a flashback from today that centers us on the heavenly victory of the exalted Christ, 14:1-5 looks forward to God's final battle on earth against death and evil. This literary "sandwich" makes it perfectly clear that today's reign of terror, described between, is but "for a short time" (12:12).

Richard Bauckham understands, then, this is a scene of holy war, each army identified by the tattoos on their foreheads (cf. 13:16-17; 14:1).[8] Mt. Zion, where the Lamb's forces muster for battle, is where David built Jerusalem, the holy city. It is the place where God brings to fulfillment the promises made to God's people. This is holy war that finally and fully will bring to realization God's promise to repair and restore creation on earth as it already has been realized in heaven.

The battle song of the Messiah's forces, sung with harp accompaniment in front of heaven's Throne, is "a new song." Its lyrics undoubtedly reprise those of the "new song" sung in heaven when the worthy Lamb took the inscrolled plan on salvation from God's hand and began to open its seven seals so to publish its glad tidings of great joy (cf. 5:9-10). It is a song of salvation sung by those "purchased from the earth," because it is they who testify to the efficacy of the Lamb's shed blood that cleanses them from sin for service of a holy God (cf. 7:14-15).

For this moment, however, these saints are envisioned as soldiers of the Lamb's army. Saints prepare themselves for holy war by abstaining from sex (14:4; cf. 1 Sam 21:5-6)—we should assume the "women" in this case are the Apocalypse's two evil women, Jezebel (2:20) and Babylon's prostitute (17:1-2)—and by intently following the Lamb *wherever* he goes (even to death). This verb "to follow," the key act of discipleship, is its only use outside of the Gospels and Acts. In this case, to follow Jesus includes confessing the truth about him (cf. 1 John 2:22-23; 4:15) and "blamelessly" following his righteous example.

The word, "blameless," doesn't mean perfect but rather without defect. In this context, John has in mind a manner of a holy life that is unmistakably Christ-like. Some interpreters have taken this to require sexual abstinence: the 144,000 must not engage in sex in order to follow Christ wholly (cf. 1 Cor 7:1-7). Within the context of John's visionary drama, however, the point is to underscore that a people's complete

---

[8] Richard Bauckham, "Revelation," in *Oxford Bible Commentary*, ed. John Barton and John Muddiman (Oxford: Oxford University Press, 2001), p. 1298.

faithfulness to Christ is the mark of holiness. Only this kind of company of disciples can effectively wage God's battle against evil on earth.

Readers of the Apocalypse already know the outcome of this holy war. The heavenly choir, which is informed with more inside information acquired with cosmic eyesight, already has celebrated God's victory over the destroyers of earth (cf. 11:17-19; 12:10-12). But it is a victory whose full effect is not yet celebrated on earth as it is in heaven. In this sense, then, the confession of a holy church, which is on earth, is profoundly hopeful, affirming God's coming victory when the heavenly company comes to earth still following the triumphant Lamb wherever he goes but now in doxology and worship.

The Church Is Catholic

The Apocalypse's narrative of God's salvation it plotted by a temporal and spatial ambivalence between what is already realized by God's people in heaven but not yet fully realized by God's people still on earth. While John's vision helps us imagine that the Lamb has already ended sin's reign, we also note that human existence remains largely unchanged and even the church's witness is sometimes compromised because unrepentant sin still remains on earth (9:20-21). The martyrs' poignant refrain, "how long?" (6:10), is still applied to creation's continuing experience of God's past judgment of evil on the Cross: when will we experience God's victory over wickedness on earth as it is in heaven? When will God make good on the prophet's promise that the apocalypse of God's salvation is "soon ... for the time is near" (1:1, 3)?

John's response to this question in chapters 11-12 retains a deep sense of the church's dual citizenship on earth and in heaven. Our exploration of this familiar theme seeks to extend the scope of the present church's catholicity to include both heaven and earth. That is, to confess the church is "catholic" recognizes both its global and cosmic dimensions (see Ephesians). In this sense, the worship practices of the heavenly church envisioned by John are "words of the prophecy" that look forward to that moment when the community of saints on earth, presently suffering and embattled (see above), will join its heavenly counterpart in unending worship of the holy Trinity. In this sense the reach and witness of God's people are as inclusive and expansive as the cosmic place created by "the Almighty, maker of heaven and earth, and of all that is, seen and unseen."

The present passage is framed by an interlude (cf. Rev 10:1–11:14) within an arresting vision of divine judgment (cf. Rev 8-11) that is brought to dramatic conclusion by a seventh trumpet fanfare (Rev 11:15-21). The final two panels of this interlude depict a civil war between God's people and God's enemies, "the Gentiles," which takes place in and around "the temple" (11:1-2). Into this war step "two" witnesses, which Torah stipulates in making God's case against evil (cf. Deut 19:15). Who are they? If the "Gentiles" are non-believers whose mission to destroy God's people takes place over a three and half month period (i.e., half the length of time according to God's inscrolled plan; so 10:1-11), then the "two witnesses" likely represent God's people over this same span of time. The misery God describes to John in 11:5-13 is the effect of a global confrontation between God's people (= two witnesses) and those who refuse to repent and remain opposed to God's gospel (= Gentiles; cf. 9:20-21).

Indeed, any definition of catholicity must include the global nature of the conflict between good and evil. Those who gloat over the bodies of martyred saints (11:7-8) and refuse them burial rights (a horrendous offense in the Jewish culture) are numbered from "the peoples, tribes, languages, and nations" (11:9-10). This snapshot of the civil war between God's people and God's enemies, and the fearful images of suffering it contains, occupies the centerpiece of the Apocalypse's pastoral message: the church bears witness to God's victory in Christ by participating in his suffering, sometimes even in his death, until his return to realize on earth what is already so in heaven. Indeed, the "hour" of destruction that brings this second horror to an end (11:13-14) gives glory "to the God of heaven" as victor.

The final trumpet fanfare does not announce a "third horror" (11:14), which is "coming soon" (and described in 12:1–19:10), but rather the decisiveness and finality of God's victory over "the Gentiles" (so 11:13): "the kingdom of the world has become the kingdom of our Lord and his Christ ... forever and always" (11:15). The lyrics of the triumphant chorus is sung by heaven's church choir (11:15-18) in worshipful praise of the Lord God Almighty whose rule over creation has been enforced by judgment (11:16-17). The judgment is just, since the punishment of the Gentiles matches their malicious crimes (11:18): those who are destroyers of the earth are themselves destroyed by earth's Creator Lord.

Although this is a heavenly scene, what is true in heaven is truth on earth, which is confirmed for all the nations to see as the Apocalypse unfolds toward its stunning conclusion: the slaughtered but exalted Lamb returns to earth to destroy the destroyers as the purifying act of the Creator who is utterly faithful to creation and to the promise of restoring it anew.

For this moment, however, the vision of the seals—a vision about the present results of Jesus's past work on the Cross—happily concludes in heaven rather than on earth: John sees the temple's open door and through it he catches a glimpse of the hope chest—the "ark of the covenant"—that contains elements of God's promise of an enduring covenant with God's people that nothing, "not death or life, not angels or rulers, not present or future things" (Rom 8:38) can or will threaten.

God's victory because of God's Christ, announced by trumpet fanfare (11:15-18), yields a salutary result in heaven where the Lord God Almighty is worshiped and God's triumph over the destroyers of earth is celebrated; but God's victory is not yet fully experienced on earth. The heavenly temple where the ark and presence of a covenant-keeping God is fully on display (11:19) is now open for the business of salvation. Here it is where the heavenly congregation gathers to experience already what its earthly congregation has not yet but soon will.

The "Then" that opens chapter 12 marks a new beginning and cast of characters. This is a vision about the present moment of God's salvation but from ground level. If the constant chants of God's victory reverberate through heaven's throne room, Christ's sacrifice for creation's salvation has a somewhat different result on earth: a spiritual war ensues between God's people and an unholy trinity that rules over God's opposition on earth.

First, a flashback that refocuses the reader on the climax of scripture's story of God's salvation. This passage is found at the pivot-point of the Apocalypse because it is the pivot-point of human history. John envisions the story of Christmas, which marks the real beginning of history's last days. The Gospel narratives of Messiah's birth (Matt 1-2; Luke 1-2) are plotted as a familiar conflict between the forces of evil (i.e., Herod, Rome) and God.[9] Here too a pregnant woman is now in labor (12:2) and about to give birth to a son (12:4-5), but is threatened by "a great fiery-red dragon" (12:3) that intends to "devour her child" (12:4).

John records this scene as heaven's way of signaling earth (12:1). The elaborate description of the pregnant woman tells nothing of her real identity. Frankly, the two most common interpretations of this woman—that she is either Mary or Eve—make little sense of this context. The personal stories of neither match the woman's characterization in 12:6, 13-16. More likely, this woman is the figuration of a community. Other entire communities, both for and against God, are personified in the Apocalypse by female characters (14:4; 17:18; 21:9-10); here too. Even the child of a pregnant woman could symbolize a people living "within" another people, as Isaiah imagined the "deliverance" of Judah (see Isa 26:17; cf. 66:7-8). In any case, the grand entrance of this stunning woman, dressed in the sun, standing on the moon, and wearing a crown of twelve stars, would seem to suggest that she stands in for God's faithful people (Israel and Church; see 12:17), which birthed and then nurtured God's Messiah for the salvation of the world.[10]

The agony she experiences giving birth may represent the heroic suffering of Israel's faithful remnant that carried God's promises forward from the exile (Micah 5:3; cf. Heb 11:29-40) as well as the earliest community of Christ's followers (for whom John writes), many of whom were martyred for their faithfulness (cf. Rev 2:8-11; 3:7-13; 6:9-11; 14:1-5). the Apocalypse has already made clear that faithfulness to God's redemptive purposes comes at a steep price; however, the wider Johannine tradition, which includes the letters of John, makes it equally clear that ultimately "the evil one does not touch God's children" (1 John 5:18).

This is an incredible promise since the portrait of the evil one presents an awe-imposing figure: a serpent of a fiery-red "power" color, seven heads each with a crown, and a vast tail that takes down a third of the sky's stars. This dragon has other names: "the old snake, who is called the devil and Satan, the deceiver of the whole world" (12:9). It is the party of God's opposition, which certainly offers stiff competition for creation's destiny. For this reason, the clipped way John reports the woman "gave birth to a son...who was snatched up to God" (12:5) creates an impression that underscores the gospel's thematic: evil, no matter how imposing and powerful it may be, does not

---

[9] The salvation myths of several cultures tell this same story of a cosmic battle between the forces of good and evil. In each case, the myth is personified by the particular history of that culture in large part to insure people their origins did not come without a fight won by their gods! See, Robert W. Wall, *Revelation*, NIBC (Peabody, MA: Hendrickson, 1991), pp. 158-9.

[10] The celestial creatures—sun, moon, stars—may symbolize creation. If so, the importance of God's people (= woman) in giving birth and caring for Messiah is understood here in creational terms, for it is the Lamb that God sends into the world to take away sin and restore all creation to its original purposes.

accomplish its malevolent purpose.[11] God has won the battle and, so it would seem, without much fuss or foment on God's part. Messiah is born to rule the nations (see 11:15), the dragon doesn't devour the child, and once finished with salvation's work, the child is snatched back to God. One and done.

The woman's flight to the desert place God has prepared for her allows her (i.e., God's people) to take refuge for the forty-two months allotted God's enemies—under the first beast's earthly rule (see 13:5)—to trample down the redemptive prospects of the unbelieving community (see 11:1-2). Christ's death ends Satan's capacity to "accuse" God's people (12:10), whatever influence this may have had on God's providential care of the covenant community (see Job's story); but Satan is granted authority to deceive the world (12:9; cf. Dan 7:25)—that is, that evil is a good or that God is not good. Once again, John envisions a clear and sharp divide between the believing and unbelieving communities, and the influence the powers and principalities of evil have on each. Drawing upon Paul's vivid imagination, a people's faithfulness to God wraps it in "the full armor of God" so that they can "extinguish the flaming arrows of the evil one" (Eph 6:13-17).

The child's return to heaven, clearly referring to the risen Jesus's exaltation, occasions a territorial war, which decides whether the evil one and its angels should have a place left in heaven (12:8). The next cast member introduced into John's visionary narrative is the archangel Michael who represents God's people in heaven's war between good and evil (12:7; cf. Dan 10:13, 21; 12:1). We already know who wins: "now salvation and power and the kingdom of our God and the authority of God's Christ have already come" (12:10). Corresponding to the victory of God's Lamb over sin (12:11), then, Michael defeats the evil dragon and its army.

But there is a price to pay: the dragon's occupation of heaven where it "accuses our brothers and sisters day and night before our God" (12:10; cf. Job 1-2; Zech 3:1) ends and it gets tossed to earth. Here's the price we pay: the dragon is seriously ticked off knowing he has only a short time to do mischief (12:12); and mischief is what the evil one will do as we will soon see. Clearly, however, the dragon's rage is not a Hollywood-motif of power but of failure. Its inability to thwart God's messianic plan of salvation (12:4-5) and corresponding defeat by Michael in heaven seal its fate. The dragon knows it's a loser, and a sore loser at that!

The relationship between Christ's death and the costly loyalty of his faithful followers unafraid to die is clear in the lyrics of this hymn. What is also made clear is the importance of this community's fearless witness: God's victory is forged by a partnership of the Lamb "and the word of their witness" (12:11); it is this solidarity of trust that exposes the evil one's deception. It is an embodied (not spoken) word of witness, especially lived by the faithful martyrs, exemplified by the slaughtered Lamb, which underwrites the truth of the gospel: "now the salvation of our God has come" (12:10).

---

[11] The verb CEB translates as "snatched up" carries the sense of an event that suddenly or abruptly occurs. The devil's surprise at finding himself on earth (12:13) may indicate that Messiah's mission was cut short, a reflection of the gospel's division of Jesus's mission into two parts: his first advent, ending in his rejection and death, inaugurates God's redemptive plan, while his second advent completes its implementation.

The prediction that the earth and sea will be the new headquarters of an awfully angry devil and its mischief elicits both heaven's celebration but also the recognition that horrors are about to be visited upon earth (12:12). The combination of "earth and the sea," which is the address of the devil's new digs, anticipates their demise in the coming age (see 21:1) when God's fiercest enemies, devil and death, already defeated by the exalted Son are then thoroughly destroyed (cf. 20:10-15). Gospel, people, gospel!

John's vision returns to elaborate the earlier sighting of the woman who had fled to the wilderness where God could care for her over an extended period of time (see 12:6). The devil's immediate reaction once realizing its sudden defeat and exile to earth is to target and pursue the woman (i.e., God's people; 12:13). The word CEB translates as "chase" connotes the intention to persecute whomever is chased—a chase scene in which the bad guy pursues the heroine to harm her. As we would expect, however, the woman is protected from "the old snake" at her desert refuge (12:14-17).

The woman's transformation into a giant "eagle" to escape the devil's grasp (12:14; cf. 12:6) recalls God's description of Israel's exodus from Egypt as a flight "on eagle's wings" (Ex 19:4). Escaping the devil's deceptions (cf. 12:9) by "eagle's wings" is a standard metaphor used of God's rescue operations, whether by miraculous deliverance or by empowering God's people to endure their trials (cf. Is 40:31). The period of safety extended the woman is again counted, "a time, times and a half time" (12:14) or "1,260 days" (12:6, since one "time" = one year according to John's apocalyptic timetable).[12]

The serpent's attempts to drown the church with a flood of deceptions come from its mouth (12:15); they are the verbal attacks that ridicule and seek to marginalize Christian faith (cf. 1 Pet 4:4). One cannot help but think of today's aggressive band of so-called "new atheists" who engage in name-calling and political tactics (rather than thoughtful discourse) to discredit the intelligence and morality of God's people. It is creation ("earth") itself that comes to the rescue by swallowing the river of deception that flows from the serpent's mouth. While this image surely recalls the Creator's use of nature to force the Pharaoh's hand in rescuing Israel from Egypt, thereby fulfilling a promise made to Sarah and Abraham, perhaps it also suggests that God's protection of the gospel's proclamation against the attacks of God's enemies results indirectly from evidence that a faithful people produces, which falsifies the serpent's deceptions. After all, the dragon's rage is directed not at God but at God's people "who keep God's commandments and hold firmly to the witness of Jesus" (12:17).

One last image in this passage that is easily missed carries forward a message for the global church. The dragon's initial failure to defeat the woman only increases its resolve to take the battle to "the rest of her children" (12:17). A tension is provoked by this refrain. On the one hand, we hear the chorus celebrate the devil's defeat in heaven and the securing of God's eternal reign; we also hear its lamentation of coming horrors for God's people on earth. But on the other hand, we also are witnesses of the ineffectiveness of God's enemies to win the ground war. But a ground war is often prolonged; and the woman's children (that's us, people!) are now engaged in the same

---

[12] See Daniel 7:25; 12:7 where it times the last days of human history just prior to the in-breaking of God's eternal age.

spiritual and intellectual struggle that shaped our ancestors. The lyric of heaven's chorus, sung loudly, is now the church's battle song: "Now the salvation and the power and the kingdom of our God and the authority of God's Messiah have come" (12:10).

The Church Is Apostolic

The number "twelve" is used throughout the Apocalypse as a symbol for God's people. Wherever the reader finds it, the covenant between God and God's people is envisioned. John's use of the number comes to a climax in his vision of the New Jerusalem come down to earth in chapter 21. The twelve tribes of God's people (7:5-8), the victorious woman (a trope for God's people) who is introduced wearing a crown of twelve stars (12:1), the 144,000 who stand with the Lamb on Jerusalem's Zion (14:1-5), the city's twelve gates and foundations (21:12-21), and the twelve different crops of fruit produced by the city's "tree of life" (22:2) use the number to symbolize God's covenant people whose enduring life with God is founded on the ministry of "the Lamb's twelve apostles" (21:14)—an image of the apostolic witness that squares with the teaching of the NT (see above 1 John 1:1-3; Eph 2:20-22).

Greg Beale notes that the city's apostolic foundation is a figuration that the "fulfillment of Israel's promises has finally come in Christ, who, together with the apostolic witness to his fulfilling work, forms the foundation of the new temple, the church, which is the new Israel."[13] Christ's promise to "those who emerge victorious" that he "will make them pillars in the temple of my God (for) the New Jerusalem that comes down out of heaven from my God" (Rev 3:12) comes to fulfillment on an apostolic foundation. Simply put, John's vision of this eschatological community envisions the nature of an apostolic church.

Along with sightings of new things and non-sightings of former things, John's vision of the New Jerusalem is introduced by an audition: he hears a commanding voice that redirects his attention to "the holy city, the New Jerusalem" (21:2). He observes the city not as a particular place but as a peculiar person beautifully adorned like a bride on her wedding day, walking down the aisle leading from heaven to earth where she and the Lamb will make their home together in a renewed creation (21:2-3; cf. Is 65:17-19). The old city, Babylon, and the prostitute who personifies its repulsive evils, are replaced by this new city, Jerusalem, and the bride who personifies its sanctified goods.

The victorious declaration of Alpha and Omega, "Look! I'm making all things new" (21:5), envelops a promise to the community who "overcomes" (2:7). This is one of the Apocalypse's catchwords, designed to attract our attention when John uses it. Recall the Lord's address of the seven congregations in chapters 2-3 when repeatedly the verbal noun, "overcomer," is used to promise salvation to all those who obey "what the Spirit is saying" and overcome evil (2:7, 11, 17, 26; 3:5, 12, 21), even as he overcame evil to broker God's salvation on their behalf (3:21; 5:5; 12:11; 17:14).

Although the prophet nowhere links the testimony of the Spirit to the church's apostolic witness, 1 John 4:1-6 does. Teachers who follow the apostolic message about

---

[13] Greg K. Beale, *The Book of Revelation*, NIGTC (Grand Rapids: Eerdmans, 1999), pp. 1070–1.

Jesus "are from God" and speak the truth. Their message functions as the community's rule of faith, so that not only is an individual's membership based upon its embrace but so also is the community's "fellowship with the Father and with his Son, Jesus Christ" (1:3). Conversely, those false prophets whose teaching is funded by the "spirit of error" lead people away from God and therefore away from eternal life that is "with the Father" (1:2; 4:6).

Those who do not belong to this people are classified by a catalog of evils (21:8). At the head of this catalog are the cowardly and faithless—doubtless meant as a warning to those believers tempted to compromise their faith for the evils of Babylon (18:4). To do so is an act of cowardice, when faith is exchanged for the niceties of the "good life" offered by the beast. The courage to resist the comforts of Babylon and follow the Lamb wherever he goes requires deep faith in the apostolic testimony: this Lamb is the risen Lord who has overcome evil for the world's salvation (cf. 3:21; 17:14).

Once before the prophet is invited by "one of seven angels" to observe the judgment of "the great prostitute" (17:1-6) only then to be given a Cook's Tour of the city she represents, evil Babylon (17:18). But this is a happier season because a new creation has dawned. This time John is invited again by "one of the seven angels" to observe the Lamb's bride, the church (21:9). Once again a reversal of expectation helps readers draw the connection: the woman John is shown is the city she represents, the New Jerusalem, which he tours "in the Spirit."

The expansive contrast between Babylon and Jerusalem could not be drawn more sharply. The holy city's vastness is everywhere observed: its great size, its high walls, its jeweled brilliance, its many gates open in every direction, its firm foundation, all built with precious materials suitable for the Creator's dwelling place. And unlike Babylon, observed as a two-dimensional city, Jerusalem is measured in three dimensions (its length, width, height are the same). Its gates also number twelve to allow entrance and support for the entirety of God's people (21:12; cf. 7:9). It's a place of great beauty, a home suitable for the Lamb's bride: God's creations are beautiful things. Streets of pure gold shining like a mirror, bejeweled foundations, decorated walls envision an apostolic city, which is a place of great beauty.

After taking notes on what he sees, John also makes the surprising observation that "I didn't see a temple in the city." John has in mind OT prophecy of New Jerusalem's temple (Is 60; Ez 40-48; Zech 14), which he interprets as fulfilled not by building a third temple (as some Zionists suppose) but as the living presence of God and the Lamb, which fills the city top to bottom (21:22; see Is 60:19-26; Ez 48:35; Zech 14:20-21). The glory of God supplies the city's electricity (21:23); there is no darkness that requires the gates to close at night for safety (21:24-5). All twelve gates remain open in every direction to welcome the Lamb's faithful people from every nation and from all directions into God's presence (21:26-27).

Precisely because this place is home to a sanctified people and off-limits to the faithless, the people who populate the New Jerusalem form a very different community, one that makes good at long last what the church confesses about itself today: we are one, holy, catholic, and apostolic.

Summary

The church has always placed John's Apocalypse last in its biblical canon. Although there are historical reasons for this, readers may think of this as strategic: the book is placed last to perform a particular role as scripture's conclusion. Its visions, formatted by the prophet into a pastoral letter, tell how the various subplots layered into the biblical story of God's salvation conclude—how a broken world is remade into a new creation, how the reign of evil is unmasked and unmade, how the Lamb's messianic death effects God's purifying judgment that clears the brush for a ransomed people—an eschatological community of overcomers—and how the Lamb returns to lead this people into the new Jerusalem where they take up residence to worship the triune God forever.

Scripture's concluding snapshot of God's people is grounded in the prophetic address of the sevenfold church in Revelation 2-3, which sets out various threats—some external (idolatry, cultural expectations) and others internal (false teachers, laxity)—to the church's solidarity with Christ and each other. The church's capacity to overcome these threats is predicated on its close and consistent attention to imitate the exalted One who addresses them.

The church's holiness is aptly envisioned by a vision of the 144,000 disciples standing with the exalted Lamb on Mt. Zion, the epicenter of God's sacred universe (Rev 14:1-5). They are those who fearlessly follow the Lamb wherever he goes, even to death at the hands of the unholy trinity (Rev 13). Holiness is presented not so much as a moral perfection but as a radical obedience to God's commandments, as non-participation in a corrupt political and economic reign of terror, as a faithful confession of God's truth, all of which are covenant-keeping practices that bear witness of a community's allegiance to God.

This chapter has presented the catholicity of God's people in a global idiom. The church gathers communicants from around the world—from "every tribe, language, people and nation"—not only to worship God forever but in fearless witness to "the Messiah born to rule the nations" to unmask the spiritual powers of death, those "destroyers of the earth" who seek to deceive the nations (Rev 11:18; 12:11). This international community therefore participates with the risen One to insure that God's promise to restore order to a broken cosmos is realized.

Finally, the church's apostolic tradition is reimagined as supplying the firm foundation of the walled residence of God's eschatological people (Rev 21:14). The twelvefold crop of the city's tree of life indicates that the community of overcomers, who inherit the promise of eternal life, do so because they have received and trusted the truth of apostolic teaching. Like the city itself, it is a word of great beauty.

Works Cited

Aageson, James W. "The PE, Apostolic Authority, and the Development of the Pauline Scriptures." In *The Pauline Canon*, edited by Stanley Porter, 5–26. Leiden: Brill, 2004.

Aageson, James W. *Paul, the Pastoral Epistles, and the Early Church*. Peabody, MA: Hendrickson, 2008.

Abraham, William J. *The Divine Inspiration of Holy Scripture*. Oxford: Oxford University Press, 1981.

Akers, Matthew. "What's in a Name? An Examination of the Usage of the Term 'Hebrew' in the Old Testament." *JETS* 55 (2012): 685–96.

Allen, David M. *Deuteronomy and Exhortation in Hebrews*, WUNT 238. Tübingen: Mohr-Siebeck, 2008.

Alter, Robert. *The Five Books of Moses*, iv–xvi. New York: Norton, 2004.

Anderson, Paul N. *The Christology of the Fourth Gospel*. Valley Forge, PA: Trinity Press International, 1996.

Aus, Roger. "Three Pillars and Three Patriarchs: A Proposal Concerning Gal 2:9." *ZNW* 70 (1979): 252–61.

Barton, John. *Holy Writings, Sacred Text: The Canon in Early Christianity*. Louisville: Westminster/John Knox, 1997.

Barton, John. "Historical-critical Approaches." In *The Cambridge Companion to Biblical Interpretation*, edited by John Barton, 10–11. Cambridge: Cambridge University Press, 1998.

Barton, John. *The Nature of Biblical Criticism*. Louisville, Westminster: John Knox, 2007.

Bassler, Jouette M. *1 Timothy, 2 Timothy, Titus*, ANTC. Nashville: Abingdon Press, 1996.

Bauckham, Richard. *Jude-2 Peter*, WBD 50. Waco: Word Books, 1983.

Bauckham, Richard. *Jude and the Relatives of Jesus in the Early Church*. Edinburgh: T&T Clark, 1990.

Bauckham, Richard. "James and the Gentiles (Acts 15:13-21)." In *History, Literature, and Society in the Book of Acts*, edited by Ben Witherington, 154–84. Cambridge: Cambridge University Press, 1996.

Bauckham, Richard. *James*. New York: Routledge, 1999.

Bauckham, Richard. "Revelation." In *Oxford Bible Commentary*, edited by John Barton and John Muddiman, 1287–306. Oxford: Oxford University Press, 2001.

Bauckham, Richard. *Jesus and the Eyewitnesses: The Gospels as Eyewitness Testimony*. Grand Rapids: Eerdmans, 2006.

Bauer, David. *The Structure of Matthew's Gospel: A Study in Literary Design*, LNTS 31. Sheffield: Sheffield Academic Press, 1989.

Beale, Greg K. *The Book of Revelation*, NIGTC. Grand Rapids: Eerdmans, 1999.

Bede, "On the Seven Catholic Epistles" (c. 700), translated by David Hurst, O.S.B., CSS 82. Kalamazoo, MI: Cistercian, 1985.

Black, C. Clifton. *Mark: Images of an Apostolic Interpreter*. Columbia: University of South Carolina Press, 1994.

Black, C. Clifton. "The First, Second, and Third Letters of John." In *New Interpreter's Bible*, volume 12, edited by Leander E. Keck, 365–78. Nashville: Abingdon Press, 1998.

Bornkamm, Günther, Gerhard Barth, and Heinz Joachim Held. *Tradition and Interpretation in Matthew*, NTL. Philadelphia: Westminster, 1963.

Bovon, François. "The Synoptic Gospels and the Non-Canonical Acts of the Apostles." In *Studies in Early Christianity*, 209–25. Grand Rapids: Baker Academic, 2003.

Bruce, F. F. *Commentary on the Epistles to the Hebrews*, NICNT. Grand Rapids: Eerdmans, 1964.

Bruce, F. F. "Some Thoughts on the Beginning of the New Testament Canon." *BJRL* 65/2 (1983): 38–9.

Brueggemann, Walter. *The Land*, 2nd ed. Minneapolis: Fortress Press, 2002.

Campenhausen, Hans von. *Ecclesiastical Authority and Spiritual Power in the Church of the First Three Centuries*. Peabody, MA: Hendrickson, [1969] 1997.

Castelo, Daniel and Robert W. Wall. "Scripture and the Church: A Précis for an Alternative Analogy." *JTI* 5/2 (2011): 197–210.

Castelo, Daniel and Robert W. Wall. *The Marks of Scripture: Rethinking the Nature of the Bible*. Grand Rapids, MI: Baker Academic, 2019.

Childs, Brevard S. "Psalm Titles and Midrashic Exegesis." *JSS* 16 (1971): 137–50.

Childs, Brevard S. *The New Testament as Canon: An Introduction*. Minneapolis: Fortress Press, 1984.

Childs, Brevard S. *Biblical Theology of the Old and New Testaments*. Minneapolis: Fortress Press, 1993.

Childs, Brevard S. *The Church's Guide for Reading Paul: The Canonical Shaping of the Pauline Corpus*. Grand Rapids: Eerdmans, 2008.

Chilton, Bruce and Craig Evans, eds. *James the Just and Christian Origins*, NovTSup 98. Leiden: Brill, 2014.

Docherty, Susan. *The Use of the Old Testament in Hebrews: A Case Study in Early Jewish Bible Interpretation*, WUNT 260. Tübingen: Mohr-Siebeck, 2009.

Dunderberg, Ismo. *Beyond Gnosticism*. New York: Columbia University Press, 2008.

Dunderberg, Ismo. "The Reception of Paul in Valentinianism." Unpublished paper presented at the annual meeting of SNTS, Berlin, 2010.

Elliott, John K. *1 Peter*, AB 37B. New York: Doubleday, 2001.

Elliott, John K. "The Early Text of the Catholic Epistles." In *The Early Text of the New Testament*, edited by Charles Hill and Michael Kruger, 204–24. Oxford: Oxford University Press, 2012.

Elliott, Neil. "Introduction to Hebrews, the General Epistles, and Revelation." In *Fortress Commentary on the Bible: New Testament*, edited by Margaret Aymer, Cynthia Briggs Kittredge, and David Sánchez, 621–4. Minneapolis: Fortress Press, 2014.

Epp, Eldon J. "Issues in the Interrelation of New Testament Textual Criticism and Canon." In *The Canon Debate*, edited by Lee Martin McDonald and James A. Sanders, 485–515. Peabody, MA: Henrickson, 2001.

Fowl, Stephen E. and Gregory Jones, *Reading in Communion*. Grand Rapids: Eerdmans, 1991.

Fowl, Stephen E. *Theological Interpretation of Scripture*. Eugene, OR: Wipf&Stock, 2009.

Fretheim, Terrence E. *Exodus*, Interp. Louisville: Westminster/John Knox, 1991.

Funk, Robert W. "The Apostolic Parousia: Form and Significance." In *Christian History and Interpretation: Essays in Honor of John Knox*, edited by William Reuben Farmer, C. F. D. Moule, and Richard R. Niebuhr, 249–68. Cambridge: Cambridge University Press, 1967.

Gallagher, Edmon L. and John D. Meade. *The Biblical Canon Lists from Early Christianity: Texts and Analysis*. Oxford: Oxford University Press, 2017.

Gamble, Harry Y. *The New Testament Canon*, GBS. Philadelphia: Fortress Press, 1985.

Gamble, Harry Y. *Books and Readers in the Early Church*. New Haven, CT: Yale University Press, 1995.

Gamble, Harry Y. "The New Testament Canon: Recent Research and the *Status Quaestionis*." In *The Canon Debate*, edited by L. McDonald and J. A. Sanders, 267–94. Peabody, MA: Hendrickson, 2002.

Gelardini, Gabrielle. "'As if by Paul?': Some Remarks on the Textual Strategy of Anonymity in Hebrews." In *The Early Reception of Paul the Second Temple Jew*, LSTS 92, edited by Isaac W. Oliver and Gabriele Boccaccini, 267–86. London: T&T Clark, 2018.

Genette, Gérard. "Introduction to the Paratext." *New Literary History* 22 (1991): 261–72.

Genette, Gérard. *Paratexts: Thresholds of Interpretation*. Cambridge: Cambridge University Press, 1997.

Goswell, Gregory. "Finding a Home for the Letter to the Hebrews." *JETS* 59 (2016): 747–60.

Graham, Susan L. "The Next Generation: Irenaeus on the Rebellion in the Desert of Paran." In *Israel in the Wilderness*, edited by Kenneth E. Pomykala, 183–99. Leiden: Brill, 2008.

Gregory, Andrew F. *The Reception of Luke and Acts in the Period before Irenaeus*, WUNT 2/169. Tübingen: Mohr Siebeck, 2003.

Gregory, Andrew F. "The Reception of Luke and Acts and the Unity of Luke-Acts." *JSNT* 29/4 (2007): 459–72.

Grünstäudl, Wolfgang and Tobias Nicklas, "Searching for Evidence: The History of Reception of the Epistles of Jude and 2 Peter." In *Reading 1-2 Peter and Jude: A Resource for Students*, SBLRBS 77, edited by Eric Mason and Troy Martin, 215–28. Atlanta: SBL, 2014.

Hahneman, Geoffrey M. *The Muratorian Fragment and the Development of the Canon*. Oxford: Oxford University Press, 1992.

Harding, Mark. *What Are They Saying about the Pastoral Epistles?* New York: Paulist Press, 2001.

Horsley, Richard. *Paul and Empire: Religion and Power in Roman Imperial Society*. Harrisburg, PA: Trinity Press International, 1997.

Hill, Charles E. *The Johannine Corpus in the Early Church*. Oxford: Oxford University Press, 2004.

Hill, Craig C. *Hellenists and Hebrews: Reappraising Division within the Earliest Church*. Minneapolis: Fortress Press, 1992.

Jenson, Robert W. *Canon and Creed*. Louisville: Westminster/John Knox, 2010.

Jenson, Robert W. *On the Inspiration of Scripture*. Delhi, NY: American Lutheran Publicity Bureau, 2012.

Johnson, Luke T. *James*, AB 37A. New York: Doubleday, 1995.

Johnson, Luke T. *Letters to Paul's Delegates*, NTC. Valley Forge, PA: Trinity Press International, 1996.

Johnson, Luke T. "Literary Criticism of Luke-Acts: Is Reception-History Pertinent?" *JSNT* 28 (2005): 159–62.

Johnson, Luke T. *Among the Gentiles: Greco-Roman Religion and Christianity*, AYBRL. New Haven: Yale University Press, 2009.

Käsemann, Ernst. "An Apologia for Primitive Christian Eschatology." In *Essays on New Testament Themes*, SBT 41, 149–68. London: SCM Press, 1964.

Knapp, Andrew. "The Role of Historical Criticism in Wesleyan Biblical Hermeneutics." In *The Usefulness of Scripture: Essays in Honor of Robert W. Wall*, edited by Daniel Castelo, Sara Koenig, and David Nienhuis, 24–46. University Park, PA: Eisenbrauns, 2018.

Knox, John. *Marcion and the New Testament: An Essay in the Early History of the Canon*. Chicago: University of Chicago Press, 1942.

Koester, Craig B. *Hebrews*, AB 36. New York: Doubleday, 2001.

Koester, Helmut. "Written Gospels or Oral Tradition?" *JBL* 113 (1994): 293–7.

Konradt, Matthias. "Der Jakobusbrief als Brief des Jakobus." In *Der Jakobusbrief. Beiträge zur Aufwertung der "strohernen Epistel,"* edited by Petra von Gemünden, Matthias Konradt, and Gerd Theißen, 16–53. Münster: Lit. verlag, 2003.

Kovacs, Judith. *1 Corinthians: Interpreted by Early Christian Commentators*, The Church's Bible. Grand Rapids: Eerdmans, 2005.

Kruger, Michael. "The Authenticity of 2 Peter," *JETS* 42 (1999): 645–71.

LaGrand, James. *The Earliest Christian Mission to "All Nations" in the Light of Matthew's Gospel*. Grand Rapids: Eerdmans, 1999.

Legaspi, Michael. *The Death of Scripture and the Rise of Biblical Studies*, OSHT. Oxford: Oxford University Press, 2011.

Levenson, Jon D. *The Hebrew Bible, The Old Testament, and Historical Criticism*. Louisville: Westminster/John Knox, 1993.

Lincoln, Andrew T. *Ephesians*, WBC 42. Dallas: Word Books, 1990.

Lincoln, Andrew T. *Hebrews: A Guide*. London: T&T Clark, 2006.

Lindars, Barnabas. *The Theology of the Letter to the Hebrews*, NTT. Cambridge: Cambridge University Press, 1991.

Lindemann, Andreas, "Die Sammlung der Paulusbriefe im 1 und 2 Jahrhundert." In *The Biblical Canons*, BETL 153, edited by J. M. Auwers and H. J. Jonge, 321–51. Leuven: Leuven University Press, 2003.

Lockett, Darian. "Reading Scripture as Canon: Theological and Historical Commitments." Unpublished paper presented to Westminster Theological Seminary, Philadelphia, 2018.

Luz, Ulrich. *Matthew 1–7: A Continental Commentary*. Translated by Wilhelm Linss. Minneapolis: Fortress Press, 1989.

Luz, Ulrich. *Matthew 1–7: A Commentary*, Hermeneia. Minneapolis: Fortress Press, 2007.

Marshall, I. Howard. *Pastoral Epistles*, ICC. London: T&T Clark, 1999.

Massaux, Édouard. *The Influence of the Gospel Saint Matthew on Christian Literature before Saint Irenaeus*, NGS 5. 5 vols, edited by Arthus J. Bellinzoni. Macon, GA: Mercer University Press, 1990.

McKnight, Scot. "A Parting within the Way: Jesus and James on Israel and Purity." In *James the Just and Christian Origins*, edited by Bruce Chilton and Craig A. Evans, 83–129. Leiden: Brill, 1999.

McDonald, Lee M. *The Biblical Canon: Its Origin, Transmission, and Authority*. Peabody, MA: Hendrickson, 2007.

McDonald, Lee M. *The Formation of the Biblical Canon*. 2 vols. London: T&T Clark, 2017.

Metzger, Bruce M. *The Canon of the New Testament*. Oxford: Clarendon Press, 1987.

Mitchell, Margaret M. *Paul, the Corinthians and the Birth of Christian Hermeneutics*. New York: Cambridge University Press, 2010.

Mitton, C. Leslie. *The Formation of the Pauline Corpus of Letters*. London: Epworth Press, 1955.

Morgan, Robert. "Made in Germany: Towards an Anglican Appropriation of an Originally Lutheran Genre." In *Aufgabe Und Durchfuhrung Einer Theologie Des Neuen Testaments*, WUNT XII-1 205, edited by Cilliers Breytenbach and Jörg Frey, 85–112. Tübingen: Mohr Siebeck, 2007.

Moule, C. F. D. *The Origin of Christology*. Cambridge: Cambridge University Press, 1977.

Mount, Christopher N. *Pauline Christianity: Luke-Acts and the Legacy of Paul*, NovTSup 104. Leiden: Brill, 2002.

Neyrey, Jerome. *2 Peter, Jude: A New Translation and Commentary*, AB 37C. New York: Doubleday, 1993.

Ngewa, Samuel. *1 and 2 Timothy and Titus*, African Bible Commentary. Grand Rapids: Zondervan, 2009.

Nicklas, Tobias, "'Der geliebte Bruder': Zur Paulusrezeption im zweiten Petrusbrief." In *Der zweite Petrusbrief und das Neue Testament*, WUNT 397, edited by Wolfgang Grünstäudl, Uta Poplutz, and Tobias Nicklas, 133–50. Tübingen: Mohr-Siebeck, 2017.

Nielson, Charles M. "Scripture in the Pastoral Epistles." *PRSt* 7 (1980): 4–23.

Niebuhr, Karl-Wilhelm and Robert W. Wall, *The Catholic Epistles and Apostolic Tradition: The New Perspective on James and Other Studies*. Waco: Baylor University Press, 2009.

Nienhuis, David R. *Not by Paul Alone*. Waco: Baylor University Press, 2007.

Nienhuis, David R. *A Concise Guide to Reading the New Testament*. Grand Rapids: Baker Academic, 2018.

Nienhuis, David R. "'From the beginning': The Formation of an Apostolic Identity in 2 Peter and 1-3 John." In *Muted Voices of the New Testament: Readings in the Catholic Epistles and Hebrews*, LNTS 565, edited by Katherine Hockey, Madison Pierce, and Francis Watson, 71–86. London: T&T Clark, 2017.

Nienhuis, David R. "Reading James, Rereading Paul." In *The Early Reception of Paul, the Second Temple Jew*, LSTS 92, edited by Lester L. Grabbe, 236–51. London: T&T Clark, 2018.

Nienhuis, David R. and Robert W. Wall. *Reading the Epistles of James, Peter, John and Jude as Scripture: The Shaping and Shape of a Canonical Collection*. Grand Rapids: Eerdmans, 2013.

Nolland, John. *The Gospel of Matthew*, NIGTC. Grand Rapids: Eerdmans, 2005.

Painter, John. *1, 2, and 3 John*, SP. Collegeville, MN: Liturgical Press, 2002.

Painter, John, *Just James: The Brother of Jesus in History and Tradition*, 2nd ed. Columbia, SC: University of South Carolina Press, 2004.

Parker, D. C. *An Introduction to the NT Manuscripts and their Texts*. Cambridge: Cambridge University Press, 2008.

Patsch, Hermann, "The Fear of Deutero-Paulinism: The Reception of Friedrich Schleiermacher's 'Critical Open Letter' Concerning 1 Timothy in the First Quinquenium." *Journal of Higher Criticism* 6 (1999): 3–31.

Pervo, Richard I. *Dating Acts: Between the Evangelists and the Apologists*. Santa Rosa, CA: Polebridge Press, 2006.

Pervo, Richard I. *The Making of Paul: Constructions of the Apostle in Early Christianity*. Minneapolis, MN: Fortress, 2010.

Pervo, Richard I. "To Have and to Have Not: Receptions of Paul in the *Acts of Paul*." Unpublished paper presented at the annual meeting of SNTS, Berlin, 2010.

Picirilli, Robert E. "Allusions to 2 Peter in the Apostolic Fathers." *JSNT* 33 (1988): 57–83.

Porter, Stanley E. "Pauline Authorship and the PE: Implications for Canon." *BBR* 5 (1995): 105–23.

Porter, Stanley E. "When and How Was the Pauline Corpus Compiled? An Assessment of Theories," in *The Pauline Canon*, edited by Stanley Porter, 95–127. Leiden: Brill, 2004.
Quinn, Jerome. "P46—The Pauline Canon." *CBQ* 36 (1974): 381–4.
Räisänen, Heikki. *Neutestamentliche Theologie?*, SB 186. Stuttgart: W. Kohlhammer, 2000.
Regev, Eyal. "Hebrews' Priestly Christology and the Understanding of the Death of Jesus: Taking the Temple Cult Seriously." Unpublished paper at the SBL annual meeting, Boston, 2017.
Riesner, Rainer. "James' Speech (Acts 15:13-21), Simeon's Hymn (Luke 2:29-32), and Luke's Sources." In *Jesus of Nazareth: Lord and Christ*, edited by Joel B. Green and Max Turner, 263–78. Grand Rapids: Eerdmans, 1994.
Rothschild, Clare K. *Hebrews as Pseudepigraphon*, WUNT 235. Tübingen: Mohr Siebeck, 2009.
Rowe, C. Kavin. *World Upside Down: Reading Acts in a Greco-Roman Age*. Oxford: Oxford University Press, 2009.
Sanders, James A. "Torah and Paul." In *God's Christ and His People: Studies in Honour of Niles Alstrup Dahl*, edited by Jacob Jervel and Wayne A. Meeks. Oslo: Universitetsforlaget, n.d.
Sanders, James A. *Canon and Community*, GBS. Philadelphia: Fortress Press, 1984.
Sanders, James A. "The Issue of Closure in the Canonical Process." In *The Canon Debate*, edited by Lee M. McDonald and James A. Sanders, 252–63. Peabody, MA: Hendrickson, 2002.
Schlossnikel, Reinhard F. *Der Brief an die Hebräer und das Corpus Paulinum*, GLB 20. Freiburg: Herder, 1991.
Schröter, Jens, *From Jesus to the New Testament (ET)*, Waco, TX: Baylor University Press, 2013.
Seitz, Christopher, "Canonical Approach." In *Dictionary for Theological Interpretation of the Bible*, edited by Kevin J. Vanhoozer, 100–2. Grand Rapids, MI: Baker Academic, 2005.
Seitz, Christopher R. *Character of Christian Scripture*, STI., Grand Rapids, MI: Baker Academic, 2011.
Smith, David E. *The Canonical Function of Acts: A Comparative Analysis*. Collegeville, MN: Liturgical Press, 2002.
Smith, D. Moody. "When Did the Gospels First Become Scripture?" *JBL* 119 (2000): 3–20.
Smith, Jonathan Z. *Imagining Religion: From Babylon to Jonestown*. Chicago: University of Chicago Press, 1982.
Spina, Frank A. "Israel as a Figure for the Church." In *The Usefulness of Scripture: Essays in Honor of Robert W. Wall*, edited by Daniel Castelo, Sara Koenig, and David Nienhuis, 3–23. University Park, PA: Eisenbrauns, 2018.
Stanton, Graham N. "The Early Reception of Matthew's Gospel: New Evidence from Papyri?" In *The Gospel of Matthew in Current Study*, edited by David E. Aune, 42–61. Grand Rapids: Eerdmans, 2001.
Stendahl, Krister. *The School of St. Matthew and Its Use of the Old Testament*. Philadelphia: Fortress Press, 1968.
Strange, W. A. *The Problem of the Text of Acts*, SNTSMS 71. Cambridge: Cambridge University Press, 1992.
Sundberg, Albert C. "Canon Muratori: A Fourth-Century List." *HTR* 66 (1973): 1–41.
Taylor, Charles. *A Secular Age*. Cambridge, MA: Harvard University Press, 2007.
Towner, Philip H. *The Goal of Our Instruction*, JSNTSup 34. Sheffield: Sheffield Academic, 1989.

Towner, Philip H. *The Letters to Timothy and Titus*, NICNT. Grand Rapids: Eerdmans, 2006.
Trobisch, David. *The First Edition of the New Testament*. Oxford: Oxford University Press, 2000.
Trobisch, David. *Paul's Letter Collection: Tracing the Origins*. Minneapolis: Fortress Press, 1994.
Trobisch, David. "Oral Performance of Biblical Texts in the Early Church." *Concordia Journal* 37 (2011): 277–84.
Tyson, Joseph B. *Marcion and Luke-Acts: A Defining Struggle*. Columbia: University of South Carolina Press, 2006.
Wall, Robert W. "Reading the New Testament in Canonical Context." In *Hearing the New Testament: Strategies for Interpretation*, edited by J. B. Green, 370–93. Grand Rapids: Eerdmans, 1995.
Wall, Robert W. *Community of the Wise: The Letter of James*, NTC. Valley Forge, PA: Trinity Press, 1997.
Wall, Robert W. "The Rule of Faith in Theological Hermeneutics" (88–107) and "Canonical Context and Canonical Conversations." (165–82). In *Between Two Horizons: Spanning New Testament Studies and Systematic Theology*, edited by J. B. Green and M. Turner. Grand Rapids: Eerdmans, 1999.
Wall, Robert W. "The Canonical Function of Second Peter." *Biblical Interpretation* 9 (2001): 64–81.
Wall, Robert W. "The Acts of the Apostles: Introduction, Commentary, and Reflections." In *The New Interpreter's Bible Commentary*, vol. 10, edited by L. E. Keck, 3–370. Nashville: Abingdon Press, 2002.
Wall, Robert W. "The Significance of a Canonical Perspective of the Church's Scriptures." In *The Canon Debate*, edited by Lee M. McDonald and James A. Sanders, 528–40. Peabody, MA: Hendrickson: 2002.
Wall, Robert W. "Toward a Unifying Theology of the Catholic Epistles: A Canonical Approach." In *Catholic Epistles and the Tradition*, BETL 176, edited by Jacques Schlosser, 43–71. Leuven: Peeters, 2004.
Wall, Robert W. "The Function of the Pastoral Letters within the Pauline Canon of the New Testament: A Canonical Approach." In *The Pauline Canon*, edited by S. E. Porter, 27–44. Leiden: Brill, 2004.
Wall, Robert W. "The Jerusalem Council (Acts 15:1-21) in Canonical Context." In *From Biblical Criticism to Biblical Faith: Essays in Honor of Lee M. McDonald*, edited by William H. Brackney and Craig E. Evans, 93–101. Atlanta: Mercer University Press, 2007.
Wall, Robert W. "Reading Paul with Acts: The Canonical Shaping of a Holy Church." In *Holiness and Ecclesiology in the New Testament*, edited by Kent E. Brower and Andy Johnson, 129–47. Grand Rapids: Eerdmans, 2007.
Wall, Robert W. "Introduction" (1–5), "A Unifying Theology of the Catholic Epistles" (13–40), "Acts and James" (127–52), "The Priority of James" (153–60). In *The Catholic Epistles and Apostolic Traditions*, edited by Karl-Wilhelm Niebuhr and R. W. Wall. Waco, TX: Baylor University Press, 2009.
Wall, Robert W. "A Canonical Approach to the Unity of Acts and Luke's Gospel." In *Rethinking the Reception and Unity of Luke-Acts*, edited by Andrew Gregory and C. Kavin Rowe, 172–91. Columbus: University of South Carolina Press, 2010.

Wall, Robert W. "The Canonical View." In *Biblical Hermeneutics: Five Views*, edited by Beth Stovell and Stanley E. Porter, 111–30. Downers Grove, IL: InterVarsity Press, 2012.

Wall, Robert W. *1-2 Timothy & Titus*, THNTC. Grand Rapids: Eerdmans, 2012.

Wall, Robert W. *Why the Church? Reframing New Testament Theology.* Nashville: Abingdon, 2015.

Wall, Robert W. "What If No 2 Peter?" In *Der zweite Petrusbrief und das Neue Testament*, WUNT 397, edited by Wolfgang Grünstäudl, Uta Poplutz, and Tobias Nicklas, 37–54. Tübingen: Mohr-Siebeck, 2017.

Wall, Robert W. and E. E. Lemcio. *The New Testament as Canon: A Reader in Canonical Criticism*, LNTS 76. Reprint. London: T&T Clark, 1992.

Walton, Steve. *Leadership and Lifestyle: The Portrait of Paul in the Miletus Speech and 1 Thessalonians*, SNTSMS 108. Cambridge: Cambridge University Press, 2000.

Watson, Francis, "The Fourfold Gospel." In *The Cambridge Companion to the Gospels*, edited by Stephen Barton, 34–52. Cambridge: Cambridge University Press, 2006.

Watson, Francis. *The Fourfold Gospel: A Theological Reading of the New Testament Portraits of Jesus*. Grand Rapids: Baker Academic, 2016.

Webster, John. *Holy Scripture: A Dogmatic Sketch*. Cambridge: Cambridge University Press, 2003.

Wenham, David. "Acts and the Pauline Corpus." In *The Book of Acts in Its Ancient Literary Setting*, edited by Bruce Winter and A. Clarke, 215–58. Grand Rapids: Eerdmans, 1993.

Wilder, Terry L. *Pseudonymity, the New Testament, and Deception: An Inquiry into Intention and Reception*. Lanham, MD: University Press of America, 2004.

Wood, Charles. *The Formation of Christian Understanding*. Philadelphia: Westminster, 1981.

Works, Carla S. *The Church in the Wilderness: Paul's use of Exodus Traditions in 1 Corinthians*, WUNT 2/379. Tübingen: Mohr-Siebeck, 2014.

Young, Francis. *The Theology of the Pastoral Epistles*, NTT. Cambridge: Cambridge University Press, 1994.

Young, Francis. "The Non-Pauline Letters." In *The Cambridge Companion to Biblical Interpretation*, edited by John Barton, 276–304. Cambridge: Cambridge University Press, 1998.

Index of Authors

Aageson, James W. 105 n.22, 122 n.60
Abraham, William J. 82 n.22
Allen, David M. 139 n.29
Alter, Robert 138 n.27
Anderson, Paul N. 36 n.22, 56 n.43
Athanasius 51, 142
Augustine xii, 150
Aus, Roger 59 n.47

Barrett, C. K. 27 n.9
Barth, Gerhard 13 n.12
Barth, Karl 2
Barton, John 9 n.4, 24 n.2, 76 n.6, 95 n.4, 107
Bassler, Jouette M. 96 n.7, 116 n.52, 117 n.57, 124 n.65
Bauckham, Richard 16 n.20, 49 n.21, 62 n.53, 63 n.56, 87, 79, 80 n.16, 80 n.18, 87, 157 n.8
Bauer, David R. 9 n.3
Baur, F. C. 67
Beale, Greg K. 163
Bede the Venerable 50 n.26, 58, 150
Black, C. Clifton 14 n.16, 48 n.20
Bokedal, Tomas 1 n.1
Bornkamm, Günther 13 n.12
Bovon, François 31
Bruce, F. F. 54, 106 n.25, 129 n.3
Brueggemann, Walter 135, 137

Cadbury, Henry J. 24, 25, 27 n.9, 35 n.19
von Campenhausen, Hans 115, 116 n.54
Cassiodorus 51 n.28
Castelo, David 3 n.2, 76 n.5
Cheung, A. 62 n.52
Childs, Brevard viii, x, 1, 2, 3, 12, 15 n.17, 15 n.18, 16 n.20, 17 n.21, 36 n.23, 65, 81, 82 n.22, 83 n.25, 95 n.6, 116 n.53, 130 n.7, 131 n.8, 132 n.10, 134–5
Chilton, Bruce 51 n.30
Claromontanus 142

Clement of Alexandria xii, 51 n.28, 76, 82, 109, 144 n.39
Clement of Rome 144 n.39
Collins, Raymond F. 96 n.7
Conzelmann, Hans 102 n.19
Cullmann, Oscar 35 n.20, 56 n.41
Cyril 142

Davids, P. 83 n.26
Delatte, A. 54
Dibelius, Martin 102 n.19
Docherty, Susan 141
Dunderberg, Ismo 108, 109–10

Elliott, John K. 68 n.60, 78 n.12
Elliott, Neil 128 n.1
Epiphanius 142
Epp, Eldon J. 46 n.12
Esler, P. 62 n.52
Eusebius xii, 44, 45, 50, 51, 76, 78 n.12, 142

Fornberg, T. 79
Fowl, Stephen E. 4, 38 n.27, 62 n.54, 96 n.9
Fretheim, Terrence E. 18 n.24
Funk, Robert W. 106

Gallagher, Edmon L. 76 n.54, 127, 142
Gamble, Harry Y. 14 n.14, 43 n.5, 105, 108 n.31, 129 n.2
Gelardini, Gabriella 131 n.8
Genette, Gérard 130, 136
Goodspeed, Edgar 54, 107
Graham, Susan L. 137 n.23, 138 n.26
Gregory, Andrew F. 24 n.1, 27
Grünstaudl, Wolfgang 78 n.9

Hagner, D. H. ix
Hahnemann, Geoffrey M. 110 n.41
Harding, Mark 96 n.7
von Harnack, Adolf 36 n.23, 75, 108, 144 n.39
Hegesippus 50, 51 n.30

Held, Heinz Joachim 13–14 n.12
Hill, Charles E. 149 n.1
Hill, Craig C. 37
Hoppin, Ruth 144 n.39

Ignatius 82
Innocent 142
Irenaeus xi, 12, 18, 27, 28–31, 49, 80, 108, 120
Isho'dad of Merv 44

Jenson, Robert W. 18 n.23, 82 n.22
Jerome xiii, 142
Jobes, Karen 64, 83 n.26
Johnson, Luke Timothy 26 n.4, 62 n.55, 96 n.7, 98, 100 n.17, 101, 102, 115 n.49, 135 n.18
Jones, Gregory 62 n.54
Justin Martyr 107

Käsemann, Ernst 81, 84, 86, 88
Knapp, Andrew 93 n.1
Knight, George W. 96 n.7
Knox, John 54, 107, 108 n.34
Koester, Craig B. 130 n.7, 132, 142 n.34
Koester, Helmut 14 n.14
Konradt, Matthias 52 n.32, 60
Kovacs, Judith L. 109
Kruger, Michael 80 n.18

Ladd, George Eldon ix
LaGrand, James 135 n.20
Lake, Kirsopp 35 n.19
Legaspi, Michael 79 n.14
Lemcio, Eugene E. 1, 53 n.35, 123 n.63
Levenson, Jon D. 95 n.5
Lincoln, Andrew T. 80 n.17, 98, 136, 144 n.39
Lindars, Barnabas 134
Lindemann, Andreas 108 n.30
Lockett, Darian 64, 83–4 n.26, 93–4 n.2
Luther, Martin 44 n.6, 53 n.34, 63, 123 n.62, 144 n.39
Luz, Ulrich 11 n.8

Malherbe, Abraham 102 n.19
Marcion 8, 28, 30, 47 n.15, 67, 75, 80, 108, 109, 110, 111, 120, 143
Marshall, I. Howard 96 n.7, 117 n.55
Massaux, Édouard 14 n.14, 15

McDonald, Lee Martin 4, 14 n.15, 127, 142 n.35
McKnight, Scot 51 n.30
Meade, John D. 76 n.7, 127, 142
Metzger, Bruce M. 44 n.7, 50 n.25, 142
Mitchell, Margaret M. 121 n.59
Milton, C. Leslie 111–12
Morgan, Robert 96 n.8
Moule, C. F. D. 10 n.8
Mounce, William D. 96 n.7
Mount, Christopher N. 27, 28, 29 n.12
Moyise, Steve 83 n.26

Neyrey, Jerome 85
Ngewa, Samuel 96 n.7, 99 n.16
Nicklas, Tobias 78 n.9, 84 n.27, 88 n.31
Niebuhr, K.-W. 26 n.7
Nielson, Charles M. 111
Nienhuis, David R. 26 n.6, 26 n.8, 42, 46 n.11, 66, 67 n.59, 69 n.61, 78 n.10, 84 n.26
Nolland, John 16 n.20

Origen xii, 51, 78 n.12

Painter, John 37 n.25, 42 n.3, 48 n.20
Pantaenus of Alexandria xii
Parker, D. C. 127, 142
Patsch, Hermann 97 n.12
Pervo, Richard I. 24, 35 n.19, 110 n.39, 120
Picirilli, Robert E. 80 n.18
Polycarp 44, 109
Pomykala, Kenneth F. 137 n.23
Porter, Stanley E. 96 n.10, 97 n.11, 105 n.22

Quinn, Jerome 110

Räisänen, Heikki 55 n.40
Reger, Eyal 132 n.12
Riesner, Rainer 38 n.27
Robinson, Anthony 75 n.3
Rothschild, Claire K. 128, 142 n.33, 145
Rowe, C. Kevin 102 n.21
Rufinus 142

Sanders, E. P. 62 n.52
Sanders, James A. viii, x, 1, 2, 3, 4, 30, 53 n.35, 57, 108 n.32, 123 n.63, 138 n.28
Schleiermacher, Friedrich 97 n.12

Schlossnikel, Reinhard F. 143
Schröter, Jens 81, 82 n.21
Seitz, Christopher R. 113 n.46, 134
Smith, D. Moody 49 n.22
Smith, David E. 28 n.9
Smith, Jonathan Z. 74
Spina, Frank A. 134 n.16
Stanton, Graham N. 12 n.10, 15
Stendahl, Krister 9
Strange, W. A. 26 n.5, 35 n.19
Stuhlhofer, Franz 76 n.6
Sundberg, Albert C. 76, 110 n.41

Tatian viii, 2, 13
Taylor, Charles 99
Tertullian xii, 27, 108, 110, 111, 120, 144 n.39
Thomassen, Einar 1 n.1
Towner, Philip H. 96 n.7, 109 n.35, 115 n.48
Trobisch, David 27 n.9, 35 n.19, 46 n.12, 53, 75 n.4, 107, 127, 142, 143

Tyconius 150
Tyson, Joseph B. 35 n.19

Valentinius 28, 108, 109, 110, 111, 120

Wall, Robert W. 26 n.7, 34 n.18, 35 n.21, 46 n.14, 47 n.16, 48 n.18, 53 n.35, 56 n.42, 76 n.5, 78 n.10, 123 n.63, 132 n.11, 149, 160 n.9
Walton, Steve 34 n.17
Watson, Francis 14 n.13
Webster, John 82 n.23
Wenham, David ix, 34 n.17
Wilder, Terry L. 98 n.13
Wilhelm-Niebuhr, Karl 1 n.1
Wolterstorff, Nicholas 79 n.15, 113
Wood, Charles 108 n.33
Works, Carla S. 140 n.31
Wrede, W. 80

Young, Francis 41 n.1, 116 n.50, 124 n.64

Index of Biblical Figures

Abraham 10, 137, 138
Apollos 144 n.39

Barnabas 144 n.39
Bathsheba 10

Cornelius 57

David 10, 132, 134

Eve 160

Herod 10, 11, 16, 17, 160

James 28, 30, 35, 37, 38, 40, 42, 44, 50, 51, 52, 54, 55, 56, 58–63, 67, 70
Jezebel 154, 157
John 35–6, 55, 56, 70, 150, 152, 158, 160
Joseph (OT) 135
Josiah 139
Jude 70

Luke 29, 31, 34, 35, 37, 42 n.2, 56, 57, 144 n.39

Mark 67
Mary 50 n.26, 160

Michael (archangel) 161
Miriam 138
Moses 16, 135, 136, 138, 139

Onesimus 107

Paul xi, xii, 29, 30, 32, 34–8, 46, 47 n.17, 50, 51, 54–9, 61, 62, 65, 67, 88, 89
   Hebrews and 128, 131, 132, 137, 140–6
   Pastoral Epistles and 96–125
Peter 33, 35, 36, 37, 38, 50, 55, 56, 57, 59, 60, 67, 70, 83
Pharoah 135, 136
Priscilla 33, 144 n.39

Rahab 10
Ruth 10

Sarah 137, 138
Silvanus 67
Simeon 38

Tamar 10
Theophilus 25, 27, 31
Timothy 39, 58, 107, 142
Titus 39

Index of Scriptures

Genesis		2 Samuel	16
2:1–3	139		
14:13	135	2 Kings	
39:14, 17	135	9	154
40:12	135		
43:32	135	2 Chronicles	8
Exodus	139	Job	
2:15	16	1–2	161
3:18	135, 136		
4:19–20(LXX)	11	Psalms	
5:2(LXX)	135	2	154
5:3	135	39:7 (LXX)	141
7:16	135	40(MT)	141
9:1, 13	135	94(LXX):7b–11	139
9:29	18		
10:3	135	1 Maccabees	
15	18, 138	2:46	37
16	138		
19:4	162	Sirach	8
19:5	18		
33:19	136	Isaiah	56
34	138	26:17	160
34:6–7	136	40	67
		40:31	162
Leviticus		60	164
17–18	63	60:3	154
		60:19–26	164
Numbers	139	65:17–19	163
13–14	137	66:7–8	160
14	139		
24:8	16	Ezekiel	
24:17	154	40–48	164
		48:35	164
Deuteronomy	139		
19:15	158	Daniel	8
29:16–29	139	7:1–8	155
30:1–14	139	7:13–14	150 n.2
32:8	139	7:25	161, 162 n.12
		10:13, 21	161
1 Samuel	135	12:1	161
21:5–6	157	12:7	162 n.12

Index of Scriptures

Hosea	16, 17	2:4–2:6	11
11:1	16	2:4	10, 11
12:9, 13	16	2:7–15	7–19
13:4	16	2:7	11
		2:8	10
Amos	38	2:9	10, 11
		2:10	11
Jonah		2:11	10, 11, 16
1:9	135	2:12	16
		2:13	10, 11, 12, 16
Micah		2:14	10, 11, 12, 16
5:3	160	2:15	12, 16
		2:16–23	9
Zechariah		2:16	11
3:1	161	2:19–21	11, 12
14	164	2:20	10, 11, 12
14:20–21	164	2:21	10, 11, 12
		2:22–23	12
Malachi	8	2:22	12
		3–4	16 n.20
Matthew	7–9, 12–15, 30,	10:7	ix
	49, 52, 61	12:28	ix
1–4	8	14:26	11
1–2	9, 10, 15,	16:28	ix
	17, 160	27:11	10 n.7
1:1–16	8	27:29	10 n.7
1:1	10, 16	27:37	10 n.7
1:2–17	9	28:15	10 n.7
1:2–16	10	28:16–20	9 n.3
1:2	10	28:19–20	10, 16
1:6	10	28:20	9
1:16	10		
1:18–20	8	Mark	x, 8, 13, 14, 15
1:18	10	9:1	ix
1:18a	9		
1:18b–25	9	Luke	x, 13, 14, 17,
1:19	11, 12		23–7, 29, 30,
1:20	12		31, 133
1:21–25	10	1–14	128
1:21	8, 10, 11, 17	1–2	160
1:22–25	8	1:1–4	95, 128
1:23	10	1:4	27
1:25	10 n.6	2:29–32	17, 38
1:38	17	4:19–20	36 n.22
1:48	17	9:27	ix
2:1–6	9, 10	10:9–11	ix
2:1	10	17:20–21	ix
2:2	10, 11	22:28–30	59 n.49

Index of Scriptures

John	ix, 13, 30, 48, 74, 149	13:47	119
		15–18	68
5:28–29	ix	15	36–40, 52 n.32, 56, 62, 66–7
10:10	ix		
11:25–26	ix	15:1–29	34, 55
14–16	33	15:1–2	57, 61 n.51
21:15–17	33	15:1	37, 60, 63
		15:4–29	50
Acts	23–40, 42 n.2, 44, 45, 51, 53, 54–64, 76, 103, 108, 142, 143	15:4–21	59
		15:4–5	57, 61
		15:4	38
		15:5	37, 38, 60
1:1–26	59 n.49	15:6–12	50
1:1	33, 54 n.37	15:6	60
1:8	37	15:7–11	57
1:12–14	70	15:9	35, 38, 57, 59
1:21–22	29, 65	15:13–29	28, 50
2:22–36	35, 56	15:13–21	60, 63
2:22	133	15:14	63
2:38	63	15:16–21	62
2:42–47	34, 55	15:19	62, 63
2:42	63	15:20–21	61
2:43–44	63	15:20	38, 57, 59, 60, 62, 63
2:47	63		
3:13	35, 56	15:21	57, 60, 63
3:19	63	15:22–29	60
3:20–23	35, 56	15:24	37, 57, 63
3:20–21	33	15:28	62
3:26	35	15:29	38, 60, 62, 63
4:10	63	16:3	39, 58
4:12	63	16:20–21	39, 58
4:19–20	56	18	33
4:24	35, 56	18:24–19:41	54 n.38
4:27	35, 56	19	10
4:30	35, 56	20:17–38	54 n.38
4:32–35	63	20:17–35	100
4:33	63	21	35, 56
6:1–8	63	21:17–26	34, 37, 55, 57
6:1	129 n.3	21:17–25	50
7:23–43	137	21:18–25	59
8	10	21:19–26	50
8:26–40	33	21:20–21	47 n.15, 61
9:15–16	34, 55, 132, 145	21:20	60
11	38	21:21–26	28, 61, 63
11:1–18	34, 55, 57	21:23–26	39, 58
12	68	21:25	60, 61, 62, 63
12:17	34, 55	24:16–21	38, 58
13:38–39	57	27	119
13:46	63	28:17–31	34

Index of Scriptures

Romans		2:16	61
1:5	104	3:28	103, 135
1:10–11	104	4:4	66
1:15	34	6:1–10	115
5:18–21	155	6:12–16	61
9–11	146 n.41	6:16	61
10:5–13	139		
10:9	xi	Ephesians	54, 115, 158
12:1	118, 124	2–3	145
16:1	115	2:8–10	118, 124
		2:13–16	135
1 Corinthians	38, 115, 128	2:20–22	163
2:13	116	3:3–4	95
4:16–17	104	6:13–17	161
5:9	xi		
7	121	Philippians	
7:1–7	157	1:1	115
9:12b–23	40	4:2–3	104
9:19–23	62		
10	137	Colossians	115
10:1–13	140	3:11	103
10:8	141	4:16	xi, 143
10:9–10	141		
15:7	59 n.49	1 Thessalonians	
16:10–11	104	3:2	104
2 Corinthians		2 Thessalonians	109
4:7	95		
9:8	118, 124	1 Timothy	93, 97, 100, 101, 102, 110 n.39, 115, 142
Galatians			
1–2	65	1:3	99
1:1	66	1:4	103
1:11–15	59 n.48	1:8–11	117
1:11–12	66	1:10–11	116, 119
1:15–16a	66	1:11–17	83 n.25
1:16b–24	66	1:12–17	97, 122
2	52 n.32, 54, 70	1:12–16	119
2:1–15	50, 53, 123	1:15	97, 119, 122
2:3–5	59 n.48	1:18–20	121
2:3	39, 58	1:20	119, 121
2:6–8	59 n.48	2:2	104, 118
2:7–10	39, 57, 61	2:2b	102
2:7	61, 70, 75	2:3–7	83 n.25, 97, 122
2:9	59, 61, 64	2:3–6	122
2:11–18	61	2:3–4	104
2:11–14	59 n.48, 61 n.51	2:4	125
2:12	61	2:5–6	104
2:15	61		

2:7	104, 119, 122, 131	1:15–18	119
2:8–15	97	2:1–7	122
2:9–15	103	2:1–2	83 n.25, 100, 120, 121, 125
2:10	118		
2:13–15a	122	2:2	117
2:15–3.1a	119, 122	2:8–20	121
3	99	2:8–13	102
3:1–16	97	2:11–13	97, 119, 122
3:1	118	2:17	119
3:5	115	2:21	118
3:15	103, 104, 115, 117, 124	3:5	118
		3:10–14	122
		3:10–13	119
3:16	111 n.43, 118, 119, 122	3:11–14	97
		3:14–4:4	116
		3:14–17	107, 121
4:7	118	3:14	107
4:8–9	122	3:15–17	18, 112
4:8	118	3:15	106, 121, 122
4:9	119	3:16–17	77
4:13	95, 117	3:16b	101, 118
4:14	116	3:17	118
4:16	117	4:9–21	119
5:1–16	103		
5:10	118	Titus	93, 97, 100, 101, 102, 110 n.39, 115
5:16	115		
5:18–19	121		
5:25	118		
6:1–2	97	1:1–3	100, 119
6:3	118	1:1	118
6:5	118	1:2–3	131, 145
6:6	118	1:3–7	97
6:11	118	1:3	83 n.25, 117, 119
6:13	104		
6:15	104	1:5	99
6:18	118	2:7	118
6:20	120, 125	2:11–14	97, 104, 111 n.43, 122
2 Timothy	54 n.38, 83 n.25, 93, 100, 101, 102, 104, 110 n.39, 142	2:14	118
		3:1	118
		3:3–7	97
		3:4–8	119
1:6–7	117	3:4–8a	122
1:6	116	3:8	118
1:7	116	3:12–14	119
1:8–12	119	3:14	118
1:9	97		
1:12–13	83 n.25	Hebrews	x, xi–xii, 74, 84 n.26, 127–46
1:13–14	100, 120, 125		
1:13	121	1–2	134

1:4–4:16	140	2:3–6	125
2:3–4	133	2:8–13	62, 63
2:5	134, 139	2:9–11	62
3–4	139	2:14–26	40, 47 n.17, 62, 63, 64, 124
3:1–4:16	138		
3:1	134	2:14–17	63
4:2–6	139	2:14	64
4:11–13	139	2:15–16	124
4:16b	138	2:15	63
5:1–11:40	138	2:18–3:7	125
5:11–6:12	141	2:18–20	63, 64
6:1	140	2:22	47, 63
10:12	141	2:26	63, 64
10:32–34	133, 136	3:1–17	124
11:29–40	160	4:6–10	67
11:35	139	5:19–20	48, 70
12:1–29	139	5:20	67
12:2–3	136		
12:27–28	139	1 Peter	44, 45 n.10, 47, 52 n.32, 56, 60, 64, 65, 68, 73, 74, 79, 83, 84, 88, 123, 125
12:28–13:21	130–1 n.7		
13:7–19	141		
13:7–17	133		
13:8	xii		
13:13	136	1:1	67, 68
13:14	xii	1:2	68
13:20–25	145	1:3	35, 56
13:22	134	1:5	85
		1:6–9	67
James	17 n.22, 42, 44 n.6, 45, 46 n.11, 49, 51, 52 n.11, 53, 54, 58–64, 65, 66, 67, 68, 74, 123 n.62	1:6	85
		1:10–12	35, 56, 68, 85
		1:17	85
		1:19	68
		1:21	35, 56
		1:22	35, 56
1:1	67	1:23–24	67
1:2–3	67	2:5	124
1:4b	140	2:12	85 n.29
1:10–11	67	2:16	68
1:12	62, 66	2:20	125
1:18	67	2:21–25	35, 56, 84
1:21	62, 63	2:22–24	85 n.29
1:22–2:26	122	2:23	85 n.29
1:25–27	62, 64	3:13–17	85
1:26	63	3:17	125
1:27	40, 59, 62, 63	3:18–22	84
2:1–7	124	3:19–20	68
2:1	63, 64, 125	3:20	68
2:2–7	63	3:21	35, 56
2:2–3	62, 64	4:4	162

Index of Scriptures

4:5	85 n.29	2:11–22	85 n.29
4:8	67	2:13	68, 69, 89
4:11	68	2:14–15	88
4:17	85 n.29, 124	2:15–16	89
4:19	35, 56	2:15	69
5:1	69	2:18–20	69
5:5–9	67	2:18	69, 89
5:12–13	67	2:19	68, 85 n.29
5:12	68	2:20–21	89
5:13	67	2:20	86, 88
		2:21	87, 88
2 Peter	x, 45 n.8, 46 n.11, 47, 48, 49, 56, 64, 65, 68, 69, 70, 73, 74, 77–89, 108, 121, 123, 125	2:24	88
		3	84
		3:1–14	83
		3:1–13	35, 56
		3:1–2	48, 68
		3:1	69, 73
		3:2–5	85 n.29
1:1	86	3:2	68, 86, 87, 89
1:2	68, 88	3:3–4	87
1:3	87, 88	3:3	69
1:4	87, 88	3:4	69
1:5–11	87	3:5–7	69
1:5	88	3:5–6	85 n.29
1:6	88	3:6	68
1:7	88	3:7	85 n.29
1:8	83, 88	3:8–13	87
1:9	87, 88	3:10–12	85 n.29
1:10	68	3:10	85 n.29
1:11	86, 88	3:11	86 n.29, 88
1:12–21	125	3:13–17	87
1:12	83, 125	3:13	86 n.29
1:16–17	87	3:14–15	77
1:16	69, 86, 87	3:14	68, 88
1:17	83, 86	3:15–16	83, 89, 107, 121
1:18	69	3:15b	106
1:19–21	83	3:16	83, 106
1:20–21	68	3:17	69, 88
2:1–3	125	3:18	68, 85 n.29, 86
2:1	69, 85 n.29, 86	4:1–6	87
2:2–3	125	5:1	87
2:2	88, 89		
2:4–5	85 n.29	1 John	44, 45 n.10, 48, 64, 65, 69, 70, 74, 83–4 n.26, 123, 125, 149
2:4	68		
2:5	68		
2:6–8	85 n.29		
2:9–10	69	1:1–4	125
2:9	68	1:1–3	36, 56, 163
2:10	89	1:1	66, 69

1:3	69	1:20	151, 152
2:15–17	69	2–3	151, 152 n.4,
2:19	69		163, 165
2:22–23	69, 157	2:1	152
2:26	69	2:2	152
2:27	69	2:4	153
3:7	69	2:5	152
4:1–6	69, 125, 163	2:6	152
4:1	69	2:7	153, 163
4:6	69	2:8–11	160
4:15	157	2:8	152
4:16–21	70	2:9–10	153
5:18	160	2:9	152
		2:10	152
2 John	48, 49, 64, 65,	2:11	153, 163
	69, 70, 74,	2:12	152
	83–4 n.26,	2:13–15	153
	123, 125, 149	2:13	152
7	69	2:16	152
		2:17	153, 163
3 John	48, 49, 64, 65,	2:18–29	153
	70, 74, 83–4	2:18	152
	n.26, 123, 125	2:19	152, 153
4	124	2:20–23	153
9	124	2:20	154, 157
10	124	2:22	152, 154
12	125	2:23	152
		2:24	154 n.5
Jude	17 n.22, 48,	2:25–28	152
	49, 70, 73	2:25	152, 154 n.5
1	70	2:26–27	154
3–4	125	2:26	152, 163
4	48	2:26a	154
20	70	2:28	154
22–23	70	2:29	151, 153
24–25	48	3:1	152
24	70	3:1a	152
		3.1b	152
Revelation (Apocalypse)		3.2	152
of John	48, 75, 149–65	3.3	152
1:1–4	95	3:5	152, 163
1:1	133, 158	3:6	151, 153
1:2	164	3:7–13	160
1:3	152, 153,	3:7	152
	158, 164	3:8–10	156
1:6	152	3:8	152
1:13–1:19	150	3:11–12	152
1:13	151, 152	3:11	152
1:19	150, 151	3:12	163

3:13	151, 152, 153	12:6	160, 162
3:15	152	12:7–9	154
3:17–18	153	12:7	161
3:20	152	12:9	156, 160,
3:21	152, 153,		161, 162
	163, 164	12:10–12	154, 158
3:22	151, 153	12:10	156, 161
4:2	150	12:11	161, 163, 165
4:6	164	12:12	157, 161, 162
5:5	163	12:13–16	160
5:6	155	12:13	161 n.11, 162
5:9–10	157	12:14–17	162
5:9	157	12:14	162
6:9–11	160	12:15	162
6:10	158	12:17	155, 160, 162
7:1–4	157	12:18	155
7:4	157	13	165
7:5–8	163	13:1–10	155
7:9	157, 164	13:1	155
7:14–15	157	13:2	155
8–11	158	13:3	155
9:20–21	155, 158, 159	13:3b–4	155
10:1–11:14	158	13:5–7	156
10:1–11	158	13:5	161
11–12	158	13:6	156
11:1–2	158, 161	13:8	155, 156 n.7
11:5–13	158	13:10	156
11:7–8	159	13:12	156
11:9–10	159	13:13	156
11:13–14	159	13:15	156
11:13	159	13:16–17	157
11:14	159	13:16	156
11:15–21	158	13:17	156
11:15–18	159	14:1–5	154, 157,
11:15	154, 159, 161		160, 163
11:16–17	159	14:1	154, 157, 165
11:17–19	158	14:4	157, 160
11:18	154, 159, 165	16:13	156
11:19	159	17:1–6	164
12–13	154	17:1–2	157
12	159	17:3	150
12:1–19:10	159	17:14	163, 164
12:1–12	157	17:18	160, 164
12:1	160, 163	18:4	164
12:2	160	19:15	154
12:3	155, 160	19:20	156
12:4–5	160, 161	20:10–15	162
12:4	160	20:10	156
12:5	154, 160	21	163

21:1	162	*Adversus haereses*	
21:2–3	163	(Irenaeus)	12, 18, 28, 30
21:2	163	Apocalypse of Peter	76
21:5	153, 163	Apocalypses of James	51 n.30
21:8	164	Apocryphon of James	51 n.30
21:9–10	160	*Apostolos*	26, 28, 42, 78
21:9	164	*Diatessaron* (Tatian)	viii, 2, 13
21:10	150	*Didache*	xi, 61 n.51, 76, 82, 101
21:12–21	163		
21:12	164	Epistle of Barnabas	xi
21:14	163, 165	*Gospel According to Judas*	xi
21:22	164	Gospel of the Hebrews	51 n.30, 52–3, 122
21:24–25	164		
21:26–27	164	Gospel of Thomas	51 n.30
22:2	153, 163	*Historia Ecclesiastica*	
22:3	153	(Eusebius)	xii, 44, 45, 50, 51 n.30
22:16–17	151		
22:16	154	*Hypotyposes* (Clement of Alexandria)	51 n.30
NON-BIBLICAL WRITINGS		Letters of Clement	xi, 76, 82
Acts of Paul and Thecla	120	Letters of Ignatius	82
Adumbrations		*Protoevangelium of James*	17 n.22
(Clement of Alexandria)	51 n.28	Pseudo-Clementines	51 n.30, 52, 122
		Shepherd of Hermas	xi, 76, 82

www.ingramcontent.com/pod-product-compliance
Lightning Source LLC
Chambersburg PA
CBHW070638300426
44111CB00013B/2150